# MODERN-DAY MIRACLES

# MODERN-DAY MIRACLES

### 50 Real-Life Stories of Divine Encounters, Supernatural Healings, Heaven and Hell Experiences, and More

ALLISON C. RESTAGNO

DESTINY IMAGE® PUBLISHERS, INC.
P.O. Box 310, Shippensburg, PA 17257-0310
*"Speaking to the Purposes of God for This Generation and for the Generations to Come."*

This book and all other Destiny Image, Revival Press, MercyPlace, Fresh Bread, Destiny Image Fiction, and Treasure House books are available at Christian bookstores and distributors worldwide.

For a U.S. bookstore nearest you, call 1-800-722-6774.
For more information on foreign distributors, call 717-532-3040.
Reach us on the Internet: www.destinyimage.com.

Trade Paper ISBN 13: 978-0-7684-3731-7
Hardcover ISBN 13: 978-0-7684-3732-4
Large Print ISBN 13: 978-0-7684-3733-1
Ebook ISBN 13: 978-0-7684-9012-1

For Worldwide Distribution, Printed in the U.S.A.

1 2 3 4 5 6 7 /15 14 13 12 11

# DEDICATION

This book is dedicated to the glory of the Lord
and in accordance with the "Great Commission"
(see Matt. 28:18-20).

# ACKNOWLEDGMENTS

I would like to take this opportunity to sincerely thank all of the wonderful story contributors who so generously volunteered their stories for inclusion in this book of 50 miracle stories for the glory and purposes of the Lord.

I would also like to extend a very special thank you to all of those contributors who have provided me with referrals for this book, including Mr. Sid Roth, Mr. Jack Olson, Mr. Bruce Van Natta, Mrs. Ellen Stevenson, Dr. Sherry Anne Lints, Dr. Theresa Veach, and Ms. Audra Rose Smith. Thank you all so very much.

Thank you also to Dr. Sherry Anne Lints, Dr. Theresa Veach, and Mrs. Carolyn Curran-Fyckes (my mother) for so generously volunteering your time and talents to writing an extra story or two each for this book. This was so highly appreciated. You are all very talented writers.

To all of those persons who have supplied books, CDs, DVDs, and other resources and teaching materials to help with this book, a big thank you goes out to those of you too. This help was absolutely invaluable, and these materials were so needed for this book project. Thank you also to my intellectual property lawyer, Mark Koch, for his invaluable and most generous advice and assistance with this book, and as well a thank you to everyone who supported or assisted with the advance ministry pre-orders for this book. Two-thousand copies of these books were ordered in about eleven weeks! That was a true miracle of the Lord!

To Pastor Rev. Evans Barning of Lamb of God Miracle Ministries, who wrote the foreword for this book, thank you ever so much. This was such an amazing blessing.

To a very special team of book endorsers: Rev. Joe Campbell, national director of development at Christians for Israel; Audra Rose Smith, producer of *The 700 Club* from the Tennessee office; Mr. Ed Epp, executive director of CBM Canada; Mrs. Vicki Schleider, co-owner and station manager of Power 93.9 FM in Brantford, Ontario, Canada; and Dr. Rev. Larry Brice, co-founder of Reachout Ministries. Thank you all so very much. Your endorsements were so wonderful, and I am truly thankful for each and every one.

Next, another huge thank you certainly goes out to two individuals who are requesting anonymity: a wonderfully generous best-selling author who paid for the editing expenses, and also to an editor friend of his, who he arranged to do the editing for this book. There are no words in our English dictionary to thank you enough for what you have done. Thank you both so very, very much, from the bottom of my heart. I just know that the Lord will repay you for your most wonderful kindness and generosity to me, and for this book. Bless you both so very much. I believe also that countless souls will come into the Kingdom as a result of how you have both heard from the Lord.

Now a word of thanks to my amazing publisher, Destiny Image, and especially to Ronda, my acquisitions agent, along with all of those persons involved in the decision-making process, and other areas of bringing this book together. You have all been amazing, and I thank you tremendously for all that you have done. You sensed the Lord in this book and brought the vision of this book to life with the aid and direction of the Lord in every step. You heard from the Lord, and now this book is here. Thank you all so very much. I have treasured my first experience with your publishing company.

Now almost last, but certainly not least, I wish to thank my sister, Bonnie, who not only was my regular office assistant with this book project but then also willingly lent her photography assistance for this book. Bonnie, you were an incredible help. This book wouldn't have been possible without your steadfast and consistent help and support. You are a fantastic sister, and I thank you and love you very much. Also I would like to make mention a very special note of thanks to my wonderful husband, who I love very much. I'm very proud of you also!

And finally, thank you to all of my family, and the many wonderful friends—including story contributors and others—who have so freely lent their support from start to the finish with this book project. Your continued prayers and many words of encouragement have been invaluable. May the Lord richly bless each and every one of you for all of your tremendous contributions. You have all been amazing, and I thank the Lord for each and every one of you!

In His Love,
Allison

# ENDORSEMENTS

The testimonies in this book will dramatically encourage and inspire each Christian reader. I was amazed at the diversity of stories in which God's miraculous power radiated in the lives of ordinary persons who were impacted in extraordinary ways. No one who reads *Modern-Day Miracles* will be left without impact upon their spiritual temperature! Thank you, Allison, for abundantly blessing the Kingdom.

Rev. Joe Campbell
National Director of Development
Christians for Israel Canada
Coordinator, Stand On Guard Prayer Canada

At a number of the most critical times in my life, I have personally experienced what can only be understood as a series of God's amazing miracles. Read this book by Allison Restagno of 50 testimonies that only God can and does do at times of need for provision, comfort, healing, encouragement, and salvation, and find your faith greatly strengthened to trust the living God for your own miracle and heart's desire!

Rev. Dr. Larry Brice
Presbyterian minister, evangelist, and television host

What a victorious collection! This is a divinely inspired set of stories. These compelling first-person accounts will stir up and renew your faith—no matter how bleak your situation looks today. This powerful book reminds me that miracles are possible, miracles are for today, and that the God behind these miracles loves us more than we can imagine. If you are holding this book, it's not by accident. I promise you, there is something in this book specifically for you.

Audra Rose Smith
Producer
*The 700 Club*—Nashville

I don't claim to understand how God's direct presence in this world intersects with so-called "natural" forces—where skill, training, hard work, and careful thought leave off and where divine healing and guidance breaks through. And yet, along with the contributors to this book, I choose to interpret much of the hope and healing in this world as straight from the hand of God. This book is a reminder that the world is full of miracles.

Ed Epp
Executive Director
CBM Canada

Only the hand of God could be behind this collection of powerfully expressed stories. These are testimonies of how ordinary lives have been and are being touched and impacted by the extraordinary, one, true living God.

These stories are little vignettes that could, in mere seconds, pull you into a saga and have you rooting for someone to just "Hang in there!" They are varied, and in them you will find yourself identifying with our humanness and rejoicing in God's faithfulness and His extravagant love for His children. Congratulations to everyone who shared their story and to Allison for compiling them so that God could receive the glory and we could all be encouraged.

Vicki Schleifer
Co-owner/Station Manager
CFWC, Power93.9FM
Brantford's Christian Radio Station

*Sing to the LORD a new song;*
*sing to the LORD, all the earth.*
*Sing to the LORD, praise His name;*
*proclaim His salvation day after day.*
*Declare His glory among the nations,*
*His marvelous deeds among all peoples.*
*For great is the LORD and most*
*worthy of praise;*
*He is to be feared above all gods.*
*For all the gods of the nations are idols,*
*but the LORD made the heavens.*
*Splendor and majesty are before Him;*
*strength and glory are in His sanctuary.*
*Ascribe to the LORD, O families of nations,*
*ascribe to the LORD glory and strength.*
*Ascribe to the LORD the glory due His name;*
*bring an offering and come into His courts.*
*Worship the LORD in the splendor of His holiness;*
*tremble before Him, all the earth.*
*Say among the nations; "The LORD reigns.*
*The world is firmly established, it cannot be moved;*
*He will judge the peoples with equity."*
*Let the Heavens rejoice, let the earth be glad;*
*let the sea resound, and all that is in it;*
*let the fields be jubilant, and everything in them.*
*Then all the trees of the forest will sing for joy;*
*they will sing before the LORD, for He comes,*
*He comes to judge the earth.*
*He will judge the world in righteousness*
*and the peoples in His truth (Psalm 96).*

# CONTENTS

## PART II: COMFORT, REASSURANCE, AND ANGELIC ENCOUNTERS

# PART V: DECLARATIONS OF GOD'S ABIDING FAITHFULNESS AND MIRACLES OF SALVATION

# FOREWORD

I have had the great privilege of witnessing firsthand the miraculous power of God in my miracle meetings in Toronto. It always gives me much joy when I see children of God giving testimony to what the Lord has done.

Revelation 12:11 states, *"And they overcame him by the blood of the Lamb, and by the word of their testimony; and they loved not their lives unto the death"* (KJV).

*Modern-Day Miracles* is a very significant work for the Body of Christ. Whether we are a new believer, a veteran of the faith, or an unbeliever, it reminds us in a very tangible way that we serve a God who is still in the miracle business. He impacts His people globally and transforms lives completely and permanently. The power within these testimonies allows us to overcome our own unbelief in the most challenging situations of our lives.

The dictionary defines miracle as: "An act or event that does not follow the laws of nature and is believed to be caused by God."[1] In fact, God acts on our behalf daily in miraculous ways. Each time we breathe His breath of life, we encounter the works of His miraculous hand. As we survey the splendor of His living creation, we see the active work of a miraculous artist, sculptor, and designer. The evidence of God's power is clearly manifested in our natural world. When we embrace the understanding that His power is available to work in our lives, we gain the ability to identify our daily miracles.

On a daily basis, God miraculously provides for and protects His children. He comforts, encourages, and demonstrates His abiding faithfulness and unfailing love to us. When we are broken and in need of physical, emotional, and spiritual healing, He rescues and restores us. Each time we experience His grace and mercy in our lives, we are impacted by His miracle of salvation.

With the understanding that God is no respecter of persons, we are then empowered by the testimonies outlined in this book to believe God in all things and to receive all that He has for us in Jesus' name.

I would strongly encourage you to read *Modern-Day Miracles* with an open mind and heart, expecting God to accomplish great and mighty things in your life—including the working of miracles.

Pastor Evans Barning
Lamb of God Miracle Ministries
Toronto, Ontario, Canada

## ENDNOTE

1. "Miracle." *Student's Oxford Canadian Dictionary,* 2nd ed. (Toronto: Oxford University Press, 2007), 674.

# INTRODUCTION

When I look back over all of the miracles that have happened as a result of putting together this book, I am truly and utterly amazed. There are so many miracles that have occurred since the start of this book, that I could—and maybe will—write a book someday on all of them that have taken place.

The first miracle that occurred with the making of this book was when I received a computer on which to write this book as a complete and total surprise, but a total and immediate answer to my prayers for one. I had prayed for a confirmation that if I was to compile these 50 miracle stories, that the Lord would make this known by giving me a computer to write this book on.

Two days later, He did.

My father, who knew nothing of this prayer, nor the feeling that I was supposed to put together this book for the Lord's glory and purposes, called and said that his company just happened to be upgrading his computer that week and asked me if I would like his "old" laptop. He wanted to give it to me for free. He just wanted to know if I needed it.

Another of several miracles occurred one day a few months after I had started working on this book. I was a bit discouraged and questioning whether I was really called to do this book and if I was even working in the right direction with compiling these 50 short miracle stories. Suddenly, after praying to the Lord for confirmation, I felt that I should go down to a local bookstore and pull out the first book on miracles and read what it said on the page that it opened up to. So I went down to that bookstore and did just that.

The first book on miracles that I pulled off of the shelf fell open to an explanation of why that author had elected to include 50 miracles in his book. Fifty, I learned in Greek, translated to the word *Pentecost*, and Pentecost, I learned that day, occurred exactly 50 days after Jesus' resurrection, and was when all of the miracles started occurring in the Book of Acts. This indeed was another confirmation that I was on track with this book. Now I understood why I had been feeling—and telling all of my family and friends for months—that I had just felt that I was to compile precisely 50 miracles for this book.

Yet another miracle, and another very special one, occurred on a day that I was praying to the Lord and asking him to meet my need for a Christian editor—and hopefully one for free—to edit this book. After seeking the Lord early in the morning, by afternoon, God provided a Christian editor for this book—for free.

Now, maybe you are wondering if you can have a miracle, or if miracles are even real, or still for today. Maybe you have picked up this book, wondering these very questions, or perhaps you are just reading this book now, because it was given to you or placed in your path somehow.

Well, I don't believe that you are reading this book by an accident. I believe that God has placed this book in your hands at this very moment in time so that you might absorb the words from these pages, and that these words would resonate with your spirit and these words would take root and grow your faith in God—a good God who has great and mighty plans for you and for your life. God, as you are about to discover, truly is the one, true, miracle-working God of yesterday, today, and tomorrow.

Just put your trust in Him, and open up your heart and your spirit to Him, as you allow the words of these testimonies to speak to you and reach you in your innermost being.

You know, I once too was lost, but now I am found. I once didn't believe, but now I believe.

All things are possible to them who believe. Just believe and have faith. This is what life is all about: coming to know God, putting your trust in Him, and letting His plans and His purposes prevail in your life.

Give Him a chance. Let Him show you who He truly is, let Him speak to your innermost spiritual being, and let Him assure you that yes, He truly is faithful, yes, He can be trusted, and yes, His word is really alive and true.

Before you start reading these pages, take a moment and pray to God to open the eyes to your heart. Believe that the Lord has good plans still for your life, and that He has had these plans yet to unfold in your life from before the foundation of the world was established.

Just believe, trust, and receive, and remember that while God does miracles to show and reveal Himself to be real and omnipresent, seek His face and not His hand.

By the end of the book, He will show you that He is real, and that He is indeed a true rewarder of those who diligently seek Him. This means seeking Him with all of your heart, mind, body, and soul. If you seek with half or three-quarters, you may never find Him.

If you dare to believe with every fiber of your being however, He *will* visit you, and He *will* speak to you. All you have to do is just believe and receive, and remember that *all glory goes to Him and is His alone.*

So turn these pages with joy, seeking with an open heart, and you will find Him. Truly you will. I just know it. I feel it in the spiritual realm. Just turn that page. Your destiny in God is waiting. Turn that page, and just believe—right now.

# PART I

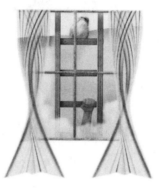

# MIRACLES OF PROVISION AND PROTECTION

*Thank the Lord! Praise His name! Tell the world what He has done. Oh how mighty He is! Sing to the Lord, for He has done wonderful things. Make known His praise around the world!*
(Isaiah 12:4-5 NLT)

# CHAPTER 1

# THE INFERNO THAT COULD HAVE BEEN, BUT GOD

## *Johnnie Pearl McNeil*

*The angel of the Lord encamps around those who fear Him, and He delivers them* (Psalm 34:7).

In the fall of 1964, when I was 10 years old, I lived with my family in a very old-framed two-bedroom house. My family consisted of my siblings, mom, dad, and grandmother. During this time of my young life, I had a very close relationship with God but had never had a personal experience of a miraculous move of God in my life or family. My family was very religious because of the upbringing of my dad and because his Mama lived with us. She instilled a lot of her religious, or should I say spiritual, values in us, along with her traditional lifestyle and practices into our family. After all, Daddy was her youngest, so she felt she still had some control over him and his family, and she did.

My grandmother would get on her knees to pray for about an hour or two every night before she went to bed and every morning before starting her day. I didn't understand why it took so long, but that was her time with God, and we didn't dare interfere. I finally found out why my grandmother stayed on her knees so long. She was praying in order for her to feel that she was not defeated by the devil.

She stayed there until she felt she had gotten through to God, which usually took about an hour or two. Seeing my grandmother praying was very common, and it rubbed off on all of us. In my house, you just didn't hop into bed without getting on your knees to pray first. This included my mom and dad. I felt very secure with God because I knew I had a praying family, especially in my grandmother.

My family was poor but very loving. We were stable and a lot of fun. We had a lot of hard times, but my grandmother was the spiritual backbone of the family.

We had two large bedrooms with two beds in each room to accommodate nine children, Mom, Dad, and a grandmother, so you can imagine we had to do some maneuvering. Our house did not have electric heat, so during the fall and winter, we used a large, wood-burning tin heater in each room. We also had a large, heavy, wood-burning iron stove in the kitchen to cook on.

My mom, dad, and younger siblings slept in the same room; I slept across the hall from my parents in between my oldest sister and my grandmother. Across the room three of my brothers slept in the other bed, two at the top and one at the bottom. Although we only had two rooms, we made do.

Since it was fall, it was starting to get cool enough some nights to have heat. Therefore, my two oldest brothers were responsible for making sure we had heat in our rooms and extra wood in case the fire got low before we went to bed. My brothers were young and never thought to check the floor under the heater to see if the heater was too close to the floor. They just made sure the room was well-heated.

No one ever thought about the fact that we were using a heater in a very old-framed house that was practically dry-rot and was a fiery death trap waiting to happen. The devil knew my dad's and brothers' lack of wisdom about the kind of heater we were using was just the thing needed to burn most, if not all, of us up while we slept.

One night my brothers made the fire as usual, and we all went to sleep, but because the floorboards were very dry, the floor caught fire in the room where my grandmother, my oldest sister, I, and my three brothers were sleeping. As dry as the weather had been and as old and rotten as the wood on the house was, there was nothing to keep that house from becoming an inferno, *but God.*

The next day, when my brothers got ready to clean the ashes from the heater and put in new wood to start another fire, they saw the big hole in the floor. They could actually see the ground and stick their heads through the floor and look under the house. The heat from the heater had burned a hole in the floor large enough for me to fit my small body through. With no one awake to put the fire out and nothing else to stop it from engulfing the house, it was evidence that God blew that fire out. If He had not done it, I do not believe I would be here today to share this with you.

When my mom, grandmother, and other siblings who were old enough to understand found out about the fire, we knew it was the hand and breath of God that had saved us from death. I interpreted this miraculous act of God as Him saying, "Not yet, I'm not ready for them now." When my dad came home from work, we told him about the fire. He was thankful to God for sparing his family. He fixed the floor and positioned the heater on a stand so that would never happen again. I think about this miraculous act of God often because again, there was no reason for this fire to go out, *but God.*

This is one of the miracles in my life.

## ABOUT THE CONTRIBUTOR

Pearl McNeil currently resides in Nashville, Tennessee. Pearl is employed both as a real-estate agent and also as a prayer counselor with a well-known Christian television ministry. She volunteers her time twice each month as a Sunday-school teacher at a girls' correctional facility, and in her spare time, she enjoys spending time with her 10-year-old niece, taking in movies and plays, and reading.

# CHAPTER 2

# RIGHT ON TIME: A TESTIMONY TO GOD'S POWER AND PROVISION

## *Michael Sampson*

*This poor man called, and the Lord heard him; He saved him out of all his troubles* (Psalm 34:6).

I am compelled to write about how God has been taking care of me and my family since I left my previous place of employment. He has done amazing things that only He could do, and it would be very wrong for me to keep silent. Honor should be given where honor is due, and I give honor to Him today.

When I left the firm in February, I was on a very good salary but had no savings due to a number of projects we'd done around the house. And there was a major tax bill due within a couple of weeks. I hoped there would be some new project work via Collaboration Success Advisors, but that didn't materialize.

A friend here in New Zealand asked me where I was at and what I was thinking of doing and then said that if I needed any money for anything, to just call and give a bank account number. I didn't ask for him to say that, but he offered, and I saw that as God's way of getting my tax bill paid. The money wasn't a gift, however, but rather an advance on some work that I would do for him and his business at some point in the future.

As time went on, there were a few projects here and there, but nothing major, and I began to doubt whether I'd done the right thing in leaving the firm, particularly when another major tax bill was sprung upon me that was due April 7. I had been told about it a year earlier but had forgotten about it, and so when it was announced by letter one Saturday morning, I felt very deeply in trouble. When the time came to pay the bill and no major projects were forthcoming, I transferred the money from my Visa card into my checking account and paid for it that way. Obviously, that meant I was paying a fairly high interest rate until the amount was settled, but I decided that it would be OK.

As funny as it might sound, one of the major ways that I found to remember to be faithful in *"the valley of the shadow of death"* (Ps. 23:4) was running. As I ran along the quiet but long back roads of the Canterbury plains, it became a time and place for prayer, for crying out to God for help, for speaking to myself, "I must remain faithful," and "I must keep on going, even when the going is hard." Words cannot express how much running has meant to me this year in keeping me following after the Lord.

As the middle of April came, and I forecast out my bills and income for the next month, it was plain to see that I had run out of money. I had exhausted my overdraft through paying for food and family expenses, and the second tax bill, plus some other bills, had drained my Visa card limit. There was no money left. There were no projects on the horizon that would fix the situation. And at times when there is nothing left and there is no hope, that's often when God decides to come through, for then it is plain that it could only have been God.

God came through in the form of an email that I received very early on April 20. Even that was amazing because I had been saying to myself, "It only takes one email." It was an inquiry about how I could help a major organization with its collaboration strategy. In the days that followed, even though it involved a trip up to the United States, the amount of money, the specific details on the dates, and the flights that I would need to take all fell into place perfectly.

Here's an example: the organization that contacted me originally requested five days of my time in New York, which was fine, but I knew that there was another organization in California that wanted me for a day. We were going to meet in June, but I'd found out that May would be better. With five days in New York, however, unless I was willing to stay over the weekend, it wasn't going to happen. And then the New York organization reduced what they wanted to four days, and from Tuesday to Friday to boot, enabling me to fly into California on a Sunday, spend Monday up in Mountain View with my client there, and then experience a too-short night on the red eye across to New York for four days. Even as I write this, I'm astounded at how only God could work all of that out.

One more example: on the Friday afternoon in New York, at about 2:00 P.M., the lead person from the organization said that we'd finish at about 3:00 P.M., the first time in the four days that we'd finish "early." At 2:11 P.M., I received an email from a law firm asking if I'd be interested in a project as an expert witness, that I'd been recommended by another analyst firm. They knew I lived in New Zealand, and they said they'd be grateful if I could call or email at some time. Now this was 6:00 A.M. on Saturday in New Zealand, so they probably didn't expect an immediate answer. We traded a few emails, and then at 2:30 P.M., I left the building I was in on Madison Avenue, walked down the street 200 meters or so, went up the elevator, and presented myself in the foyer of the law firm. "Here I am, let's talk," I said.

As we sat down to speak, what they wanted in an "expert" aligned precisely with the financial modeling work I'd done at Telecom New Zealand in the mid-1990s, on exactly the same technology, and more. Only God could have arranged that—a law firm I'd never heard of, the background required, the timing on that Friday, and the fact that I was actually there in New York—incredible.

And going forward, there are more projects springing up, new opportunities that look ripe to come to fruition, and I praise God for His faithfulness to me and my family. Kurt, another friend down here who goes to the same church as us, once asked me how I got contracts for my business. "God brings them when I need them," was my honest answer. And I recounted to him the numerous times in my business life that He has brought projects and clients at just the right time. And even before then, God was faithful to provide the financing for my Master of Commerce in the early 1990s via winning an essay competition (which paid for the first year of the degree) and then winning a scholarship that I had no idea I was in the running for, which paid for the second year. Incredible—just incredible. It can only be God.

Here are the words of a song I wrote, inspired by Psalm 78:72:

*Give me an undivided heart, that I may walk in Your path,*
*Give me an undivided heart, and show the way.*
*Give me an undivided heart, that I may fear Your name.*
*Give me an undivided heart.*

*Give me an undivided heart, that I may walk in Your light,*
*Give me an undivided heart, so I won't stray.*
*Give me an undivided heart, that I may fear Your name.*
*Give me an undivided heart.*

*Give me an undivided heart, that I may walk in Your love,*
*Give me an undivided heart, my Lord, I pray.*
*Give me an undivided heart, that I may fear Your name.*
*Give me an undivided heart.*

(If you want the tune, you'll have to Skype me for a rendition.)

He is faithful. He works in ways that I cannot explain so that the glory goes to Him. If you are in trouble, lift your eyes to Him, lift your voice to Him, and cry out for His help.

# ABOUT THE CONTRIBUTOR

Michael Sampson is a Christian husband, father, and businessman in New Zealand. He has been married to his high school sweetheart, Katrina, for 15 years, and together they have 9 children, whom they home school. Michael, Katrina, and family attend the Darfield Baptist Church on the Canterbury Plains of New Zealand.

Michael runs The Michael Sampson Company, a collaboration strategy firm focused on helping organizations improve the performance of distributed teams. Michael is the author of books on collaboration tools and approaches, runs workshops, speaks at conferences, and consults with clients from around the world.

To learn more about Michael's company, please go to his Website, www.michaelsampson.net, or to send him an email, please contact him at: michael@michaelsampson.net.

# CHAPTER 3

# NIGHT OF A MILLION MIRACLES

## Rev. Paul Estabrooks and Open Doors Ministries

*Call unto Me, and I will answer thee, and shew thee great and mighty things, which thou knowest not*
(Jeremiah 33:3 KJV).

*Time* magazine called it, "The largest operation of its kind in the history of China."[1] But for me, June 18, 1981, was simply the most exciting day of my life. I was one of 20 men who delivered one million Chinese Bibles in one night. It was called Project Pearl.

Our 100-foot miracle tugboat, *Michael*, lumbered along at the sleepy speed of three knots. It towed the semi-submersible barge, Gabriella, loaded with 232 tons of Chinese Bibles.

As we headed due west toward the coast of China that afternoon, the sunset was one of the most beautiful I can remember. The sea was proverbially as smooth as glass.

By nine o'clock, we were weaving our way in the dark through a maze of anchored Chinese navy ships. When we arrived at the pre-appointed beach, there were thousands of local Christians waiting in the darkness.

The cardboard boxes of Bibles were waterproofed in 232 one-ton blocks that could float. We towed them with small rubber boats toward the shore. The Chinese believers came out in the water—some up to their necks. We threw them the lines, and they pulled the blocks up onto the beach. They cut them open with shears and handed the boxes of Bibles to one another up the sand to the tree line.

Two hours later, we left with one million Bibles in the care of Chinese believers. They promised to circulate them across the entire country. In some cases, that process took five years.

But what I now remember most is not just that evening of delivery. Those two hours were also the fastest of my life. What I will never forget is the commitment and sacrifice that was behind the whole project, as well as the many miracles God performed to enable us to accomplish it.

Shortly after the request for one million Bibles was received from China, we sent our Chinese colleague, Joseph Lee, to ask many questions of those who made that request.

There were five house church leaders at that meeting in the southern coastal city of Swatow, today known as Shantou. Joseph's first question was, "Do you men know how many a million Bibles are?" He described the weight and space dimensions.

The men responded, "Yes, we know, and we're prepared for them. We have a plan and a place. You just bring them."

Joseph continued, "Do you know what could happen if you are discovered with even a portion of one million Bibles?"

They smiled, and one responded, "Brother Joseph, all five of us have been in prison for many years for our faith in Jesus. And we are willing to die if one million brothers and sisters can have a copy of God's Word."

Joseph reported back to us with tears in his eyes. He whispered, "I couldn't ask them any more questions."

Later, six of us on the project leadership team met in Hong Kong to pray and plan. Those house church leaders who requested the Bibles also promised to pray and fast for 24 hours while we met.

We began with devotions. The one leading turned to Ephesians 1:18-21. He read the passage and said, "If we are ever going to accomplish this project, it will only be in God's power. That power *'which He exerted in Christ when He raised Him from the dead...'* (Eph. 1:20)." The meeting became inspired and continued for two more days as we formulated an exciting plan for a night delivery by tugboats and specially designed barges.

Later we received a message from the Chinese believers. They said, "While we were in an all-night prayer meeting, God gave us a Scripture for you. It is Ephesians 1:20." I thought, *What coincidence.*

A month later, the same six people were meeting for the second time in Manila, Philippines. This time our devotional was from Exodus 14 when the Egyptians were sorry they let the Israelis leave and began to chase them:

> *Then the angel of God who had been travelling in front of Israel's army, withdrew and went behind them. The pillar of cloud also moved from in front and stood behind them, coming between the armies of Egypt and Israel. Throughout the night the cloud brought darkness to the one side and light to the other side; so neither went near the other all night long* (Exodus 14:19-20).

We later named the tugboat and the barge after the only two angels whose names are mentioned in the Scriptures.

Again a message came from China. "While we were in an all-night prayer meeting, God gave us a Scripture for you. Exodus 14:19-20." I promised the Lord to never again call His messages, His timing, or His appointments and plans a "coincidence." In fact, now I actually look for them.

The greatest test of faith was finding the tugboat. God provided us with a talented missionary who was an experienced sea captain. He and I searched everywhere, we thought, for a tugboat that was powerful enough to tow 232 tons, had a high bow for ocean travel, and was able to accommodate a crew of 20 men. We could not find a suitable vessel, and our deadline was fast approaching.

Meanwhile, our leader, Brother David, was on an author's speaking tour in New Zealand. There he met a committed intercessor named Eddie who promised to pray all night, if necessary, asking God for direction to the right vessel. They prayed passionately, and late in the evening, Eddie received a vision.

He excitedly told Brother David, "I saw this sandy shoreline with green trees behind and a tall building with pastel-colored vertical stripes. In front of it on the sand was the tugboat up on jacks."

David, now even more excited than Eddie, queried, "Where is it?"

Eddie countered, "That's the only thing the Lord didn't show me."

The next day Brother David was to return to the Philippines. An airport strike at the Auckland airport caused a delay, so he and his wife were being rerouted via Singapore on Singapore Airlines. This would require an extra night's layover—at the airline's expense.

Brother David was not impressed because he wanted to get back immediately for the project supervision. On the plane, his wife, Julie, casually asked, "Don't you think the Lord is in this change of airlines somehow?"

David suddenly realized that the captain and I had not looked for a tugboat in Singapore, since none were advertised there. Immediately after the plane landed, he and Julie jumped in a cab and shouted, "Take us to the river." It was just an hour before sundown when they raced along the highway across from the water.

As they looked across the river, they saw the sandy shoreline with green trees behind and a tall building with pastel-colored vertical stripes. And there on the sand, propped up on jacks, were not one but two tugboats.

It turned out they were brand new, having been built for an Indonesian company that went bankrupt. The captain declared them perfect for the project.

Brother David and I negotiated with the owners for one. Their final price was a $100,000 deposit (all the money we had in the bank at the time) and $380,000 due in 30 days—the time required to out-fit the vessel. If we did not come up with the balance in 30 days, we would forfeit our deposit. It was a big step of faith but was necessary if we were to meet our schedule for the project anyway.

God laid on the heart of Pastor Chuck Smith from Calvary Chapel, Costa Mesa, California, to call at that time for a project update. He took the need to his church board, and the following week we received a check from that one church for $380,000.

I've written a book to share all the directions God gave us and all the miracles He provided to see this project accomplished (*Night of a Million Miracles: The Inside Story of Project Pearl*, Open Doors International). I can testify it is God alone who should receive all the glory.

Our human frailty and inexperience was highlighted one night en route to China when we almost ran into our own barge with the tugboat.

What about the results? This is the most exciting part of all. Project Pearl Bibles have been seen all across China. One of them was received by a young man who had been praying for a Bible for three years. After reading it through three times in three weeks, he felt God calling him to become one of the itinerant evangelists preaching in China's countryside. Today he pastors a network of house churches that has grown to over 400,000 members. He has since received many Bibles from Open Doors for his churches, but he personally used that Project Pearl Bible for 15 years.

## Wet Bibles

Some of the boxes of Bibles did get wet during the very physical and demanding off-loading procedure. Four hours after leaving the beach that night of delivery, a patrol of Chinese police came by and found some boxes of Bibles stashed under the trees. They had not yet been transferred to the numerous storage areas. The police tried unsuccessfully to burn the Bibles, and then, in frustration, threw them into the water. The next morning, fishermen plucked these floating volumes out of the sea and put them on the roofs of their homes to dry. Later they sold them to Christians in the area.

One well-known Chinese Christian leader acknowledged receiving "wet" Bibles from Project Pearl in his book titled, *The Heavenly Man*. Brother Yun sent a personal message via a friend that stated, "A big 'Thank You' to Brother David and team who risked their lives for Project Pearl. And thank you so much for your great concern and love for the house church in China."

## Perfume Bibles

Peter Xu, the leader of the Born-Again Movement—one of the largest house church networks in China—visited the U.S. office of Open Doors a few years ago. When he saw a sample of a Project Pearl Bible on a shelf, he animatedly shared his Project Pearl experiences.

After the delivery, Bibles were stored in depositories in southern China. Peter Xu sent three men every month by train or bus to the depository contacts to bring back about a thousand Bibles per trip for his growing house church movement. One month, local police discovered the three men with their Bible load. The police threw the thousand Project Pearl Bibles into the cesspool of the public latrine, and the three men were interrogated and jailed for the weekend.

Monday they were released and commanded to return straight home and never return. Instead they waited inside the latrine until darkness fell. Then they climbed down into the filthy cesspool of human waste, carefully retrieving each of the foul-smelling books. They washed them off under the local water tap and carried them home. There they dried them out, sprayed them with perfume, and circulated them through the network. Such was the hunger and importance of every copy of God's Word.

Project Pearl also had an impact on the future printing of Bibles inside China, which continues today. Shortly after the project was completed, China's Three Self Patriotic Movement announced the first official printing of Bibles inside the country. In his book, *Jesus in Beijing*, noted author and China watcher, David Aikman, wrote, "[Project] Pearl had a major long-term impact on the overall availability of Bibles in China."

But far more important are the personal evaluations from Chinese believers: "These gifts were more precious than gold."

A Chinese lady wrote to Brother Andrew thanking him for the first Bible she received (from Project Pearl) in answer to many years of prayer, which strengthened and deepened her faith. She continued:

> But please remember that hundreds of thousands more remain without the Bible. They need to be fed with the Word of God. May the grace of our Lord be with you and your mission so that many more Bibles can be delivered to meet the needs of our brothers and sisters inside China.

As a bottom line, I can say that through it all, God was faithful. It was His plan, His project, and therefore His accomplishment. And how exciting to be on His team. Membership is open to everyone.

## ABOUT THE CONTRIBUTOR

Paul Estabrooks is a veteran foreign missionary with a deep concern for Christians in restricted countries. He has completed 30 years of ministry to persecuted Christians with Open Doors International. He is currently serving as a Minister-at-Large. He was coordinator of Project Pearl, the secretive delivery of one million Chinese Bibles in one night in June 1981. Paul is the author of four books and a large number of booklets. One book is a major training manual used around the world by Open Doors titled *Standing Strong Through the Storm (SSTS)*. He can be contacted at paule@od.org.

An estimated 100 million Christians worldwide suffer interrogation, arrest, and even death for their faith in Christ, with millions more facing discrimination and alienation. Open Doors supports and strengthens believers in the world's most difficult areas through Bible and Christian literature distribution, leadership training and assistance, Christian community development, prayer and presence ministry, and advocacy on behalf of suffering believers. For more information, go to www.OpenDoors.org.

## ENDNOTE

1. "Risky Rendezvous in Swatow," *Time* (October 19, 1981), 109.

# CHAPTER 4

# WALL OF STONE

## *Jack E. Olson*

*Trust in the Lord with all your heart and lean not on your own understanding; in all your ways acknowledge Him, and He will make your paths straight* (Proverbs 3:5-6).

I knew the voice was real. It came booming into my ears, over the top of my dream, and jarred me awake. "When you say I don't love you, you are mistaken."

I turned and looked at my wife. She was sleeping soundly, as if nothing had happened. I placed my hand on her shoulder and gave her a shake.

"Doreen, did you hear that?"

"Huh, hear what?" She turned and peeked at me through mostly shut eyes.

"I just heard a voice. It sounded something like a trumpet blast, only deeper. I was in the middle of a dream and it woke me up. It said, 'When you say I don't love you, you are mistaken.' I think it was God."

I had lost my job two years previously. Our situation continued to worsen. Shortly after hearing the voice, we were down to a few dollars and a half tank of gas. The bank was foreclosing on our home.

With no money, there was nowhere we could move, no way to store furniture. I was 60 years old, and without a degree, no one would hire me. We would lose the home where we'd raised our five children and lived for 27 years. All would be lost: home, furniture, automobile, and personal things.

We prayed often and trusted God to deliver us. But things only got worse. We had seen others rescued miraculously, but not us. People showed up at their doorsteps with money saying, "The Lord told me to give you this." And it would be precisely what they had prayed for. But that never happened to us.

We were sitting together on the step into a garage that I had converted into a family room. We were talking about all these things and decided that we had been abandoned.

"God doesn't love us anymore," Doreen said.

"I guess you're right."

We went to bed dejected, hopeless.

But God did love us. He told us so—vocally.

The next day, a Friday, I went to see about a job at a conveyor company. The marketing director took me to lunch and offered me his job. But when he had finished telling me about the company, it was clear that there was no way I could fit in with their ethics and continue to honor God, my loving Father.

Driving away, I was completely discouraged, sort of in a daze, watching the buildings drift by as I proceeded home to give my wife some more bad news. We were against a wall of stone.

Then I saw a business I recognized. I had been on that street once before many years ago. *I know the man who owns that,* I thought.

The door was open; there were lots of desks in a big office. I walked in and through a doorway into a very dirty production area. There was one old man there. "Is this owned by a man named Ron?" I asked.

"Yeah, Ron Baldwin. Here's his number."

When I got home, I told Doreen the bad news and called Ron. He recognized my name immediately. "I tried to call you a couple of months ago," he said. "If you're not doing anything, why don't you come to my office for about an hour right now, and we'll get acquainted again?"

I got there at about 2:00 P.M. We talked until 6:00, and he decided we should get together. Although we couldn't decide what that should be about, we agreed to agree. Saturday, we talked from 8:00 A.M. until 4:00 P.M. I would return on Monday and check out the market for a line of fishing tackle products he'd accumulated.

Finally, there was some good news for Doreen. In my haste to tell her, it seemed that all the stoplights were against me and stayed red forever. I hope I didn't offend anyone with my wild driving (an old man driving like a kid).

When I saw Ron on Monday, I had to admit that I couldn't afford gas to get back the next day. He gave me $2,000. I got home before noon with literature to study and a lot of library work to do. I love to see my sweetheart smile. "But," she asked, "what do we do about the foreclosure? The bank has sent it to their attorney."

That same Monday, I had an afternoon meeting with a company I had started a couple of years previously with a former employee. There was a fellow there who had helped us write our memorandum. After the meeting, he said he would like to have some of my stock. Tuesday morning, I met him, and he offered me $8,500 for 10,000 shares of my stock.

Sunday night we were nearly penniless, but by Tuesday evening, I had deposited $10,500.

Wednesday morning, these words popped into my mind (sometimes God speaks that way): "Go withdraw six thousand dollars."

"But, Lord, you know those checks couldn't possibly have cleared."

"Do it."

There was some hesitation at the bank, but within an hour, I had the cash.

"Now, get on your good clothes and get to the mortgage bank fast."

No argument that time. As it turned out, I was just in time, almost to the minute, to save myself $1,500 in legal fees.

And the two years of trials were over.

He really does love us, just as He said.

Since then, doors have been opened to us that we couldn't have imagined.

I stand in awe at His timing and orchestration of events. All that time, when I was alone and discouraged, He was leading—preparing me to trust more fully.

Sometimes we feel ashamed of our fears. But God knows. After all, Jesus became a man to experience our trials, hunger, and pains so that He could be our advocate before God. He even calls us brothers. He agonized on the cross to make that possible, to make us good enough to stand confidently before God.

He loves you, too. You are not reading this by accident, anymore than I passed that business by accident, or did any of the other things.

You don't need to be good, either. He understands. All you need is to say, "Thank You, Jesus, for sacrificing Yourself for my punishment. I accept that. Thank You for wanting me to live forever with You. You really do love me. I love You, too."

You just heard the voice of God in your heart.

## ABOUT THE CONTRIBUTOR

Jack E. Olson was formerly an atheist and involved in psychic phenomenon and eastern teachings. It was due to a statement made by an atheist scientist that Jack decided to read the Bible. By the end of the first four books of Moses, Jack realized that God is alive and is exactly who the Bible claims Him to be. It was at this turning point that three things occurred. One, Jack recalls that he wanted to "get on the rooftops and shout to the world, 'Wake up. Jesus is Savior. Eternal life is available.'" Two, Jack's life then started to become a catalog of miracles. Three, he then decided to write down the miracles that he had received, and soon found himself writing for others. That then became a ministry with a name "The Word of Our Testimony," which Mr. Olson still runs today.

To hear more testimonies, or to contact "The Word of Our Testimony," and/or to purchase any of Jack's books, please go to www. olsonhouse.org. There you will find a wealth of information to put you on the path to true healing, deliverance, and success.

# CHAPTER 5

# THE SEVENTY DOLLAR
# TELEVISION STATION MIRACLE

## *The testimony of Pat Robertson, as written by Allison C. Restagno*

*The dictionary defines "miracle" as "a marvelous event manifesting a supernatural act of God." "Faith," according to Hebrews 11:1, "is the evidence of things not seen." And, as James 2:20 (KJV) further states, "Faith without works is dead."*

It is with faith in the Lord Jesus Christ, and through stepping out with that faith, that the miracle of CBN was born. Through prayer and fasting, the Lord had prepared me with a revelation of His plan for this television station: "You must claim the airwaves from the prince of the power of the air, and give them to the Prince of peace." So in 1959, after hearing from the Lord, I proclaimed my faith and set about in deed to what the Lord had instructed me to do.

I rented a 5x7 U-Haul trailer for our meager belongings, and with my family and our few material goods attached to the back of our used DeSoto automobile given to us by my wife's father, we headed out to Virginia to "our promised land."

I had only $70.00 in my pocket at the time, but I also had enough faith that the Lord was going to move and that He would orchestrate our path. In the natural, this $70.00 would never have been enough to live on, much less support a family of five and find more permanent shelter (we only had a temporary place to stay at the time when setting out on this journey), but my focus was faith in a miracle-working God.

Needless to say, I had no capital. For months I had not even been in communication with the owner of the television station which the Lord was prompting me to purchase, but I was operating in a spiritual realm…by faith, not by sight. With a firm and unshakable belief that the Lord was guiding my steps and that the Holy Spirit was instructing me to do so, I wrote to the owner to obtain a purchase price for his station.

The station was indeed for sale for $50,000, and the price of the additional station equipment was $25,000. God, however, had already given me a purchase price. His number was $37,000.

Although I had only that $70.00 in my wallet, the Lord allowed me (by faith and a miraculous move of the Spirit) to negotiate the purchase of that station. God supernaturally opened up the windows of Heaven and poured out what He had in his hands. He had opened a way where there seemed to be no way, and The Christian Broadcasting Network (CBN) was born by faith. Faith in combination with works makes way for God's miraculous power to come alive!

That is the story of how CBN came into being in 1960. CBN was the first Christian television network established in the United States, and today is one of the world's largest television ministries, producing programming seen in 200 nations and heard in 70 languages including Russian, Arabic, Spanish, French, and Chinese. CBN's flagship program, *The 700 Club*, can be seen in 97 percent of television markets across the United States and is one of the longest running religious television shows that reaches an average of one million American viewers daily. All praise be to God!

## ABOUT THE CONTRIBUTOR

Pat Robertson is the founder of CBN, a multi-national Christian media giant that produces television programs such as *The 700 Club, CBN NewsWatch, Christian World News, The 700 Club Interactive*, among other programming. CBN programs are seen by millions of daily viewers from around the globe, and they are bearing much fruit and harvest, in these endtimes. If you would like to know more about CBN, the gift of salvation, and/or contact CBN for any other reason, please go to www.cbn.com. Pat Robertson is also a best-selling author of numerous books and teaching materials, including his *New York Times* best-selling book, *Miracles Can Be Yours Today*, published by Integrity Publishers, 2006.

CHAPTER 6

# A Miraculous Light in the Arabian Desert

## *Ema Paul Boghossian*

*But without faith it is impossible to please Him; for he that
cometh to God must believe that He is, and that He is a
rewarder of them that diligently seek Him*
(Hebrews 11:6 KJV).

Iraq, Baghdad, in February 1991. The war raged after Iraq invaded Kuwait, and soon images of destruction could be seen everywhere in the city. Bombings, killings, and bloodbaths were the sole theme in the media. Warning sirens sounded throughout the day, and the smell of death filled every alley. Thick, dark clouds dominated the city skyline, delivering black rain and fumes from the battlefield.

Life was paralyzed in Baghdad, with its five million residents. There was no electricity and no water, shops were closed, and no civilian vehicles were on the streets. The safest place to be was a shelter core in our house under the stairwells. Sleeping for a few hours without being called to the shelter was sort of a dream for us.

That was the scene when my brother, a freshly graduated doctor, was serving in the Iraqi military during the second Gulf war. He was the only doctor remaining in his unit on the front lines in Kuwait, while most of his mates chose to escape that hell or got killed.

In Baghdad, the whole family was following every bit of news about the war, searching for any person who could get us any piece of information about my brother. Was he alive? Injured? Dead or captured? It seemed that news was more important than our own survival dilemma at that time.

Media reports showed how the Iraqi military was being hard hit and brutally destroyed, not only on the battlefields but also in every city and on each road they could be found on, whether in Kuwait or in Iraq. Weeks passed, and we had no clue of my brother's whereabouts.

In the midst of this entire dilemma, I was not taken by all that devastation. I was a newly born-again Christian, so I decided not to listen anymore to what the media had to offer but turn instead to the Lord and seek His help. Those very first sermons at the church were echoing in my ears, as this was my first genuine experience and direct encounter with God. But like a small, innocent child, I believed in all I had heard in the past about God and that He could do anything, including bringing my brother safely to Baghdad. He is the God of living miracles and is still very much in business.

So, I started praying and interceding for my brother continuously, and within a few days, the Lord reminded me of how Jericho's walls fell down and God delivered His people after seven days of fasting and praying. He encouraged me to put His words on the line, saying, "This was not only for Jericho but can also be for you." I trusted His words and took a step in faith to pull up myself and ask my family to pray and fast for seven days for my brother to return home. We read this Bible story over and over, and there was a noticeable disbelief in the air, questioning if fasting and praying for seven days would really bring back our brother. It sounded foolish and naïve.

But it seemed that we did not have any other option to choose from. Hence we decided to fast and pray for seven days and wait for the Lord. This was a great challenge to my family. It was not easy at all for us simply to believe that a Bible story and mimicking some words written a few thousand years ago would save our brother.

But the Lord was continuously whispering in my ears, saying, "Your brother will come back safe, trust me."

We started fasting and praying, but the news was so disappointing. We could turn the television on for two or three hours a day when the generator was working. All we could see were coalition forces pounding the Iraqi military. It looked like a living hell. Many were discouraged, and some gave up on God, but a few, me included, were walking the opposite direction. Our faith was growing. And we trusted our God to bring my brother home safe and sound. It was His promise.

Days passed so slowly; each hour felt like a year. We continued fasting and praying. When the seventh day arrived, I have to be honest—I was very nervous about what would happen. Every single member of my family was waiting and questioning, "What will Ema's God do? Will he really come back home?"

That day was the longest of my entire life. The clock hands in the family room were not moving at their normal pace on that day. My worry and concern were increasing, but so was my faith. I knew that the Lord had a good purpose and plan, even if my brother did not show up that day. But I kept hanging on that tiny string of hope and reminding myself of God's promise.

The atmosphere was heating up, and tension and frustration were obvious on everyone's face. I felt like they were accusing me. "Where is your God? The day is almost over." At that moment, I never thought of myself or how embarrassing the situation would be for me. I never thought of my credibility. All I was thinking of was the Lord, His reputation, and His credibility. What would my family say about Him?

Immediately, I went up to my bedroom and stared through the little window to the sky, saying, "Lord, I know You can do it. I know You promised me, and You keep your promises. It was Your voice I heard and not mine. It is not for my pride, neither for my brother, although You know how much I love him, but it is for Your name's sake, Your glory. All I want is my family to see what You can do with their own eyes. Let it be a testimony of how great You are. Let Your name be glorified. Please, Lord, witness for Yourself. Do it, oh Lord."

Before long, there was somebody gently knocking on the main entrance door, and within a few seconds, I heard them all screaming, "He is here." My brother came back home. I wanted to see him, but I decided to stay in my bedroom for few more minutes to thank the Lord for this miracle. No words at this point could describe my feelings, nor express my gratitude to the Lord.

All I could see in the family room when I went down was a weak, skinny, and half-dead body of someone who looked like my brother. It took us some time to believe this man was really my brother. But it was not a dream; it was real, and he was alive.

Everyone spontaneously started moving in every direction to do something for him; he was so weak that he could barely hold a cup of water. My mother helped him change his filthy uniform and then to take a bath. He rested for the day while I was leading my family in lifting thankful prayers to let the Lord know how grateful we were for this miracle. We all decided to fast and pray for another seven days just to thank the Lord for saving my brother and bringing him back safe and sound from the valley of death.

The next day my brother was able to tell us how he came back home, walking from Kuwait to Baghdad. Countless miracles took place during his journey; his shelter one day was targeted, and everyone around him was either dead or severely injured, but he was not scratched. On his way back, there was a little shining light that looked like a star guiding him through the Arabian deserts, and soon enough multitudes of soldiers were following him and saying, "We know that your God will save you, so we decided to follow your footsteps."

The coalition air forces at that time were pounding the Iraqi military personnel even when they were pulling back after they surrendered; the target clearly was not to destroy the Iraqi army only, but also to kill as many soldiers as possible. My brother told us stories of how he and his followers were walking among the mines, dead bodies, and bloody streets with no water and food supplies, fearing they might perish before anyone could find them. But always, day and night, that little shining star was there giving them hope and leading them to safety.

This is a story that changed our lives forever, and since that day I've decided to look for the shining star in every situation in my life. We've been through so many challenging times and trials, but in every single situation, my heart was drawn to God, my eyes were searching for the shining star, and my faith was growing in His promise, believing that *"all things work for the good for those who love Him"* (Rom. 8:28). I know that God will *"never leave nor forsake"* His children (see Heb. 13:5).

Psalm 23 is now engraved in my heart, and since that day, I have never ceased worshiping and praising this mighty, omnipotent, and omnipresent Lord. His little shining star was and still is leading my path. His Holy Spirit is my strength, counsel, and guidance in every step in my life.

I encourage every person reading this story not to give up on God. You might be going through tough times, a hopeless situation in your eyes, physically, emotionally, financially, or otherwise, but *faith* is the key to overcome all that, and here are some practical steps to win your *battle*:

- Believe that God knows all you are going through.

- Allow Him to help and guide you through His Spirit.

- Trust that He is in control.

- Turn to God in every situation in your life.

- Listen and follow God's words carefully.

- Earn the victorious life God has promised you.

## (Believe—Allow—Trust—Turn—Listen—Earn)

The words in Hebrews 11:6 are absolutely true: *"And without faith it is impossible to please God, because anyone who comes to Him must believe that He exists and that He rewards those who earnestly seek Him."* What else can any believer seek more than pleasing God?

Hebrews 11:1 says, *"Faith is being sure of what we hope for and certain of what we do not see."* If God said it, then He knows it, and He means it. If God said it, then believe it and follow it.

Arthur Ashe is said to have remarked, "Happiness keeps you sweet, trials keep you strong, sorrow keeps you human, failure keeps you humble, and success keeps you glowing, but only faith and attitude keep you going."

## ABOUT THE CONTRIBUTOR

Ema Paul Boghossian, originally from Armenia, immigrated with her family to Canada from Dubai in 2006. Before coming to Canada, Ema was employed in Dubai both as an elementary school coordinator and also as a piano and ballet instructor. Since coming to Canada with her husband and their three children, she has been actively engaged in volunteering both her talents and skills at her home church of Bethel Gospel Tabernacle, a large Pentecostal Assemblies of Canada affiliated church, located in Hamilton, Ontario, Canada.

## CHAPTER 7

# SHIELDED BY GOD'S GRACE

## *Blair Bartlett*

*Every word of God is pure: He is a shield unto them that put their trust in Him* (Proverbs 30:5 KJV).

Do you believe in miracles? We do. My wife and I have been Christians since early childhood. Throughout the years, we have been truly amazed in God's faithfulness toward us and how He has kept His loving, protective hands upon us.

Over and over, He has manifested himself in various ways, which confirms to us that there is indeed a loving and benevolent God who watches over those who serve Him. Psalm 139:13-16 eloquently states:

> *For You created my inmost being; You knit me together in my mother's womb. I praise You because I am fearfully and wonderfully made; Your works are wonderful, I know that full well. My frame was not hidden from You when I was made in the secret place. When I was woven together in the depths of the earth, Your eyes saw my unformed body. All the days ordained for me were written in Your book before one of them came to be.*

On December 15, 2004, my wife and I were in a horrific motor vehicle accident, and by all accounts, we should have been seriously injured, if not killed. Instead, by the grace and mercy of God, we miraculously escaped from our demolished 1995 Windstar minivan with no broken bones, no internal injuries, and no cuts that needed stitches. Surely the Lord had his hand upon us.

The night before the accident, I worked a 12-hour shift at my place of employment and knocked off work the morning of the 15th. After I had a nap, we departed for a day of Christmas shopping up in Moncton, New Brunswick. (We had been planning to go up there in previous weeks and take my parents along, but the weather wasn't the best, so we stayed put. We finally left on the 15th, but for some reason I did not feel like inviting my parents along, so we went by ourselves.)

I was still tired and sleepy, so my wife did the driving while I slept in the front passenger seat. We were traveling along a four-lane divided highway at approximately 110 kilometers (about 68 miles) per hour when my wife became drowsy because of the heat. She closed her eyes for an instant, and we drifted over to the left-hand shoulder. My wife came to when she heard the sound of gravel and also the sound of the van hitting a metal highway marker.

She tried to get the van under control but veered to the right, crossed both lanes, went down an incline, and according to paramedic Keith Jarvis, rolled the van at least once or twice and hit a rock wall head on. The distance between the damaged highway marker and where we ended up at was approximately 70 paces or so. Another 10 seconds farther down on the road we could have gone off a bridge and fallen into a steep ravine.

Damage to the van was substantial. The windshield was shattered, the rear window was smashed out, four side windows were smashed out, three out of four tires blew, both air bags deployed, and the van's frame twisted and dented beyond repair.

When all mayhem was breaking loose all around us, I can truthfully say before God that I did not see any damage being done nor did I hear any damage being done. I also did not feel any kind of impact whatsoever when we crashed into the rock wall. To me it was as if we just pulled over and parked.

The only thing that I remember about it is my wife calling my name, opening my eyes, and seeing that we were heading precariously close toward a rock face that seemed to be almost right on top of us. I remember thinking that we were going to be killed, yet I had complete peace of mind about it. I always believed that our lives can be snuffed out without warning, so I always made it a point to be sure that I was right with the Lord.

The next thing that I remember is realizing that we were stopped. I turned to my wife and asked her if she was OK and tried to reassure her. She had blood on her face, and I asked her where the cell phone was. (We had purchased the cell phone several weeks before that in case of an emergency.) She replied that it was in her purse, and I retrieved it.

At that time, I spotted a gentleman walking toward us, and when he reached the van, I handed him our cell phone and asked him to call 911. When he was calling, I started to move around a little bit to see if there was anything broken. I had a drop of blood on the front of my nose, a few little specks on my hands where the glass sprayed, and a little bit of discomfort below in my lower back on the left side, but other than that I felt OK.

Being truly amazed that we survived this harrowing ordeal, I got out and took several photographs of the wreckage. The bystanders were starting to get concerned about me walking around, so I sat back down in the van, and one of them covered me with a blanket in case of shock. They were also looking after my wife. In hardly any time at all the Mounties, the fire department, and the paramedics arrived.

I informed one of the paramedics that I had already been walking around, but he advised me to be on the safe side, I should have a cervical collar on and be strapped securely on a spine board. Not wanting to take any chances in case complications set in, I concurred, and they did the same with my wife. We were transported in separate ambulances to the Sussex health center, which was only around 10 kilometers away. While there, they examined us, took blood pressures, took X-rays, and administered tetanus shots because of the broken glass. The X-rays came back negative for any broken bones. They kept us for observation for a few hours and then discharged us with a clean bill of health. However, they did prescribe an ointment for the bruise on my wife's cheek.

Victims have been in lesser accidents and fared much worse, even to the point of losing their lives. Since our mishap, there have been six people killed in four separate accidents in our area. The latest was a schoolteacher driving home from a March Break trip. According to newspaper reports, the accident was possibly caused by driver's fatigue, and it happened just a few minutes from where we had our accident. More chillingly, it happened at the same time of morning (around 10:30), under the same road conditions.

A friend of ours who is a deputy sheriff down in Maine told us that anytime he responded to an accident that involved a van rolling over, it was "bad." Occasionally they would find a "breather" (someone still living), but not always. Another individual who was a registered nurse and paramedic, also believed that we were "divinely protected" that day. This is not the only time that the Lord has protected us on the highway. Less than two years ago, we were heading to Hampton Bible Camp to volunteer our services for a week. My wife was driving, and I had a strong inclination to advise her to reduce her speed in case a deer ran across the road in front of us. I let her know what I was thinking, and she slowed down. No more than five minutes later, a deer ran across the road only a few feet away from us. That was the first time in all these years driving along that particular stretch of highway that we ever saw a deer.

Coincidence? You decide.

As Christians, we do not understand why things happen, but at the same time we should remember Romans 8:28, *"And we know that God causes all things to work together for good to those who love God, to those who are called according to His purpose."* We believe that the Lord spared us to be a witness to Him and to bring Him the glory that

He deserves. If our testimony encourages just one person, it will be worth it all.

## About the Contributor

Blair and Beth Bartlett reside in Saint John, New Brunswick, Canada, where Blair is currently employed as a heavy equipment operator at Irving Pulp & Paper. They are the proud parents of four children: Ben, age 24, Nathaniel, 21, Rebecca, 20, and Zechariah, 18.

The Bartlett family attends Forest Hills Baptist Church, where Beth is actively engaged in deaf ministry as an interpreter. Both Blair and Beth volunteer at Hampton Bible Camp in the summers, faithfully serving as kitchen staff. Beth and Blair are looking forward to celebrating their 25th year wedding anniversary this year.

# CHAPTER 8

# ALONG LIFE'S ROAD WITH GOD

## *Doug Fyckes*

*The Lord will watch over your coming and going both now and forevermore* (Psalm 121:8).

## Traveling Mercies and Protection

Over many years, my walk with God has matured slowly, bit by bit. I have witnessed many miracles. Why me? I'm certainly in no way perfect or close to it. Jesus was the only perfect man on this earth. Because of Him, I, as well as countless people over generations, have seen God work in our lives. Why? The answer is: all we have to do is ask. The following four short stories are only a few of the many miracles that I and my family have experienced. These stories all have one common theme: God's protection.

Praise the Lord.

Sound like a worn-out phrase? We need to think again before taking this statement for granted. God does inhabit praise. If we want God's closeness, love, protection, and provision, then we need to praise Him and draw Him close regularly and give Him our time in thought, prayer, and deeds.

# One Foggy Night

From 1975 to 1980, my wife and I lived in London, Ontario. My employer's Canadian Head Office was located in Markham, Ontario. However, my job took me through most of southwestern Ontario.

On a winter evening, during the late 1970s, I was driving from London to Markham to attend a sales meeting scheduled for the following morning. I was traveling at about 100 km per hour, just enjoying the peaceful highway drive without the noise and traffic congestion of the city. The night was fairly clear, except for a few light fog patches.

A sign on the 401 highway let me know that I was approaching the exit for Mississauga Road. At that same time, I saw a fog patch in the distance ahead. Usually once one enters a fog patch, visibility becomes more difficult and patchy, but generally fairly easy to pass through. However, this time, I felt something tell me to slow down. I kept feeling that constant nudge to drop my speed, and not by just a bit. I knew that I had to decrease my speed drastically. This was one of the thickest fog patches I've ever seen on a road. It looked like a big, thick, white cloud.

I heeded the inner warning to slow down and hit the brakes, and my speed dropped to about 30 km/hr. As soon as I entered the fog, I saw a person lying on the road. An ambulance and several police cars were also present. My heart started pounding from the shock of this sudden appearance. Because I had slowed down, I was able to change lanes and pass by the accident, avoiding devastating results. Had I not slowed down, I would have run over the person on the road and possibly even hit a police officer or paramedic. They were in the exact lane that I had been in when I was approaching the fog. There would have been absolutely no way that I could have avoided hitting them or going out of control in an attempt to avoid the collision.

I realized that this was the Holy Spirit speaking to me telling me to slow down quickly. God protected the people on the road as well as me. When we feel something nudging us, we need to listen. This is one way that God speaks to us.

When Jesus told His disciples that He would be going to Heaven to be with His Father, He also said that He would be leaving the Holy Spirit with them until His return. He said, *"And I will pray the Father, and He shall give you another Comforter, that He may abide with you forever"* (John 14:16 KJV). The Holy Spirit, the Comforter, protects us, comforts us, and speaks to us, through that "still small voice" as He guides us through life. We need to be sensitive to His leading and allow Him entrance into our lives by walking with Him daily through prayer and deeds.

## Spinout

At the end of a very busy winter's day in 1990, I looked out the window of my office in Scarborough to see how the weather was for the drive home. Snow was beginning to come down very steadily. It had been snowing lightly all day, but the snowflakes were getting larger and heavier by the minute. Knowing what the traffic situation would probably become within a short while, I decided it would be safer to leave for home as soon as possible.

I got into my Taurus station wagon and headed westward along the 401 highway to Burlington, Ontario. By the time I reached the 427 highway, night was beginning to set in. As I came down the ramp onto the 427, I could see that this highway had not been plowed as well as the 401. I remembered being told that station wagons have a tendency to fishtail more easily than cars, so since this was my first station wagon, I decided to reduce my speed. Most of the other vehicles were traveling at 80 km/hr on this 100 km/hr highway. I moved to the slow lane and traveled at 50 km/hr. The ruts in the road were now about eight inches deep, and some near the exits appeared even deeper, made by the heavy trucks coming on and off the 427 highway.

Suddenly, without warning, my wheels got caught in cross-over ruts, and the back end of the station wagon began to spin out uncontrollably. The 427 was very heavily traveled. Cars filled all of the lanes. My chances of hitting another car or being hit were extremely high. I did everything I could to correct the steering, but the station wagon just kept spinning around, around, and around. All I could see were headlights, the guardrail, rear lights, more headlights, the guardrail, and again more rear lights. This went on as the car spun around three and a half times, each time changing lanes from the slow lane toward the fast lane. I could see the guardrail getting closer upon each revolution and was sure that on the last turn the car was going to hit it.

As this was happening, I called out to Jesus and asked Him to help me and to save me from hitting any other vehicle or the guardrail. Miraculously, my car moved away from the guardrail and came to a stop in the middle of the highway, facing backward, with four sets of headlights, stopped, side by side in a row facing me. I had missed the guardrail and hit no other vehicle.

No one can convince me that the Lord doesn't answer prayers. The car was sliding quickly into the fast lanes, where the snow had been well packed down because of the heavy traffic passing over it. At the speed I was approaching the guardrail, with each turn, under normal conditions, I should have hit it hard. Praise the Lord for being with me and answering my prayer.

*Draw near to God and He will draw near to you* (James 4:8).

## Unending Air Supply

It was another one of those rushed days. I prepared for an important meeting in Toronto. Everything had to be ready and perfect. I left myself enough time to prevent being late. In fact, I even allowed extra time, knowing that it was impossible to predict how long it would take to get to Toronto. Just one stalled car or accident could add substantial time to the trip.

It was 1994, and the day was perfect, bright, and sunny. The roads were dry. My Dodge was all shined up. I was happy, because I was driving my five-speed manual transmission and was sitting in a comfortable bucket seat. Wow, what a way to go.

I left Burlington, Ontario, just after lunch and was on the Queen Elizabeth Way, heading for Toronto, within a few minutes. For the first 20 minutes or so, everything was peaceful and uneventful. Then, without warning, the car began to shake and shudder. I could hear a constant and loud thud, thud, thud. I knew I had a tire that was losing air quickly.

I had to get to my appointment on time. Why did this have to happen now? Any other day would have been better. In 1994, I had no cell phone and couldn't call ahead to say that I would be late. Couldn't this have happened on the way home?

Time was running out for this tire by the second. I had to do something immediately. Without any hesitation, I called upon Jesus and asked for help. I prayed, "Lord, please help me with this tire and keep it filled with air. I'll look at it when I reach my destination, but please get me there."

The thud, thud, thud stopped as quickly as it had begun. The shaking of the car stopped right after. Within about five seconds, everything returned to normal. I thanked Jesus for His help and just continued driving to Toronto without stopping to check the tire.

I arrived at my destination on time, attended the meeting, returned to the car focused on what had transpired at the meeting, and completely forgot to look at the tire. I started the car, pulled out of the parking spot, and drove all the way home without any car trouble at all.

When I arrived home, I parked the car, went into the house, had supper, spent time with my wife and children, completed some paperwork in my office, and went to bed, without thinking about or even remembering the tire problem.

The next morning when I left for work, I noticed that I had a flat tire, the same one I suspected had given me problems the day before on the highway. Yes, it was the right front tire. I took off the wheel and replaced it with the spare. I then had a good look at the tire. It literally had a slit in the sidewall that was about three and one half inches long. The tire looked as if it had been slit with a knife. The cut was all the way through the tire. Not only would this tire not be roadworthy, but with the condition it was in, it would be impossible to hold any air even for a fraction of a second. The tire was finished. How could I have driven on this tire? How did I ever get home safely? How did it hold air?

Jesus had the answer. We need to trust Him and call upon Him for everything. Praise God from whom all blessings flow.

*For with God nothing will be impossible* (Luke 1:37 NKJV).

## Deciding to Take a Different Way Home, Really?

Wow, was it ever cold. It was a January evening during 1996. The temperature had dropped to –23ºC. I didn't really want to go out to see any client in that bone-chilling temperature. My 1992 Dodge Caravan was a great vehicle and proved to be very reliable. It was comfortable and produced lots of heat, even in those cold temperatures. Getting to and from the van and waiting for it to heat up and clear the frost from the windows was not exactly what I had in mind as having a good time.

Unfortunately, I had to leave after supper. Once the van was warmed up, it didn't seem to be such a big deal anymore. However, I always had, and still do have, concerns about car breakdowns on extremely cold or hot days. I left my home in Burlington, Ontario, and headed straight to Toronto for an appointment. Except for the frigid temperature, the evening was very clear. The Queen Elizabeth Way was moving at a good pace. Maybe it was because there were very few of us foolhardy people on the roads. I transferred onto the 403 highway. Again the roads were exceptionally clear. Very few cars were passing in comparison to an average evening.

Just as I was approaching the exit for Erin Mills, the van began to sputter. I knew that the engine was starved of fuel. Could this be a fuel pump problem? I had enough gas, or at least that is what the fuel gauge indicated. My vehicle was dying quickly. What should I do? I was in the center lane. Thankfully, there weren't too many other cars on the road, so I was able to cut across into the right lane quickly. By now I was very close to the exit ramp. I sent up a prayer: "Lord, please help me to get off this highway and to still have enough momentum to keep going far enough to get onto the exit ramp."

I reached the ramp and had enough speed left to get about one quarter of the way up the ramp before I had to pull onto the shoulder of the ramp. There the van died. There was no way I could get it started. I was very concerned, knowing that I was inadequately dressed for a long walk in –23°C. I decided that the best decision would be to stay with the van and hope that I would be able to flag someone down to help. Every car on the highway passed by my exit.

I sat there and prayed: "Lord, please let someone stop on this ramp and take me to a garage or at least to a phone so I can get help." I didn't have a cell phone at this point. I would have to guess that no more than two to three minutes passed by, and then a tow truck came up the ramp and stopped to help. What a relief. When I told the driver what appeared to be the problem, he asked me if I used gas line antifreeze at my last fill up. I hadn't put any in. He took me to the nearest gas station, where I purchased it. Upon my return, I put two bottles in the tank. After waiting about ten minutes, I tried to start the van. After a few tries, the engine started, and I had no problems from that point on. I now carry the gas line antifreeze in my vehicle at all times.

The tow truck driver not only took me to a gas station, but he also went out of his way to bring me back to my van and then waited with me until the van started. Not too many people would literally go that extra mile. Some people would say that encountering the tow truck driver was quite a coincidence. I know it wasn't a coincidence because of what the driver told me next when I thanked him for all he had done. He said that he had just finished work and was on his way home. He pointed out that this was not his usual choice of route. He said that, for some reason, at the last moment he decided to take a different way home that evening, which meant taking the Erin Mills exit off the 403 highway. I knew then that his decision to change his route was under the direct influence of the Holy Spirit. The timing of his decision would have been at the time I prayed and asked the Lord for help.

Jesus said, *"And whatever you ask in My name, that I will do, that the Father may be glorified in the Son"* (John 14:13 KJV). God does hear our prayers. Imagine the possibilities of what could happen if we gave God more of our time, more of our thought, and more of our money and had regular fellowship with Him in prayer. We would see His hand at work in our lives every moment of the day.

My prayer is that these writings will be a blessing to you, encourage you, and bring you into a closer relationship with our Heavenly Father, His Son, and the Holy Spirit.

## ABOUT THE CONTRIBUTOR

Doug Fyckes resides in Burlington, Ontario. He is married and has three daughters, as well as one grandson. He has been working in financial planning with a major investment firm for the past 17 years. Doug has a great love for music. He has been a church organist, music teacher, and a performer on the accordion, piano, and organ. He currently attends Bethel Gospel Tabernacle, a Pentecostal church in Hamilton.

# CHAPTER 9

# GOD'S SUPERNATURAL PROVISION

## *Evangelist Glennis Alleyne*

*But my God shall supply all your need according to His riches in glory by Christ Jesus* (Philippians 4:19 KJV).

Let me introduce myself to you, the reader. My name is Evangelist Glennis Alleyne. God called me to ministry in 1994 after giving my life to Him in 1985. But like Jonah, instead of obeying, I ran, and what a run it has been. When you realize that God's hand is upon you and He has chosen you to do a work for Him, you will have no rest or enjoy any other thing in life until you do what the Master called you to do.

I must say the road to my calling has not been an easy one. Every day you are faced with one thing or another, but the greatest joy is in knowing that God is riding along with you on this wonderful and beautiful journey to cause you to be victorious. I am presently embarking on my women's ministry, which will start in spring of this year. God has given me a heart of compassion to reach out to women, and I know by His grace it will be a ministry that is going to make a difference in women's lives.

First I would like to give thanks to Almighty God, my beloved Heavenly Father and Master of my life, for without Him I am nothing. It is because of His great love, mercy, and grace toward me that I can write this beautiful testimony about His supernatural provision. I want others to know that no matter what situation or circumstance we face in life, God will always come through for us as long as we put our trust in Him and take Him at His Word.

I woke up this morning and was lying in bed, thanking God for favoring me with life to see another day and meditating on His goodness and mercies toward me. The phone rang, and it was one of my former co-workers, calling to tell me that our vacation pay did not come through. I was a bit upset, because I was depending on this money for the weekend to purchase some things that I needed as well as to buy something to eat. Since I had no other means of getting money, I arose from bed after chatting with her and went to God in prayer. While on my knees, I meditated on His goodness and promises to me and kept believing that He would provide for me and left it at that. After praying, I got up and went to take my shower and prepare for work.

As I was walking to the bus stop, the enemy came up with lies about what I should do and say when I got to work. I just ignored him and kept repeating God's promises and faithfulness to me. What a struggle it was to really keep trusting God to provide. The Holy Spirit then reminded me of what God had done for me in the past, and it stirred my spirit up more. I became like a warrior waiting to destroy the enemy when he came again with his lies.

When the bus came and I boarded, I was still thinking about the money and how I would get something to eat. I thought about borrowing some money from one of my co-workers, but I said, "No, I will not do that. If it means fasting for today, I will do it, but I know that the God I serve will provide for me. How He is going to do it is His business, not mine." After I got off the bus and while walking to my workplace, the enemy showed up again with his lies. I just ignored him and started to sing to the Lord and felt really happy. Of course, it wasn't easy, but I had to do it with every fiber in me so as not to cave in to the onslaught of the enemy and his lies. I got to my workplace, and when I went into the lunchroom, there on the table was a spread of so much food to eat: pizzas, chocolate cake, bread, you name it. I nearly dropped in shock. One of my co-workers had decided to treat us all to breakfast, and there was so much food to choose from. Because I had nothing to eat and wanted a coffee, I decided to just have some orange juice and a piece of muffin.

I started work, and while I was at my cash register, a customer who I had checked out the previous week came with her husband to pay for items they had purchased. It was a large purchase, so while I was busy wrapping her dishes, she asked if I would like a coffee. I said yes. I couldn't believe it. She went to get it for me while I finished wrapping her purchase. Wow, God sure did answer my prayer, even down to me having the coffee I had desired to have. When it was time to go on my break, I went and feasted on the coffee the customer had bought for me and the other food that was provided for me by God.

What a meal it was. While I ate, I thanked and praised Him for His awesomeness and provision for me. Trust me, that meal is one that I will never forget until He returns. Every bite I took had a very delicious and unique taste because it was provided for me from my Heavenly Father. Does He ever know how to prepare tasty dishes! Give Him praise.

The entire day I spent rejoicing and giving God thanks and praise for the way He provided for me. It made me realize that God is the only one who makes provision for His children. All we have to do is go to Him and put our requests in for what we need. Even though He knows our needs, we must still let Him know. Yes, He provides for the sparrow. What about us, His own creation in His image and likeness? What wouldn't He do for us, His children, as long as we cry out to Him? On that day, He showed me that He is the great provider. I know that there is nothing that I am in need of that will not be given to me as long as it lines up with His word. To God be the glory. Great things He has done and is doing.

## ABOUT THE CONTRIBUTOR

Glennis Alleyne currently resides in Woodbridge, Ontario, Canada, with her family. She is currently employed in retail and also has been ordained as a minister of the gospel. She has a tremendous heart for reaching out to aid women and children especially, and as such has future plans of one day establishing both a women's ministry as well as a children's home in Africa.

# CHAPTER 10

# TRUSTING DAY BY DAY

## *Rev. Homer Cantelon and Mrs. Shirley Cantelon*

*Let your conversion be without covetousness; and be content
with such things as ye have: for He hath said, I will never
leave thee, nor forsake thee* (Hebrews 13:5 KJV).

A Scripture that changed our lives was made very real to us when
we were pastors of a small church in Alberta, Canada.

Financial times were hard for all the world following the Second
World War, and many of the rural churches would not have had a
pastor had not some men who felt the call of God stepped in, in spite
of small or no salaries these churches provided. Such was our case.

My wife and I had a struggle making ends meet feeding a family,
and operating a car for visitation. We had to pray for God's provision
daily. That is when the following Scripture we read in our Family
Bible reading gripped us.

Proverbs 30 verses 7 and 8 (KJV) read:

*Two things have I required of Thee; deny them not before I die,
Remove far from me vanity and lies. Give me neither poverty*

*nor riches but feed me with food convenient for me lest I be full and deny Thee and say "who is the Lord?" or lest I be poor and steal and take the name of the Lord in vain.*

From that day on, the Lord provided for our needs but did not prosper us with worldly goods. We had enough.

We were reminded of those verses many, many times. We were on our way to a farm house, a distance away, to perform a house wedding. On the way my wife said, "My I wish we had some chicken. I crave some meat today."

When we returned to the parsonage, there on the table sat two plump chickens, all cleansed and ready for the oven.

When our car needed a repair and we had no money, someone came up our driveway and in an envelope was the exact amount the new parts cost.

When we were on our way to another small church for an afternoon service, a storm was so bad we could not see in front of us, but we drove on until suddenly the car stopped. I got out to see what I could do and there right in front of me, was a stalled car, which I would have ploughed into had I gone on.

One morning after we prayed for our children, we included a request that God would provide our food for the day. Our son answered a rap at the door, and there was a lady with several bags of groceries. Our son took one of the bags but when he reached for the other, the lady was gone. We tried to find out who it was but my son said it was not anyone from our church. He thought it was an angel. He verifies that to this day.

All these experiences and some not mentioned only strengthened my faith in the fact God cares about His children. Even the smallest things in our lives are important to Him. The Word tell us to cast all our care upon Him because He cares for you.

## ABOUT THE CONTRIBUTORS

Rev. Homer Cantelon and his wife Shirley Cantelon, pastored for over sixty years and have been in retirement for ten years.

Rev. Cantelon is Pastor Emeritus at Bethel Gospel Tabernacle in Hamilton, Ontario, Canada, and they reside in Stoney Creek, Ontario.

Rev. Cantelon and his wife Shirley have three children, two of whom are in ministry. They also have been blessed with seven grand-children, and thirteen great-grandchildren, of whom four are also serving in ministry.

CHAPTER 11

# AMID PERILS OFTEN

## *Rev. Stanley Hoffman*

*Because thou hast made the LORD, which is my refuge, even the most High, thy habitation; There shall no evil befall thee, neither shall any plague come nigh they dwelling. For He shall give His angels charge over thee, to keep thee in all thy ways*
(Psalm 91:9-11 KJV).

While serving as missionaries in Uganda during the years 1983 to 1989, Marion and I found ourselves amid perils often where God protected us as He did the apostle Paul in the first century. A civil war was raging during those years that eventually claimed a million lives. Screams that we heard at night meant someone was being robbed and killed if they resisted. No one dared travel or walk after dark. Roadblocks were manned by ruthless soldiers or rebels. We would approach them with fear and trembling, not knowing what they would demand. Once we were commandeered into the bush where only with the help of the Lord did we survive the ordeal when others in similar circumstances did not. During one of the coups, shots were fired at us as we stood on our patio in front of the house. Bullets whistled by us, hitting the floor and a flowerpot near us. The city of Kampala became quite lawless, in a scale second only to Beirut.

Dogs added to the nightly ruckus of Kampala. They would commence as soon as it was dark and carry on until well after midnight.

They would bark, howl, whine, growl, yelp, and yap continuously for hours on end. Besides gunfire and barking dogs, there was also the music blaring forth from local pubs. Every weekend it was enough to keep us awake all night. It also provided good cover for thieves, who would strike more often when the disco music was booming into the night skies from giant speakers.

Whenever we heard gunshots nearby, a question would come to our minds, "Will we be attacked as well?" I'd assure Marion that God would protect us. But she wanted God to give her that assurance. On one particular night, she prayed and asked God for a sign of His protection over us and our possessions.

That very night, just after midnight, the watchman saw animals enter our compound. (When he described them to me later, they fit those of horses, which he had never seen before.) They each carried a rider. Several stayed at the gate, while the rest proceeded on up toward the house. As they drew near to where he was sitting, he rose up to stop them. They vanished. He sat back down, and the horsemen reappeared, only this time they were stacked two deep. He arose and was about to call me when they disappeared again.

When daylight came, he asked for an interpretation of what he had seen. I told him he'd had a vision. God had revealed to him that guardian angels were encamped about us. There were more than enough to protect us. I told him he should not be afraid but know he was not alone out there at night. They were watching with him.

And Marion had her sign, the confirmation she sought.

There were times I would go on safari up country for seminars without Marion. She was either busy with something at home or did not feel up to another trip so soon after one we had just completed. Leaving her alone was not the best thing to do, but there was not any other choice. The work was young, and I needed to be out in the field. What helped was that she believed in God's protection and stood firmly on what Psalm 91 says. This made it possible for us to be separated for days on end.

While I was away in southwestern Uganda for a week, Marion had two callers one night. She was awakened at 4:30 A.M. by the watchman tapping on the guestroom window. He did not come to her window, as it faces the gate. He told her that there were two men with guns outside the gate. Marion looked out her window and saw them. Then the outside security light revealed them crawling over the gate and dropping inside the compound.

She grabbed the whistle lying beside her bed and proceeded quickly to the kitchen, which faces the house above us. There they have a security guard on duty at night. She started to blow her whistle as loudly as she was able, hoping that the guard above would hear and come to her assistance, but there was no response.

Returning to the bedroom, she looked out and saw them crouched over, moving up toward the house. She moved from room to room, praying for the Lord's assistance and protection.

In the meantime, our watchman was peeking around the corner of the garage and watching the two gunmen. When they got midway to the house from the gate, they stopped suddenly. Then, turning abruptly, they ran back to the gate, climbed over it, and disappeared into the night. What had happened? Why had they turned and fled?

When I returned from my safari a few days later, Marion told me what had taken place. It was a miracle that we escaped being robbed and her getting molested. "Thank You, Lord, for watching over her and our home," I prayed. "Who but You could have assisted her?"

That night I found myself standing in front of the house at the bottom of the steps. I saw four figures in white poised between me and the gate. They faced it as if watching for something. I stared at them so as to discover who they might be when they began to fade away. Then I spied two other figures. These were black, coming up and over the gate and into the yard. They approached the house in a crouched position.

When they were about midway to the house, the white figures reappeared to stand in front of the two in black. They halted and then turned and fled. The figures in white remained and were totally visible. When it dawned on me that these were angels, I began praising the Lord and shouting, "Hallelujah. Hallelujah."

I wanted to run to them and thank them. But I could not move. I increased my efforts, while at the same time still shouting out my praises and thanksgiving to them. Then I heard Marion calling me. She wanted to know what the matter was, as I was thrashing about and groaning out loud.

I'd had a vision. The Lord revealed to me what happened the night the two gunmen had come to rob. They turned and fled the compound because of the guardian angels standing watch. They must have seen them. And I too had the privilege of looking upon four of our guardian angels on duty here at Muyenga. Hallelujah. Praise the Lord.

## About the Contributor

Stanley W. Hoffman grew up on a Canadian farm in Saskatchewan. Stanley then attended Alberta Bible Institute, where he graduated with a bachelor of theology degree. It was there that he met Marion Schwartz, whom he married in 1956. Stanley and Marion Hoffman have been abundantly blessed with three children, ten grandchildren, as well as one great-grandchild. They have dedicated their lives to fulfilling the call of God. They have pastored churches and served as missionaries for over 40 years in various countries in Africa. Their miracle story shared in this book was excerpted from Stanley's well-respected and much-noted book, *Amid Perils Often*, which offers readers a full account of the Hoffmans' six years of perils in Uganda.

CHAPTER 12

# GOD'S WORK GOD'S WAY

## *Dr. Don Kantel of Iris Ministries*

*But seek first His kingdom and His righteousness, and all these things will be given to you as well* (Matthew 6:33).

I guess it's only natural to question the supernatural. Sometimes we doubt ourselves, wondering if we really saw or experienced what we thought we did. Sometimes we doubt our sources. Maybe the reports were exaggerated, wishful thinking, or based on coincidence or misinformation. But the truth is that we often actually doubt God Himself. Our Western mindset has convinced us that we live in a natural, cause-and-effect universe and that the supernatural isn't real, that true miracles not only don't happen, they *can't* happen. This anti-supernatural mindset is what the Bible calls *unbelief.* It was enough to prevent Jesus from doing many miracles in Nazareth; and it's enough to limit the Spirit of God's activity in the Western world today. In Africa, where I serve with Iris Ministries, there is a different prevailing mindset. Of course, the objective reality doesn't differ from one culture to another, but cultural and religious beliefs do vary widely. Hundreds of millions of people in sub-Saharan Africa believe that reality is basically spiritual and that spirits control or influence the natural realm. The problem is that the spiritual powers most Africans traditionally believe in are evil, deceptive, tormenting, and demonic. Millions of Africans live in superstition and fear; and most have still never been introduced to their loving Heavenly Father and the Lord Jesus Christ, who died and rose again to release us from bondage to evil and death.

In his landmark study, *Christianizing the Roman Empire*, Yale professor and secular historian Ramsay MacMullen concluded that the two most convincing evidences for the veracity of the Christian message in the first centuries after Christ were the love and care the young Church demonstrated for those in need and the abundant accounts of supernatural miracles.[1] And interestingly, during the early stages of the Reformation in the sixteenth century, the Catholic Church challenged the credibility of the Reformers' message not so much on doctrinal grounds but by saying, "Show us your miracles."

When we tell Africans about Jesus and God's love for them, the only question they really need answered is *which* spiritual reality is more powerful—which should they give their life to? It is very like the situation Elijah faced when confronted by the prophets of Baal. This is God's battle, as it clearly was in Elijah's case also, and only God can answer the ultimate question in a man's heart. And one of the reasons there is such an abundant spiritual harvest taking place in Africa today is that God is regularly confirming His Word and His witness by supernatural signs and wonders, just as in the Book of Acts.

Along the same lines, Randy Clark shared an account while speaking at the Tenth Anniversary "Catch the Fire" Conference at Toronto Airport Christian Fellowship on October 10, 2003. Clark related that earlier that year he had been approached in Las Vegas by what he described as an "evangelical, non-charismatic mission-ary" who'd been sent from the Sinai Peninsula as a delegate for the evangelical missionaries in the region who had just been gathered in a conference. As the missionaries had been talking together about their work, they had made a startling discovery. Reflecting on their ministry experience in that region, which ranged from 2 to 22 years in length, they realized "not one of them had ever seen a Muslim accept Jesus Christ who hadn't first seen a healing or a miracle or had an angelic visitation." When they realized that, they concluded that their traditional missions approach wasn't working and they needed help to discover how to tap into more of the power of God.

In our own work in Africa over the years, the Lord has confirmed His word and His reality with signs and wonders on a regular basis. Our experience is that these moments when "Heaven invades earth" are more "normal" when we are breaking new ground for the gospel. As the church becomes established in an area, these kinds of dramatic demonstrations of super-nature seem to become somewhat less frequent, though they never cease (thankfully), and we continue to pray in faith for the impossible. This is likely because God uses the miraculous as a dramatic demonstration of His reality to call people out of spiritual darkness. Once converted, the journey to maturity has more to do with personal spiritual discipline and building our relationship of faith and love with God. We are meant to walk more by faith and less by sight, whereas the realm of the miraculous is more in the realm of experience, of sight.

In the annals of Iris Ministries, there were many instances of the dead being raised in the early years—more than 50, in fact. There have been dramatic healings numbering in the many hundreds—including blind eyes being opened, deaf hearing, dumb speaking, and many forms of lameness and deformity being supernaturally healed. These wonderful divine interventions continue to occur with some regularity, though in general, they seem to be more prevalent when we're taking new territory for the Lord. I have witnessed a few of these miracles close enough that I have absolutely no doubt about what I saw. I was two feet from a blind man and watched his milky pupils change to a solid color, and he could suddenly see clearly. I've watched the indescribable excitement in young village children when one of their friends who had been totally deaf from birth could suddenly hear and repeat sounds and words. I've held a boy's badly broken forearm and watched the arm straighten and be completely healed.

Of course, there have been thousands of testimonies of headaches and pains in legs, stomachs, and backs healed in response to believing prayer. We thank God for every such instance, but admittedly these are more difficult to verify objectively. The same is true of women and couples who receive prayer to conceive. We've had the joy of dedicating a number of babies who have come in seeming response to such prayer, but it's next to impossible to "prove" conclusively that these are supernaturally aided conceptions.

There have been a few amazing stories of supernatural multiplication over the years in Iris Ministries, as well. Most have had to do with food, though one of the most memorable had to do with the supernatural multiplication of wrapped Christmas gifts for children, each containing exactly what the waiting child had requested when asked. In my own work with Iris, I've seen food unmistakably multiplied on three occasions. The most recent of these took place in May 2007. Because of the number of witnesses to what took place, it's this account that I'd like to share here.

Over the past few years, the Lord has led me step by step to establish a transformational model for bringing the reality of His Kingdom into the spiritual darkness of traditional African villages. It's now called the "Mieze Model," after the name of the village in northern Mozambique where the model was first developed. For a description and pictures of the Mieze Model, please see www.harvestinafrica.com.

The Mieze Model focuses on impoverished village children as its primary beneficiaries and agents of change. As our ministry there was getting started, the Lord supernaturally multiplied food for these village children on two occasions in late 2006 and early 2007. The first time was so completely unexpected that the Mozambican pastor, Joao Juma, and I were the only ones who realized what had happened, and we were both stunned into silence. The second time, we recognized what was taking place and couldn't contain our excitement. I wrote enthusiastically about these remarkable events to our own friends and supporters, one of whom was John Arnott, the recognized leader of the Toronto Blessing Renewal. As it happened, John's daughter, Vicki (whom I didn't know at the time), was organizing a large group to visit Iris Ministries at our base in Pemba, Mozambique. After reading my account of the multiplication of food for children, John put Vicki in touch with me by email. I remember Vicki asking if I thought God would do it again at Mieze during their visit. My response was simply to encourage her to spend half a day there with her team to meet the children and to organize games and activities for them.

As a result, on a Saturday morning in May 2007, I took Vicki Arnott and her group out to Mieze for a visit. They had been playing games with the kids for a couple of hours when it occurred to Vicki to ask me when the kids would be going home for lunch. I explained that these kids were so poor many would only have one meal of boiled rice a day or perhaps every other day. Vicki began to weep and asked if we could provide some kind of a snack for the kids if she gave me some money. She specifically mentioned a bottle of Coke and something to eat for each one. So we sent several teenagers to the local market with the money I was given. I had done a quick head count and guesstimated there were about 100 kids present. The instructions to our shoppers were to get five cases of Cokes (120 bottles), at least 100 buns, and as much fruit as possible with whatever money was left.

When the teenagers returned with their purchases on their heads, we gathered the children in the church building for their surprise treat. There were 120 bottles of Coke, 110 plain buns, and what looked like about 60 bananas. But when all the children crowded into the little church building and sat down, it suddenly seemed like God had supernaturally multiplied the kids this time. There were well over 200 of them. During a time of lively worship led by Pastor Juma, my mind was racing to figure out what to do. I decided we could pair the kids up and give one bottle of Coke to each two kids. That worked well, and we had three bottles left over. That meant we had 234 kids. I then asked the visiting team to break the buns in half and give a half to each child. I knew that would still leave us short a few, but I figured it would more or less work out. The visitors fanned out among the crowd of kids with their armloads of buns, giving a half to each waiting child.

Pastor Juma and I watched from the front, and our jaws began to drop as we realized the visitors had worked their way most of the way through the crowd and still seemed to be holding as many buns in their arms as when they started. They got all the way to the back of the building and turned around to face us. All 234 children had received some bread when there shouldn't actually have been enough to go around; and all the visiting team still had armloads of buns. So we signaled them to work their way from the back up to the front again giving out more buns, as long as the supply continued. Again, every child received more bread, and the team members all still had their arms full of buns when they reached the front. What an awesome God we serve.

Then Pastor Juma announced that the children would leave by the small side door and each would receive a banana as they left. My heart sank at those words because there were only sixty to seventy bananas in the basket at most, not even enough for a third of the kids. Nonetheless, Pastor Juma began enthusiastically handing the bananas to the children one by one, and he was quickly joined by a few of the visitors. Then he stepped back and watched with me as the visitors continued to give out the bananas. We watched 80 kids go by...100 kids...125 kids.... God was doing it again—150 kids...200 kids...230 kids. And we jumped into each other's arms for joy as we watched Vicki Arnott pick up the last banana and hand it to the last child to go out the door. Exactly 234 bananas, one for each child. Vicki later said she thought she had seen it all during the heyday of the Toronto Renewal, but she'd never experienced anything like this.

The next day, my wife and I visited the Mieze church for the Sunday service. Four hours of energetic worship with 350 African brothers and sisters in a building built for 100 to 125 is an experience to remember. We especially watched the offering with fascination. A few people brought some small coins, but most brought fruit or vegetables. And there were three live chickens added to the mountain of produce. Then Pastor Juma announced that the entire offering would be given to the Iris Pemba Base as a love-gift from the Mieze church. What grace and generosity from people who live in such poverty and are always in need themselves. Is this why God chose to perform such a remarkable miracle in this forgotten and out-of-the-way place? I spoke about what had happened there the day before...and not surprisingly, the church was noticeably even more packed with children than usual. The people shouted their praises. *He* had not forgotten them. The children were the most enthusiastic of all, and we commissioned about 200 of them, who have experienced God's supernatural provision, to be witnesses and evangelists to all their friends and neighbors throughout their village.

The Mieze church has continued to grow in response to many, many demonstrations of the love of God for his precious people there. In 2009, we built a wonderful new church and community building accommodating 1,000 or more. We also began a new children's evangelistic program on Saturday mornings, which is regularly drawing as many as 500 children from nominally Muslim families. And we learned that a Muslim father in the village had recently gathered his 10 children and three wives outside their mud and bamboo hut and given his children his permission to become as involved in the life of the church as they wanted because he'd been watching closely for several weeks and he'd seen nothing but good coming from it.

And these precious Mozambican children—many of whom have only rags for clothes and have never been to school—now live in a relationship of faith and trust in God that often challenges and encourages me. Because of what they have experienced, they place no limitations on their faith in God. They know He can do *anything*; and everything He does is good. The superstition and hopelessness of the past is gone, and they now live in the lively expectancy of God's Jeremiah 29:11 promise of *"hope and a future"* for their lives. And, because these children are "the least of the least" in the world's eyes, only Jesus will receive the glory for what He has done and continues to do in Mieze and the surrounding district.

## ABOUT THE CONTRIBUTOR

Dr. Don Kantel was founding president of St. Stephen's University in New Brunswick, Canada. For the past several years, he and his wife, Elizabeth, have served as missionaries with Iris Ministries in northern Mozambique. Their Canadian home is on Prince Edward Island.

Iris Ministries focuses on evangelism, church-planting, and ministry to the poor...and especially to orphans and vulnerable children. Iris is actively ministering in several countries in Africa—notably Mozambique, South Africa, Malawi, and Sudan—and in several other needy regions of the world, including Brazil, India, and Indonesia. Iris has planted over 10,000 churches in the past 15 years and currently cares for over 6,000 needy children. For further information about Iris Ministries, please see www.irismin.com. For more information about Don Kantel and the work at Mieze, please see www.harvestinafrica.com.

## ENDNOTE

1. Ramsay MacMullen, *Christianizing the Roman Empire (A.D. 100–400)* (New Haven, CT: Yale University Press, 1984).

# CHAPTER 13

# SAVED FROM A WATERY GRAVE

## *Testimony of David Blatchford, as written and provided by Jack Olson*

*He stilled the storm to a whisper; the waves of the sea were hushed. They were glad when it grew calm, and He guided them to their desired haven. Let them give thanks to the Lord for His unfailing love and His wonderful deeds for men* (Psalm 107:29-31).

We saw the reflection of our running lights about 20 feet above us. The wave crashed down on the boat, hurling all of us to the transom, into a heap of bodies. Then there was a loud bump. The force of that wave had slammed us down about 30 feet to the bottom.

The day had begun as a perfect day for boating in late July. The winds were out of the southwest at about five to ten miles per hour. The sky was a beautiful shade of blue with a few puffy white clouds.

We had three people on board that day: my brother, a friend, and me. It was a stoutly built 1952, 30-foot cabin cruiser that my friend and I had bought in the spring  Throughout the better part of the season, we were renovating and repairing the old boat, which needed a lot of TLC. Finally, we were ready to take her out on a fishing trip. We checked out everything and found it satisfactory, fueled up, and were on our way. We had decided to head out to West

Sister Island. We used a canal that reached out to Lake Erie. Nothing could have been better. The weather was perfect, and we were setting out, doing the thing we liked best in a place of our choosing. That was perfect, too.

Lake Erie opened up, and we were on our way. This island was about 20 miles out. Keep in mind that we had a very old boat with a strong engine. However, the top speed was about nine miles per hour. We had a semi-distribution hull, and they are noted for creeping through the water. It took three hours to arrive at the island. The lake had low, rolling waves, perfect boating conditions.

Arriving at Sister Island, we got right to fishing. After being there for about 45 minutes, we noticed some ominous clouds low on the southeast horizon. The clouds got our attention. They were growing and coming right at us about 30 to 35 miles per hour, according to my dead reckoning, and they were turning pea green. Barometric pressure dropped quickly, meaning we were in for a bad storm. Little did we know how bad.

We knew we couldn't outrun it, so we decided to move the boat to the lee side of the island for protection. We used a double anchor to hold the boat close to the island, away from rougher water and the rocks that surrounded the island. By dark, we were being tossed about on eight-foot waves, driven by a 52-knot gale driving hail through an ink-black sky.

The danger was even more serious because we had to keep the engine going to hold our position. If it stopped, it would have to cool for half an hour before it could be started (it had a warped head). In that time, we would either drift into the rocks or out into the storm's fury and capsize. We had four bilge pumps going and bailing the whole time. We couldn't let the water reach the engine's air intake.

About 1:30 A.M., the storm had calmed somewhat, so we moved the boat out a little to test the lake on the other side of the island, thinking we might try to run back to the marina. We had just cleared the island, when suddenly, there before us, was the biggest wave I'd ever seen. It drove us to the bottom, but we popped back up. Water was coming in so fast we were afraid of sinking backward, but amazingly, although it sputtered a few times, the engine was still turning and we were able to get to the wheel and maneuver back to the lee of the island, hoping to assess the damage. With four bilge pumps and three men bailing, the water was still too deep to see where it was coming in, and it was rising, getting closer to the carburetor. There seemed to be nothing else but to risk the rocks and run to the island.

Then my friend, Dave, did a strange thing. He had brought his new guitar with him and sat down and started picking and singing gospel songs. I sat and joined in. My brother thought we had gone crazy. He was sure we were about to die.

As we sang praises to God, Dave had an inspiration, most likely from God. He said, "We have one more pump we're not using." He got up, disconnected the intake water hose, which pulls water in to cool the engine, and set it in the boat. The engine then pulled its cooling water out of the boat instead of from the lake and dumped it into the lake. We were soon able to see the leaks and stuff them with sheets and pillowcases. This was just in time, as the water had risen within half an inch of flooding the carburetor. Four hours later, the storm calmed, and we were able to limp back to the marina.

My wife had called the Coast Guard the previous day. They told her they were not going out into that storm. If we weren't back in the morning, she should call back. So she prayed and went to bed. In spite of the intensity of the storm, she had a feeling of peace, as if there was no need for concern.

In the morning, still unworried, she drove to the marina. There, as God worked it out, she pulled up to our dock as we were coming down the canal.

We inspected the boat at the dock. The hand of God was clearly upon us during that journey. The boat needed 32-3/4 × 12-inch bolts to repair the keel. The boat was built with an inside and outside hull, and a very heavy keel. That keel was split nearly end to end, separating the outer hull. Moreover, we were just a half gallon from being adrift in a seriously damaged boat. And how else could the engine not have swamped when we were driven to the bottom with over a foot of water splashing around inside?

That night five or six people had died in the storm on a brand new 42-foot Chris Craft cruiser. A 100-foot-long cargo hauler had snapped like a matchstick. We found out later that a tornado had taken a large swath of West Sister Island. We had, indeed, been saved from a watery grave.

## ABOUT THE CONTRIBUTOR

David Blatchford is retired as a professional carpenter, and resides in Bailey, Colorado, with his wife, Dorine, who is working as a respiratory therapist. They have three adult children, five grandchildren, and one great-grandchild.

In David's spare time, he enjoys oil painting, especially of painting wildlife landscapes. The Blatchfords currently attend Faith Bible Chapel in Arvada, Colorado.

His Website is www.olsonhouse.org.

# PART II

# COMFORT, REASSURANCE, AND ANGELIC ENCOUNTERS

*Clap your hands, all you nations; shout to God with cries of joy. How awesome is the LORD Most High, the great King over all the earth!* (Psalm 47:1-2)

# CHAPTER 14

# Hope Beyond Reason

## *Pastor Dave Hess*

*...He shall give His angels charge concerning thee: and in their hands they shall bear thee up, lest at any time thou dash thy foot against a stone* (Matthew 4:6b KJV).

In November of 1997, my world came to an abrupt halt. An aggressive strain of leukemia immobilized my immune system. Told by health professionals that I may have weeks to live, we went to prayer.

Actually, we went to war.

From a place of rest in our Father's presence, we were empowered to resist the physical and spiritual attacks being assailed against me. We soon discovered that we were not alone in this fight. Not only were there brothers and sisters standing with us, but here were also angelic servants sent to help us.

Here is the account of one such warrior sent on one of the most difficult days of my six-month hospital stay.

That evening I slept restlessly. At 3:00 A.M. I awoke, unable to continue sleeping.

There is a song that had come to mean a lot to me. I appreciated the music of Kirk Franklin, and found one of his songs, "My Life is in Your Hands," especially uplifting.

I believe I wore out that CD within the first few days. It ministered life and hope to me in the middle of a very dark time. I memorized the words, singing them to myself whenever fear came to visit.

And so, this night at 3 A.M., exhausted in body and soul, I began to be afraid. According to the Bible, fear is not just an emotion; it's a spirit. And this evil spirit of fear wanted to take me on a dark, distorted carnival ride. Pictures began to flash through my mind. I saw my wife, Sheri, sitting alone at home, mustering all her courage as she paid the bills and attempted to hold the family together. I saw my daughter Bethany in her wedding gown, walking down the aisle—alone. I saw my sons, Ben and Brandon, playing pick-up football in the backyard—alone.

"They are alone. And you are gone," this insidious spirit whispered in my ear.

These haunting thoughts clutched at my mind, feverishly trying to shut the door of hope. So I began to sing Kirk's song of victory:

> *I know that I can make it, I know that I can stand.*
> *No matter what may come my way, my life is in His hands.*
> *With Jesus I can make it, With Jesus I can stand.*
> *No matter what may come my way, my life is in Your hands.*[1]

I sang it softly but firmly. And then I choked on the words—and on the thoughts.

I was alone in the room, with only a small light bulb glowing under my bed. Fighting back tears, I attempted to sing again, with no success.

Then the door to my room opened. Someone was walking toward my bed, singing in a soothing voice. And she was singing *my song*.

As she stood beside my bed, I saw in the dim light what appeared to be a stately African American woman. I don't remember much about her facial features, but I will never forget her eyes. They were courageous eyes, brimming with a supernatural strength.

As I looked into them, I felt as if I was receiving a courage transfusion.

She placed her hands behind my head and gently lifted it from the pillow.

And then she sang to me:

*With Jesus you can make it, With Jesus you can stand.*
*No matter what may come your way, your life is in His hands...*

She was singing my song, singing it when I could no longer find the strength to sing.

Then she prayed for me, speaking in a language I had never heard before. And courage flooded my heart. When she had finished, she gently placed my head back on the pillow, turned, and left the room.

As I lay there, my body began reverberating with hope. Something had happened. The skirmish with fear had ended. The assaulting thoughts had ceased. The words of David rose up in me:

*"My soul finds rest in God alone; my salvation comes from Him"* (Ps. 62:1). I was experiencing that "peace that passes all understanding," and it felt good.

Sometime later, Rosemary, my nurse, came into the room. She was startled to see that I was awake. She was even more startled at my countenance, commenting that I was "glowing."

I told her about my night visitor, describing her appearance.

Rosemary informed me that her pharmacy cart had been parked beside my door for the past several hours, as she worked her way down the hall distributing pills to the patients. She had seen no other people pass by. "Besides," she ended emphatically, "we don't have any African American nurses on duty tonight."

Slightly puzzled, I thought, *Imagine that. Someone woke up in the middle of the night and came here just to sing me a song.*

I couldn't wait to tell Sheri the next day. She was equally bewildered at my encounter with the unexpected night visitor. Then, as we opened that day's bundle of letters, we found a card from some of our pastor friends. They told us that they were praying for us, mentioning that one of their church members had seen a vision as the church was in prayer that Sunday morning. This woman had written a description of the vision on an offering envelope, which they included in their card.

As I read this woman's words, I began to tremble inside. She wrote:

> As we were praying for Dave, I saw that the Lord sent an angel to him in the night. The angel walked into his room, stood by his bed, and lifted his head from the pillow, cradling it like a mother would do to her child. The angel then ministered to him, giving him gifts of courage straight from the Father.

Though I know they surround us, I had never seen an angel before. "*Thousands upon thousands*" of them gather "*in joyful assembly*," the Bible says (Heb. 12:22). They have been commissioned by the Lord to "*guard [us] in all of [our] ways*" and to "*lift [us] up in their hands*" (Ps. 91:11-12). Though we may not always see them, they are constantly present, on assignment as servants sent by our loving King to help us. And He is opening our eyes and awakening our senses to know that we are never forsaken. It would be foolish to worship angels; only Jesus is worthy of our worship. But it is equally foolish to ignore them, when we desperately need their help.

That day I was learning to welcome them, and even expect their help.

## ABOUT THE CONTRIBUTOR

Dave Hess is the senior pastor of Christ Community Church in Camp Hill, Pennsylvania. He and his wife, Sheri, have been married for 32 years. They have three adult children, one daughter-in-love, one son-in-love, and one grandson. This story is an excerpt from Dave's book, *Hope Beyond Reason* (Destiny Image). You may contact Dave at Christ Community Church, 1201 Slate Hill Road, Camp Hill, Pennsylvania 17011, via phone at: 717-761-2933, or via email at: senior.pastor@christcc.org.

## ENDNOTE

1. Kirk Franklin, "My Life Is in Your Hands," copyright 2008, Lilly Mack Publishing (Admin. at EMICMG-Publishing.com). International Copyright secured. All rights reserved. Used by permission.

# CHAPTER 15

# SAVED BY ANGELS

## BRUCE VAN NATTA

*For the kingdom of God is not a matter of talk but of power*
(1 Corinthians 4:20).

The events of November 16, 2006, changed my life forever. There has been no way to turn back or forget what happened that day; it will be with me as long as I live. Many of us can think of defining moments in our life. Sometimes they are marked by tragedy, other times by triumph, but rarely by both. This was one of those uncommon days.

I was a self-employed diesel mechanic who went around doing on-site repairs. This particular day I was at a customer's shop about 45 minutes from my home. The vehicle I was working on was a Peterbilt logging truck. I had worked nearly 12 hours that day in order to complete my portion of the engine repairs and was just finishing up. I had been working with the driver of the truck, and after we got the engine put back together, we started it to check it over and test the repairs. The rest of the truck was not completely back together, but the things that were left to do, the driver planned on finishing the next day.

I began to put my tools back into the toolboxes on my service truck as the semi engine ran up to operating temperature. The driver asked me, since I was there, if I could also diagnose a nonrelated oil leak before I left. I was in a hurry to get home but thought that this task would only take a few extra minutes.

I rolled underneath the front of the truck feet first on a creeper and started wiping off the area that appeared to be leaking. All of a sudden, the truck fell off the jack and crushed me against the concrete floor. The front axle had come down across my midsection like a blunt guillotine, nearly cutting me in two. From my viewpoint, it looked and felt like I was cut in half. In a moment of panic, I tried to bench press the ten thousand plus pound mass off of me.

When reality set in, I realized the gravity of the situation and called out, "God help me," twice. I listened as the truck driver called 911. When he got off the phone I begged him to shut the engine off because the vibration of the engine directly above me was transmitted through the axle and right into my body. Small amounts of blood started to come out of my mouth when I tried to talk.

I watched as the driver repositioned the jack and raised the truck up off of my body. I was scared of it falling again and wanted to get out from underneath that truck in the worst way. The large chrome front bumper was just behind my head, and I reached both hands back and grabbed the bottom of it. It took everything I had to pull myself out to the point that at least my head was out from underneath the truck. I stayed conscious long enough to see the first person who responded to the 911 call.

The next thing I remember was being at least 10 to 15 feet above the scene looking down at myself and the whole situation. The strangest part about my "out of body" experience was feeling like I was just an observer to what was happening below me. It was as if I were watching a movie. I felt no emotion, only a sense of peace. At one point I heard one man say to another that there was no way I was going to live, and it didn't matter to me one way or another.

From my viewpoint above I could tell that my body was still under the truck for the most part, but my head was sticking out from under the front bumper. I could see that my eyes were closed and my head was turned toward the driver's side of the truck. The man I had been working with was on his knees above me and was crying and patting me on the head as he was talking to me. I could hear and understand every word he said.

The most incredible thing wasn't that I was having this experience, but what I saw next. On either side of us were twin angels, also on their knees and facing the front of the truck. From my vantage point in the ceiling I was looking from above and behind them. The driver of the truck is over six feet tall, and yet the heads of these angels were at least a foot and a half taller than his head. If they would have been standing up, I think they would have been close to eight feet tall. They had very broad shoulders and looked to be extremely muscular. There were no wings. Each angel had his arms under the truck angled toward my body.

The angels had ringlets of long, blond hair that went at least halfway down their backs. They were wearing what looked like either white or ivory-colored robes. It was hard to tell because there was a yellowish light surrounding each angel. They seemed to be glowing. I also noticed that the robe fabric was very unusual. It was a woven material, but the thread size was very large, like miniature rope. It appeared to be very strong and durable. The angels never moved; they were as steady as statues. I couldn't see their faces because my view was from behind them, but from what I could see they were identical in appearance.

## Life or Death

More people began to come to the scene of the accident, and I continued to watch from above. A red-haired emergency worker arrived, talked to someone, and walked up the driver's side of the truck. She moved the truck driver I had been working with out of the way and asked him my name. She held my head, patted my cheeks, and told me to open my eyes. She kept repeating herself in a loud voice, and the next thing I knew I was no longer watching from above, but was looking at her through my own eyes. She told me that it was very important for me to keep my eyes open. I thought about what she was saying and realized that I had been out of my body until she got me to open my eyes. This made me believe that what she said was true and important. I was on the verge of life and death. Then I thought about the angels I had seen. I looked where they had been, but I could see nothing there now with my human eyes.

As I lay there, I heard a voice in my head telling me to shut my eyes and just give up. When I did shut my eyes, the incredible pain stopped, and I could feel my spirit drifting away from my body. But there was also another voice; this one was quieter, more of a whisper. It told me that if I wanted to live, I would have to fight, and it would be a hard fight. It was almost as if the red-haired emergency worker could hear that voice, too, because she then asked me what I had to fight for. All I could think of was my wife and four children. These two voices or conflicting thoughts volleyed back and forth in my head a handful of times.

If we think of that old cartoon with the devil on one shoulder and an angel on the other, we can use it to picture what was happening. The louder voice that was telling me to give up and die was not from God, but the whispering voice that told me to fight was. As always, the devil's voice promotes death, and God's voice promotes life. It's also interesting to note that God will always tell us the truth. He warned me that it was going to be a hard fight, and it has been. It seems that most often the right choice is not the easiest option.

I was transported by ambulance to a local hospital and then flown to our state's largest trauma center. I stayed awake the whole time, fighting to hang on and refusing to close my eyes. When the emergency doctors scanned my body, they were astounded. There were so many injuries that they couldn't decide where to start or what to do. They had given me several units of blood, but it just kept leaking out into my stomach cavity. As they were sliding me back in for another CAT scan, everything started to go dim for me, and although I hadn't been able to talk for quite awhile, the Lord gave me the strength to tell them that I was going to die and they had to do something right now. The doctors told me several weeks later that as soon as I said that my blood pressure dropped out of sight. They removed me from the machine and rushed me to the operating room.

The doctors operated on me only long enough to reattach the veins and arteries that had been severed. The head trauma surgeon had been called in from home and told my family that in all his years as a trauma doctor, he had never seen anybody traumatized like that and be alive. He told my family that he was going to cross his fingers and wait at least six hours to see if I was still alive before he would operate on me again. My wife told him that he could cross his fingers but that she and others were going to pray for my life.

The prayers were answered, and the doctors resumed operating on me the next morning. They had to remove most of my small intestine and perform various other repairs to combat my several internal injuries. They decided not to do anything with the two vertebrae that were spider-cracked in my spine. They would try to let them heal on their own.

The next thing I remember was waking up a few weeks later. I had had three operations during that time, and my wife never left my side. The night of my accident she was at our children's school for parent-teacher conferences. When she got home and heard the news, she dropped to her knees and turned it all over to God, knowing that He would give her the strength to get through whatever lay ahead. The only thing she took with her to the hospital that night was her Bible.

To everyone's amazement I was sent home a little more than a month after the accident. But after a few days, I was back in the hospital with severe complications stemming from a damaged pancreas and spleen.

I spent a few more weeks in the hospital, but got out long enough to spend the Christmas holidays at home. Then I returned to the hospital. This cycle repeated itself a few times, and then the doctors decided that they would have to perform another major operation. They had to remove another section of my small intestine that died and was closed almost completely off.

We were told that an adult needs a minimum of 100 cm of small intestine to be able to live by eating food. I was already down to this critical minimum length before my fourth operation, and then they removed more. Before the accident I weighed over 180 pounds; three months afterward, I was already down to 126 pounds because of the inadequate amount of small intestine left in my body.

## More Miracles

Nine months after the accident, I was at the hospital for some tests in preparation for my fifth operation. While performing the procedure, the radiologist and his supervisor concluded that I had at least one third, or around 200 cm of small intestine. (We have since found out that there is even more, about half that again, or closer to 300 cm.) When they looked at the doctor's notes from the previous operations, they found that they had recorded a total length of 100 centimeters several times during the first three operations and this was before removing more in my fourth operation. It was hard for them to believe the head of the trauma department and other doctors had made multiple mistakes on my chart and in their calculations, since these men are at the top of their field.

I fully believe that they didn't make any mistakes, and here is why. What the radiologist didn't know was that several people had been praying for me and that a man named Bruce Carlson had flown in from New York to pray over me after my fourth operation. This man has often displayed the gift of healing, and the Lord has used him to heal hundreds of people. The Bible tells us that we as Christians are to pray for sick people to be healed. Sometimes God chooses not to heal someone in the method or timetable that we want, but that is His decision, not ours. As believers, we are told to pray with expectation, and the results are up to God.

When Bruce Carlson prayed over me that day, he put one of his palms on my forehead. He asked the Lord to answer all of the prayers that people had been praying for me, and when he said that, I felt something like electricity flowing from his palm and into my body. He prayed for my small intestine to supernaturally grow in length in the name of Jesus, and as he did, I could feel something wiggle around inside my stomach. I can't honestly say that I knew for sure my intestine had lengthened until the radiologist told me a few months later.

It has now been three years since my accident, and I have almost no side effects or physical problems at this point, despite the tremendous amount of trauma that my body incurred. My weight has also climbed back up to about 170 pounds, thanks to the added intestine.

Now that more time has passed, the doctors have told me just what a miracle it is that I am alive. They said that because of the artery and the veins that were completely severed, I should have bled to death internally in about eight to ten minutes. Rather, it was over two and a half hours from the point I was injured until they started to operate on me. They also told me that I am the only case that they have ever had at the hospital or anywhere else (that they know of) that has sustained these injuries and lived. All other cases have come in dead on arrival. I told my doctors that I know why I am still alive. I got to see the two angels that saved my life.

## His Will Be Done

I believe that the Lord allowed my accident to happen so that His plans would be accomplished in the end, and so that His name would be glorified through it. Right from the beginning of this nightmare, my wife and I have clung to the promise that God gives us in Romans 8:28, *"And we know that in all things God works for the good of those who love Him, who have been called according to His purpose."*

It is too early to see all of the good things that God has planned to come out of this tragedy, but we can already see some things clearly. We have seen our faith grow by leaps and bounds due to this event. We are now closer to the Lord than we have ever been. Our family is more compassionate to the needs and problems of others. I have become more patient than I used to be. Our home church has rallied together to support our family in a way that many senior members of the church have told us has never happened in the past. Some people who were not involved actively in church or prayer life have been drawn back to the Lord again or for the first time. It has been said that the accident has caused a small revival in our community.

When I tell people about seeing the angels who saved my life, it has permanently affected some of them. It makes it hard for even skeptics to argue the reality of these miracles when they are shown the medical facts. More than once I have seen people break down in tears after hearing this story because it touches them deep inside. People are affected when confronted with the truth of God's reality, His mercy, and His love. Because of this fact and because Lori and I wanted to be obedient to what God was telling us, we have gone into full-time ministry. What a blessing it is to now see God do miracles in other people's lives. It is clear to us that although this accident started out as a tragedy, the Lord has used it to bring triumph for His kingdom.

## ABOUT THE CONTRIBUTOR

Bruce and Lori Van Natta and their four children live in central Wisconsin but now travel around the world after founding Sweet Bread Ministries. Invite Bruce to your church, conference, seminar, or other special event to hear about how God saved him despite a sinful past. His true-life story stirs the faith of any believer and brings unbelievers to a place where they can accept Christ. People are compelled to consider the reality of God, angels, healing, and most importantly, their salvation. Many people report being healed of all kinds of sicknesses, diseases, addictions, and emotional issues after attending one of Bruce's meetings.

His book *Saved by Angels to Share How God Talks to Everyday People* (Destiny Image) details the complete story of Bruce's miracle and the ways in which our Lord wants to communicate with us on a daily basis. You can get the book in most bookstores, or on the Web. For more information about the ministry or book, go to sweetbreadministries.com, or call 715-213-6116.

# CHAPTER 16

# A RIDE OF GRACE

## *Joe Cardinal*

*Your word is a lamp to my feet and a light to my path*
(Psalm 119:105).

It was a beautiful late summer afternoon on August 25, 2008, and I was returning from a trip to Lake Placid, one of New York's most beautiful areas, on my Harley Davidson motorcycle. I had stopped to call my wife about two hours from home at about 5:00 P.M. to let her know I would be home in two hours. After grabbing a cup of coffee and bundling up for the cool ride home, I was approaching the community of Gabriels when I was following a pickup truck on the two-lane highway who signaled a right-hand turn into an intersecting road.

As I slowed down to approximately 45 miles per hour to allow the truck to make its turn, I noticed a car to my right waiting to enter traffic. As an experienced rider, your first thought is for that vehicle to stay where it is, as we are aware drivers don't see motorcycles. Continuing on as the truck made its turn, I began to accelerate, and I noticed that the car had pulled out and was directly in front of me. There was approximately 20 feet to make a decision. All I could do was lay the bike on its side and leave the rest up to God.

There was no pain or discomfort, just the knowledge that I had a bad crash as I lay there looking at the sky. As I lay there, a gentleman came up to me and asked me my name; he was unable to see my eyes—because of my goggles that were strapped on under my helmet—to know if I was conscious or alive. He asked my name, and when I told him, "Joe Cardinal," he responded, "Fabian Hart; don't try to move."

I said, "I know you."

His response was, "You have to turn your head slightly or you're going to choke to death on the blood."

Several weeks later, I was told that at the time of my accident, Fabian and his wife were eating ice cream cones at a famous shop two miles back. He said to his wife, "There is something wrong!" Immediately throwing their ice cream cones away, they came back upon the accident where I was laying on the hood of the car. He climbed up on the hood of the car, not knowing if I was still alive.

God had intervened in their travels and sent them back, thus saving my life. To them I owe my life, as well as two ice-cream cones!

The next thing I recall was the EMTs beginning to cut away my clothing. As they proceeded to cut through my jacket, they told me they had to cut through my jeans as well, and my last response was, "Don't cut them; they are my best pair."

Three weeks later, I came to consciousness in the ICU of Fletcher Allen Medical Center in Burlington, Vermont. As I began to recollect my thoughts as to what had occurred, I realized I was unable to move and was connected to every kind of machine imaginable and that my jaw was completely wired shut. I had a retainer collar on my neck, a cast on my left hand, and a metal stabilizer between my left shoulder and elbow. Despite my condition, I had an uncommon peace; it was God's grace. My wife began to tell me what had occurred from the time I lost consciousness.

As I gradually began recovery and became aware of my condition, I was surrounded by my family: my wife, Elaine, who was constantly at my side, my son, Justin, his wife, Julie, my beautiful grandchildren, Sydney, who was four, and Asher, who was one, my son, Cody, and his wife, Lida, and a constant rotation of dear friends from our local church. My wife told me about the three weeks that were lost to me. The night of the accident, she had realized that I was running very late and had become quite concerned and contacted local police agencies.

She had not been called about the accident and was finally able to reach state police, who informed her of what had occurred at around eleven o'clock. She was later told that I had lain on the roof of the car for over three hours, and the concern at the time was merely keeping me alive. This was one accident I should not have survived, but God had other plans for me. They then transported me to Burlington Medical Center after doing everything they could. I required numerous blood transfusions and facial reconstruction the first couple days after arriving.

Approximately one week later, they reconstructed my pelvis. I had shattered my face nearly in half, crushing my chin, losing seven teeth, splitting my palate, and crushing my cheekbone. My right jaw was broken in three pieces and pushed back into my ear canal. The miracle of modern medicine meant they could reconstruct my face through the inside of my mouth, leaving no facial scars, with the exception of a small scar on my chin. It took eleven hours of surgery with metal being placed in my chin, my right cheek, and my palate.

The pelvic surgery required 21 hours of surgery to replace what was now missing. A chain was used to reinforce the front of my pelvis with pins and rods and numerous screws of varying lengths of up to one foot to reattach the bones in the rear of my hips. The doctors said it looked like a sledgehammer had taken out my pelvis. I also suffered extensive nerve damage to my right leg with loss of feeling of the leg and foot. The doctors told me they did not know if I would ever walk again. Miraculously, I had no internal injuries. As I lay there in recovery, my only thoughts were, *God I am so thankful to still be alive* and this was, again, God's grace.

There was such a tranquility that was uncommon to my nature; God was doing something to my spiritual heart as well as my body. My wife told me the first words out of my mouth were, "God's grace is good." She was amazed at my calmness and acceptance of my situation, and she wondered if I would be upset that I would probably never ride again and that my Harley—my pride and joy—was destroyed.

As the days progressed, she noticed that my eyes were extremely dilated and I could not follow her walking around the room. She requested an eye exam if at all possible, and with great difficulty, it was accomplished. The eye doctor at the hospital told me that I had lost 90 percent of my optical nerves and that there was no correction surgery or healing that would change my sight. His words were, "You're better than a blind man. At least you won't run into walls." My wife thought this was rather harsh, and after returning to my room, asked me what my feelings were. My words were, "It doesn't sound too good, but we will just trust God."

Again, I marveled at the peace I had in the situation. God's amazing grace was working in my life through this whole process. As weeks went by, the healing of my wounds were nothing short of miraculous. The nurses and doctors were amazed at my progress of healing of wounds and of bone. I would tell them that God was healing me. As the machines and tubes came out, I began to be aware of my limitations. I had suffered a severe infection in one of my wounds requiring a special machine and bed. The bed was like lying on a cloud, and I was so grateful.

As I lay there unable to do anything, my desire was to be able to at least watch television, and I prayed for this. A couple of nights later, as I was listening to television, unable to see anything more than lines, I fell asleep with it on. I woke about 2:00 A.M. When I looked around the room, I noticed that I could see what was on the television. I grabbed the boom the television was mounted on and pulled it to me and yelled quite loudly, "My God, I can see television." This brought the nurses running. They were amazed that I had gained enough sight to see television. My reply was, "God had granted my prayer."

During my entire stay at the hospital, many friends and family came nearly every weekend. The nurses were amazed at the peacefulness and the joy both Elaine and I expressed and commented on it. They were also surprised as well at the amount of visitors I always had and the joy that was always present.

A very special couple in our lives from Canada came every weekend. They would bring Tim Horton's coffee and doughnuts, which of course I was unable to have but which were enjoyed by the staff and my visitors. Their thoughtfulness was cherished, as they knew how much I liked Tim Horton's. My wife was constantly by my side from nine in the morning till sometimes one the next morning. She had such a joy and caring attitude week after week. The staff commented on this also.

There was a constant flow of cards, letters, and gifts, and my room became the center of attention for the floor. Even though I had been a Christian for the past 25 years I sometimes would grumble and complain and be judgmental. My wife would comment on this. These thoughts were no longer in my heart. Even with my new vision limitations, I saw everything in a whole new light. The nursing staff came to us the day we were getting ready to leave with a card signed by all shifts with little notes from each one. It was amazing; God had touched every one of their lives through us. We gave them a beautiful plant that had been given to us as a gift for their staff room.

I was transported in early November to a local nursing home rehabilitation unit in my hometown of Massena, New York. There I began the strenuous physical therapy to learn how to move my upper body, sit up, eat, and shower again. During this time, my daughter-in-law would come during the week with my grandchildren and spend a couple of hours. This was priceless to me. My granddaughter, Sydney, had to teach me to color again, which was ironic, because I had taught her how to color as she was growing up. We had many special moments. Again, this new nursing staff marveled at my contentment and the tenderness between my wife and me. On the day that I left to be transported to my final therapy unit for acute rehabilitation, the staff all came in to say good-bye and thanked us for touching their lives. As December approached and I arrived at this new rehabilitation unit, I faced the reality and difficulty of trying to walk again and to dress.

It was more difficult than I ever imagined. I was supposed to be there three to four weeks, and I told my therapists that I would be home before Christmas, which was in three weeks, and they told me they did not think that would happen. As I said this, I recalled the doctors telling me I may never walk again due to the extensive nerve damage to my right leg and the total loss of use of my right foot. I now understood what they meant. It would take me at least a half hour to dress, and I had to use a special device for pulling up clothes and my right sock. This was a challenge with my limited vision; it was difficult for me to see things without a great deal of light. But my determination was always there, and God kept my spirits positive.

Thanksgiving was always a special time for our family, and I wanted so very much to be with my family for the holiday, which was 30 miles away. By hard work and the grace of God, I was able to go and be with my family. I especially enjoyed my time with the grandchildren. I came home for the first time on December 17. This was one week before Christmas. Friends had constructed a handicap ramp. I walked up the ramp with my walker and into my home. It was a shock walking into such a familiar environment that I had been living in for 20 years.

It has been over a year now since coming home, and there have been many trials, more surgeries, additional therapy, and difficult times, but that constant thankfulness to God for sparing my life has remained. I walk slowly with a cane now, my vision is the same, but I have a greater purpose, and His faithfulness has taken care of every need. The world needs to know of our God and His amazing grace. I believe my purpose now is to tell people that God's grace through

Jesus Christ will take them through any situation, not necessarily out of the situation but through it and with greater victory.

## ABOUT THE CONTRIBUTOR

Joe and Elaine Cardinal live in Massena, New York, a small village across from Cornwall Ontario on the Saint Lawrence. He is a retired firefighter, and Elaine is soon to retire as an orthodontic assistant. They have two children. Justin is a Bible college instructor who, with his wife, Julie, and their two children, Sydney and Asher, lives in Portland, Oregon. Cody is a freelance graphic artist, and his wife Lida recently graduated from university. She works with the disabled. They reside in Bombay, New York. Joe and Elaine have been serving at New Testament Church since 1984. They may be reached by contacting the church at 315-769-9951 or at the church's Website: ntcmassena.com.

# CHAPTER 17

# NEVER ALONE

## *Hilda Fyckes*

*And behold I am with thee, and will keep thee in all places whither thou goeth, and will bring thee again into this land; for I will not leave thee, until I have done that which I have spoken to thee of* (Genesis 28:15 KJV).

I remember that I got up sometime during the night and didn't feel very well. Somehow, I must have made my way into the kitchen, but I don't remember walking there.

I do remember thinking that it must have been breakfast time, as there were already dishes laid out, but I couldn't remember setting the table.

I wasn't feeling well, and I knew that I should go and lie down. So I tried to get up from my walker. I tried to go from the kitchen and make my way back to my bedroom, but I couldn't. When I tried to stand up, I knew I was too ill to make it to my bedroom, and so I prayed. I remember saying, "Lord I don't know how I'm going to get back to bed. I need Your help."

Then the next thing that I can recall is lying diagonally across my bed on top of the sheets. I remember feeling that something had happened that I wasn't quite aware of. I couldn't remember ever leaving the kitchen and making my way back to my bed.

As I woke up, I heard a voice say, "I am with you." I thought that I still must have been dreaming, but I knew in my heart that I had heard that voice. So to me then I knew that it was a miracle that I was back in my bedroom and lying on my bed.

I then tried to get out of bed, but I couldn't, so I called for advice and was immediately instructed to hang up and call 911 to get an ambulance to take me to the hospital without delay. I called the ambulance, but at this point, I was really getting worried, as I was going in-and-out of knowing what was going on around me now.

A few minutes later—which seemed like an eternity for me—the ambulance arrived. They checked my blood pressure, which was 195 over something or other, I think, and they also checked my pulse, which the young attendant said was "going crazy."

I told them though that I didn't really want to go to the hospital and that I would be all right at home, if I just rested for a bit. But they wouldn't simply hear of it. The young ambulance attendant said there was no way that they were going to leave me at my apartment without taking me to the hospital. He told me that he couldn't take that responsibility if anything should happen to me. So, I went with them to the hospital, which was only about a five-minute ride away.

When I arrived, I remember my doctor coming up to me and asking why I was there. I told him that I didn't know (I guess at that point I was still coming in and out of my awareness of what was going on).

So, then they ordered a scan. The doctor showed me a picture of the scan, and explained that the little dots that could be seen were mini-strokes that they thought I'd had. The only thing was, I knew that I'd had two mini-strokes in Montreal. They couldn't tell if I had had another mini-stroke or if the ones that they saw on the scan were the ones that I'd had from when I lived in Montreal. They did tell me that I didn't have a big stroke, though. That was good news.

Looking back on that day, I was convinced that I got help from above. I clearly heard, "I am with you," that day in my bedroom as I was just waking up. Even now when there are times that I am upset, all of a sudden, I get a peaceful feeling. I just know that the things that I am worrying about are not going to happen.

I've been really blessed over the years, too. I have been alone, but yet I have always felt that I've had someone watching over me. There have been so many times I can recall when I've been protected. There was even an incident last year when a car came racing by when I was crossing the street. I felt the brush of the car against the back of my jacket, but I was not hurt. I should have been killed, I think. But I know that I am still here for a reason. I remember having so much peace when that happened that day. I wouldn't normally have peace. Usually I would have been quite upset. But I was able to keep walking to the store and go on as if nothing had happened.

God has really blessed me, and I'm very thankful for that.

One day when I was starting to doubt if I had really heard that voice, "I am with you," God reminded me of a friend who had told me that the same thing had happened to her. She had also heard the words, "I am with you," when she couldn't get out of bed one day.

At the time, I thought that maybe she was dreaming. But now I realize that she wasn't. After I started to wonder if I had also really heard the words, "I am with you," I suddenly heard a verse, "Genesis 28:15." So, I went to look it up. It was so unusual, because I had never heard a verse come to me like this before, and I was not one to memorize Bible verses, so I knew that it must have been God speaking to me.

When I went to look it up, I was astonished as to what it said. It had the same words, "I am with you." I still remember that because this was very unusual. If I would have memorized any verses of Scripture, they would have likely been from the Psalms or the New Testament. So, I knew that I had heard, "I am with you." This is often what comes back to me now if I am upset. It helps reassure me that all is well, and that Jesus indeed is watching over me.

One thing I know for sure is that I can always place my trust in the Lord.

## ABOUT THE CONTRIBUTOR

Hilda Fyckes is a very active senior in her community. She currently resides in Milton, Ontario, Canada, where she has lived since moving from Montreal, Canada, several years ago. She has two children, six grandchildren, and three great-grandchildren. She is looking forward to the celebration of her 94th birthday in the spring of 2011.

# CHAPTER 18

# Reassurance Through the Fluttering Sounds of Angels' Wings

## *Cynthia Nixon*

*For our light and momentary troubles are achieving for us an
eternal glory that far out-weighs them all. So, we fix our eyes
not on what is seen, but on what is unseen. For what is seen
is temporary, but what is unseen is eternal*
(2 Corinthians 4:17-18).

The first congregation my husband and I attended was led in worship by a small group who had a distinct anointing. This caused me many times to come right into the throne room of God. We both attended ministry training school there and began participating in the music. It seemed to reach a high place in the spirit that opened into the Heavenlies. One Christmas, I distinctly felt that some of the same angels that were at Bethlehem to welcome the Savior Yeshua were listening to and enjoying the autoharp outreach at the mall.

After two years of schooling, there was a time of waiting on the Lord for His plans. Soon there was given to me a vision of 24 little books. As I looked into them, the pages were empty, but in my spirit I knew that they were to be written in from Heaven. During the next few months, I was asked to write a newsletter for all the nursery parents. The pastor's wife thought it should be called "Heavenly Tribune." These short teachings on colorful picture stationery went out to over 100 families for nearly two years. Thoughts of Heaven were on my mind continually because I had lost two little ones before birth and I yearned to meet them someday.

One day the name of our ministry, *Crowns of Glory!*, was dropped into my heart. I had been compiling a little book for one of the nursery parents whose daughter had lost many abilities due to a genetic problem. Their children had come to pet our animals, and it brought them joy to see themselves in a book with a poem about the outing. Close to seven years later, in 2002, our first little book, *Heavenly Hope*, was printed. The format included quaint old Scripture pictures with poems that would appeal to tender hearts.

As time went on, the books grew in length, but always with teachings that pointed to Heaven. They can only be written after a distinct "dimensional" message is put on my heart catching an element of "higher life." This consistently includes a practical thought with a spiritual emphasis followed by scriptural references that make the teachings foundationally sound. The Lord had told us to raise sheep, and so our book *The Nature of the Lamb* was given. *"The Lamb which is in the midst of the throne shall feed them, and shall lead them"* (Rev. 7:17 KJV). Others include *The HIGH Way of Holiness* and *Kings and Priests Forever*. A beautiful thank you came from a believer who had comforted his wife in Israel while passing by continually reading *Ways of the Ancient of Days*.

One evening several years ago, a pastor had asked, "Who has seen angels?" My hand went up, but I was not aware that this was a gift until a friend told me that she never had seen them. With that, I began to ponder any contact and knew only that certain times when I was struggling spiritually I could feel a hand on my shoulder. The warm weight was so comforting. It could lift me immediately into the spirit realm. It also made me know that this particular angel was very big if his hand rested on my shoulder. It was at this same church that Roland Buck came to visit and where I first read his book *Angels on Assignment.* When we were given the name *"Crowns of Glory!,"* our rural home was within ten miles of the church where he had been visited by angels.

There were seven messages that the angels had reported to him from Heaven that were important for the church to teach. When it was time to write the twelfth in our series of books, I was led to include these messages. This 100-page little book is a children's curriculum that helps one imagine what a Bride of Christ would put in her *Heavenly Hope Chest.* The chests themselves include miniature items that teach about specific principles of eternal life that would prepare one for living in Heaven. In the book, there are pictures of each item and questions that are answered by verses of Scripture. When teaching about the seven candlesticks, the Spirit made it clear that each candle was to represent a message that the angels had brought to the church.

After many months of work, the accompanying book was finally printed and packaged for those on our mailing list. In spite of all the production detail, in a moment I was brought back to God's greater perspective by a strong angelic presence. I was spiritually quickened, sensed a flurry of wings, and then heard, "We'll take it from here." Selah. It took me a few moments to realize that the Lord wanted to use *Crowns of Glory!* Ministry to publish these vital truths and for His messengers to distribute them in a different way. All glory to God!

We are waiting on the Lord for the completion of his books, with 18 written so far. These currently go to Jerusalem, Judaea, Samaria, and the uttermost parts of the earth. It was made clear by His Spirit that we were not to use radio, television, newspaper, or magazine to advertise. More recently, a strong anointing conveyed that we would not be using the usual ways for distributing these publications. The admonition to trust Him came the very week I received the email from Allison Restagno saying she was given the name of *Crowns of Glory!* during her prayer time. In faith, she sought us out and asked me to contribute a story. Praise Yah. The Heavenly messengers may again be able to take God's precious words and share them by means of this miracle.

## ABOUT THE CONTRIBUTOR

*Crowns of Glory!* is called to help believers establish an eternal worldview, seeing themselves as *"strangers and pilgrims on the earth"* (Heb. 11:133b KJV).

We pray that the streams the Lord Yeshua pours through us will always be as pure and refreshing as the crystal river of water of life flowing from the throne of God and the Lamb. May His healing waters flow into every area of your life.

Robert and Cynthia Nixon, www.crowns.org.

*"Thou shalt also be a crown of glory in the hand of the LORD"* (Isaiah 62:3 KJV).

# CHAPTER 19

# THE LEAR JET LANDING WITHOUT BRAKES

## *Diana Burgess*

*The name of the LORD is a strong tower; the righteous run to it and are safe* (Proverbs 18:10).

Until that fateful day in August 2002, my life seemed perfect. God blessed me with a wonderful husband and two beautiful children, along with a rewarding career. I was the chief flight nurse for an international critical care air ambulance. I balanced my work responsibilities with those of a wife, mother, church member, praise team vocalist, aerobics instructor, and sports enthusiast. I never slowed down, always tried to remain in control, and often gave thanks to God for my blessings, all the while not acknowledging I was trying to do it all my way in my own power.

Just four months prior in April, we celebrated my 40th birthday. Friends and family members alike took turns telling hilarious stories of moments we had shared while playfully pointing out my unique personality traits. My children reminisced about the times God gave me the wisdom I prayed for and I strategically detected things that seemed amiss or when one of them was "stretching the truth." Co-workers described the precision with which I would conduct medical transports across the globe, using a certain tone of voice and not-so-subtle look to get my point across—even to those who didn't understand English. I was notorious for speaking English—in whatever accent was appropriate for the country—slowly, deliberately, and very loudly. My older sister's gift to me summed up the sentiments that evening. It was a key chain inscribed with the words, "I'm not bossy; I just have better ideas."

In essence, I knew Jesus as my savior and espoused Him to be my Lord without truly relinquishing control. I sat on the throne of my life, making decisions and setting goals. As a believer, I possessed the very power living inside me that raised Jesus Christ from the dead yet chose not to tap into it but instead relied on my own strength and abilities. I had even read the warnings in God's Holy Word the Bible, stating how God opposes the proud and exalts or lifts up the humble. James 4:6 states, *"But He gives us more grace. That is why Scripture says: 'God opposes the proud but gives grace to the humble.'"* As often happens in life, God chose to teach me this powerful truth in a most unusual and very painful way.

It was a beautiful, sunny day as we touched down on the 6,000-foot runway in Marco Island, Florida, in our medically outfitted Lear Jet. My captain, Miles, along with the first officer, Jim, and I were on a routine mission to transport a 76-year-old woman and her husband to their home in Lexington, Kentucky. The patient, suffering from lung cancer, had signed do-not-resuscitate papers, so I was the only medical crewmember onboard that fateful day. We normally flew with at least two. My patient also chose to sit up for the flight instead of reclining on the stretcher, which forced me to sit forward in the cabin on the jump seat instead of on the rear bench seat, where I sat most of the time.

After placing my patient on oxygen and attaching heart and vital sign monitors, I secured myself into the jump seat adjacent to the cockpit and directly behind my co-pilot. The flight proved uneventful, and I shared pleasant conversation with my patient and her husband, a former WWII pilot, while closely monitoring her cardiac rhythm, oxygen levels, and other vital signs. We were 20 minutes out of Lexington when we began our gradual descent. I heard my captain and co-pilot progress through their landing sequence checklist and obtain clearance from the control tower. I secured all my equipment and verified that my patient and her husband remained secured under their seatbelts.

We touched down at one o'clock in the afternoon on the Friday of Labor Day weekend, going 150 mph. I did not feel the normal sense of slowing down, and I heard my pilot exclaim, "No brakes, no brakes. Brake me." From my vantage point, I could see Miles standing up on the brakes with all of his might. I didn't panic, as I knew we had a backup system on board this aircraft, the reverse thrusters. When engaged, they force the thrust of the engine to change from back to front, providing drag, thus allowing the aircraft to slow forward momentum. I watched as my captain deployed them, but quickly realized they too had failed. He valiantly tried once more but to no avail. I heard my co-pilot, Jim, shout, "We need to slow down. Deploying emergency brake." This proved too little too late, but it did change our trajectory.

Jim firmly announced, "Hold on, hold on," as we careened off the end of the runway, off a 60-foot cliff out of control, heading into a ditch. The change in direction resulting from using the emergency brake helped us miss a cement pole, but instead we smashed into a wooden ILS structure. The impact of hitting the ILS tower tore away our right wing and half of our onboard fuel supply. The out-of-control aircraft slammed into the side of a deep ditch, shearing off our landing gear. Now fully ablaze, we skidded on the belly of the aircraft across six lanes of the only major highway in the area. We finally came to an abrupt stop in the emergency lane. The force of the impact shot up my legs and spine, sending excruciating pain throughout my body.

I was shaken, writhing in pain, and battling unconsciousness but was able to somehow survey the situation. Years of training and experience proved helpful in maintaining my calm. My captain, Miles, was draped over the yoke, unconscious, with blood oozing down his forehead. My patient was slumped forward and nonresponsive, as was her husband, sitting just behind her. A wooden partition separated me from my co-pilot, but I could hear him moaning.

"Jimmy, Jimmy, are you all right?" I begged.

"No, Di," he answered. "I think I broke my back; I can't move my legs."

By now I smelled and saw intense smoke. Witnesses said the flames were shooting 100 feet into the air. Realizing we were trapped inside a blazing inferno, I knew I had to act quickly. The door was right in front of me. I unlatched my seatbelt and tried to stand and open it. Brave people outside the plane also tried to open the door—one man actually broke his hand in the process—but they were unable to get it open. It was mechanically geared in a locked position to prevent it from opening in flight.

I couldn't stand, and I didn't understand why. Intense fear racked my mind as I frantically tried once more to stand and open the door. I couldn't. What I didn't know at the time was that the impact shoved my lower leg bones up behind my upper leg bones, shearing away all the supporting ligaments and causing posterior knee dislocation. In the process, the major arteries supplying blood to my lower legs ruptured, causing me to hemorrhage internally. I also fractured a vertebra in my upper back, collapsing my right lung and rendering me critically injured.

I was on the verge of panic, realizing we were trapped and would possibly burn to death or at least die of smoke inhalation. At that very moment, realizing I could do nothing in my own strength, I stopped struggling and cried out, "Dear God, in Jesus' name, please save us, please save us now." I kept reciting this prayer, accepting there was nothing else I could do.

In Second Corinthians it says, *"My strength is sufficient for you, for My power is made perfect in your weakness."* His Word is truth. In that moment, my captain awoke. He felt someone gently shaking him and heard a soft voice saying, "Open the door, Miles." He also heard me praying, so he knew it wasn't my voice that spoke to him. He got up from the cockpit and stumbled back a few feet, lifted open the door, and fell out onto the grassy knoll. The bystanders who had valiantly attempted to open the door from the outside now began pulling us from the wreckage.

My patient was pulled out first, followed by her husband. The man who pulled me out said he could not see me sitting two feet inside the aircraft because of the thick black smoke, but he could hear me praying. He stepped inside, lifted me into his arms, and carried me out.

I saw my co-pilot trapped in the cockpit and begged, "Please someone save him."

An off-duty firefighter working as an airport security officer came on the scene. He was also a horse jockey and thus had a small stature. He stepped inside, wrapped his arms around my massive six-foot, 270-pound co-pilot and pulled him out like he was a rag doll. Ironically, he had failed a strength agility test just weeks prior at the fire department. During this time, an on-duty firefighter dressed in his full gear arrived and stuck his upper body inside the aircraft to help extricate my co-pilot. He received second-degree burns across the back of his neck in the process.

My patient died at the scene, and my co-pilot, captain, and the patient's husband were transported to the emergency room by ambulance. But I was flown by a medical helicopter to a level one trauma center, as my injuries were assessed to be most life threatening. Within an hour, I had gone through numerous tests, revealing I needed immediate surgery. I had to sign a consent form stating they were going to use one of my veins to try and reestablish blood flow to my legs, but if unsuccessful, they might need to amputate. I lay there on the stretcher battling shock and facing the fact I had no control of the situation.

My son called the hospital at that very moment, and my nurse, Lee, got me the phone. I heard my 19-year-old six-foot-two-inch hockey player sobbing on the other end begging, "Please, Mom, tell me you're OK. I need you. Please don't die." He then told me the prayer chain at church had started and that everyone was praying for me. Instantly, warmth flooded my body. It was the peace that passes all understanding as promised in Philippians 4:7.

While the surgical staff hurried about to get me ready, I asked if we could pray. You could have heard a pin drop. I am not sure if my prayer was even audible, but I asked God to please be with me as I went into surgery and if it be His will, could I have my legs when I came out. If not, I asked that He please give me the grace to handle it. That is the last thing I can remember for over a week. I underwent 13 hours of surgery. I received over ten units of blood and almost died several times. I was admitted into the intensive care for seven days, sedated on a ventilator, battling lung and kidney failure, a bleeding disorder, and a temperature of 104. Any of these complications could have killed me, and the combination statistically should have, but thankfully God had other plans.

I awoke with my husband at my bedside and ten-pound fixator rods protruding from my ankles to my hips, stabilizing my legs. The pain I experienced could only be described as intense electrical shock and scalding burning sensations shooting through my legs. Both sides of my lower legs were filleted open. Every time I moved, the metal rods screwed into my leg bones rubbed against my skin, causing discomfort. The nursing staff medicated me as much as was possible, and my family and friends prayed with me, read Scripture verses to me, and played praise worship music to help relax me. Numerous physicians managed my care and informed me I would need multiple surgeries to repair the damage to my knees, and if I ever walked again, it would be with a limp. My family and several close friends took turns keeping vigilance at my bedside and helping care for me the entire time I was in the hospital in Kentucky.

After three weeks, I begged my husband to take me home to Florida. After a second surgery, I was flown back on another air medical aircraft and admitted to a local trauma center near my home in St. Petersburg, Florida. I spent another two and a half weeks there, receiving therapy and undergoing yet more surgery. Finally, I came home, and my family cared for me around the clock. I also attended outpatient therapy three times a week. For close to two years, I struggled through difficult and painful therapy. I made slow but steady progress while battling frustration and depression. Being reliant on others for everything proved extremely difficult for me. I had always been the caregiver, and now I was the one in need of constant care.

It was apparent once again to me that I could not get through this difficult situation in my own strength. I decided to pray for God's grace, not for an entire day, but for the next 60 seconds. I needed help just to get me through an exercise or feeling of despair. I found solace as I daily read God's Word and claimed His many promises, such as:

*For I know the plans I have for you declares the Lord. Plans to prosper you and not to harm you, plans to give you hope and a future* (Jeremiah 29:11 KJV).

*My grace is sufficient for you, for My power is made perfect in weakness* (2 Corinthians 12:9 KJV).

*Call upon Me in the day of trouble; I will deliver you, and you shall glorify Me* (Psalm 50:15 KJV).

*Call to Me, and I will answer you, and show you great and mighty things, which you do not know* (Jeremiah 33:3 KJV).

*"Cry aloud to our God in your trouble"* and then *"Give thanks to the Lord for His goodness,"* (Psalm 107:8 KJV).

*O Lord my God, I cried out to you, and you healed me* (Psalm 30:2 KJV).

*Dear friends, do not be surprised at the painful trial you are suffering, as though something strange were happening to you. But rejoice that you participate in the sufferings of Christ, so that you may be overjoyed when His glory is revealed* (1 Peter 3:12-13 KJV).

*I can do all things through Christ which strengthens me* (Philippians 4:13 KJV).

Holding fast to God's Word reminded me that if the God who parted the Red Sea, walked on water, healed the deaf and blind, rose from the dead, and saved me from a burning aircraft decided I would walk, I'd walk. And, if He decided I would run, then I would run. I also felt depression and sadness flee each time I turned on the television and sang contemporary praise music. I recalled how King Saul would call for David to come play his harp when he was emotionally and spiritually tormented, and then, his entire mood would transform. God's gift of music is powerful and a wonderful source of blessing and healing. The Bible tells us in Philippians 4:4 to *"rejoice in the Lord always."* We are to rejoice or give thanks, not necessarily for all the difficult circumstances surrounding our situation, but for God's faithfulness and promise to never leave us nor forsake us (see Deut. 31:6).

I also held tight to Romans 8:28, *"And we know that all things [even a plane crash] work together for good to them that love God, to them who are the called according to His purpose."* I came to understand "good" did not mean my physical pleasure, worldly wealth, or high status, but instead to be transformed more into the image of Christ my Lord and Savior. *That* was the very purpose of my creation in the first place, to glorify God in all things. He used the most difficult experience I had ever been through to conform me, mold me, and make me to be more like Jesus. God took away my control, pride, and impatience and replaced it with sweet fruits of the Spirit such as peace, mercy, longsuffering, patience, goodness, and joy. I wasn't always happy to be suffering, but God's joy flooded my soul. When I chose to praise God and count my blessings instead of focus on the negative and my pain, my spirit lightened. I believe I had a choice, and I chose joy.

God's grace proved sufficient, just as He promised. He met my every need. I learned how to let go and let God. He met my physical, financial, emotional, and spiritual needs. I saw firsthand the importance of the church, the Body of Christ. Fellow believers became the hands and feet of Jesus as they brought food, provided transportation, cleaned my house, cut my hair, performed massages, donated money, and visited me. A local church held a spaghetti dinner fundraiser where I shared the story of my miraculous survival for the first time. It was emotional, yet very therapeutic as I recalled all the specific miraculous details that God arranged to create the huge, amazing miracle of my survival. Not only did I survive, but I also thrived and regained almost all of my strength. I did lose a job I loved and mourned the loss of my career. I was also left with horrific scars on my legs, which caused people to stop and stare.

My daughter wrote me a poem for Mother's Day, which finally changed the way I looked at my scars. It was entitled, "My Mom, the Portrait of Beauty." A portion of that poem that Mallory wrote was:

> When I look into my mother's face, I see a woman created in the image of God. I see the structure of her face shaped by His very hand. Eyes of warmth, cheeks of laughter, a smile of compassion, ears ever ready to listen, and soft flowing hair that shapes the face of beauty.

> When I look into my mother's face, I don't see wrinkles. Instead, I see the lines of laughter that trace out the years of a life lived happily. I see the most beautiful legs anyone could ask for. I don't see the scars left from surgeries. Instead, I see the thumbprints of God's protection and provision. I see a reflection of the marks on my Lord's hands and feet, and become even more aware of the likeness of her to my Savior.

The precious gift of her words helped change my perspective. My ugly scars truly were the result of God's miraculous intervention in my life. Something tragic and painful could be used for God's glory. They gave me a unique opportunity to share with all who asked about them the amazing story of God's divine miracle in my life. As soon as someone heard I had survived a fatal plane crash, I had their full attention.

I began sharing my story at churches, ladies groups, schools, and civic functions. Each time I told the intricate details surrounding my survival and recovery, lives were touched. Once I was asked to share it with the senior class of nursing students at St. Petersburg College of Nursing, where I had graduated in 1982. After that, they asked me to speak at several of their graduations. Eventually, I began working at the college and now serve as an adjunct clinical instructor. Although I miss my flight-nurse job, I adore being an educator. I love teaching students, sharing my experiences, and inspiring them to be the best they can be. I remind them that nursing is a career God calls you to, where you can touch someone in their darkest hour of need not only physically but emotionally and spiritually as well.

I can honestly say that I would not change the few years of struggle and pain I have endured, because of all that I, as well as my family, have gained. In a small way, I better understand pain and realize that Christ suffered pain willingly and ultimately died and rose again to save us from our sins. I stand in awe that He has chosen me to be one of His very own and has called me to share my story so that others might be drawn closer to Him. I now have a unique opportunity to serve Him in a different yet more powerful way. I praise Him for being the God who is the same yesterday, today, and forever. Although He chose in love to change my path, my character, my goals, and my ambitions through a difficult trial, praise God, He remains the same, and I can trust Him always.

## ABOUT THE CONTRIBUTOR

Diana Burgess is a critical care flight nurse who, since surviving a deadly plane crash, began teaching nursing at a local college. She is happily married to her high school sweetheart. They have a son and daughter, who are both married as well. Diana travels sharing the miraculous story of her survival and recovery from life-threatening and devastating injuries as well as the many things God taught her through this difficult ordeal. She can be reached through her Website at http://www.dianaburgess.com or via email at flydi21@hotmail.com.

# CHAPTER 20

# THE MIRACLE OF THE WORD

## *Dr. Theresa Veach*

*In the beginning was the Word, and the Word was with God,
and the Word was God* (John 1:1 KJV).

If I absolutely had to choose one verse from Holy Scripture that is my favorite, it would be: *"In the beginning was the Word, and the Word was with God and the Word was God"* (John 1:1 KJV). In a way, John says it all with this one statement. God is the Word, the one and only Word. The Word always has been and always will be. Every single thing that has ever been made was made by and through this one Word—this one Word. Wow. It just doesn't get any better than that.

I like to think of this one Word as simple, maybe even so simple it is only one syllable, one breath. In its utter simplicity, the Word is mightier than a thousand tongues and so good—so very, very good. Now let me take a moment to note something here: the Word can be mighty and the Word can be good only if the Word is alive, and yes, my dear friend, the Word is indeed alive.

Ever since I became a believer in Jesus (Yeshua) as the One True God, I somehow also came to know, at least intellectually, that His Holy written Word is very different from all other written texts. I know that it is different if only for the simple fact that it was penned by over 40 different authors over the course of thousands of years and yet every theme, every symbol, and every story is so intricately woven into one message that its design staggers the human mind. If those facts alone weren't enough to make me a believer in our Bible as inspired through and through by none other than our Lord's Holy Spirit Himself, then the miracles I have experienced by the reading of His Word surely did.

The first miracle I received through our Lord's Holy Word happened during a time of need for physical and emotional healing. I had been so sick that I had not left the house for many months. I had been to numerous physicians, and no one could definitively diagnose me. I thought that life as I knew it was over. I would spend hours laying on the sofa or in bed thinking of how it used to be when I was able to work as a licensed psychologist and have the blessing of being instrumental in the healing of others. Now it felt that there was no one who could possibly help me in my own healing.

It was in the early spring when I received the telephone call. I remember it was in the spring because my husband had bought a new car for me in December, and by the time I had received the telephone call it was springtime, and I had still not even sat in the car, let alone driven it. As usual, we let the answering machine pick up the call. It was a patient of mine, a dear young woman who I had not seen in many months. My husband asked me if I wanted him to tell her that I was too sick to take the call. Somehow, deep down in my spirit, I knew my Lord was telling me to take the call. I slowly got off the sofa and stood up, no small feat in and of itself.

She was in dire need. She was scheduled to have surgery the next day and desperately needed me to be with her after surgery. Again, I could hear my Lord speaking to me, "Go. Be with her, and I will be with you." I told her with all certainty that I would be there for her in the morning.

*What in the world had I promised her?*

I knew my Lord had told me what to do. I knew I was going to be obedient. This meant only one thing: my Lord was going to miraculously heal me in the night. I was going to wake up good as new—or at least well enough to go to the hospital for an hour or two.

I woke up the next morning. I wasn't healed. I could barely move. I went downstairs and reached for my Bible. I didn't know where to turn. I didn't know what passage to find. I just opened it and began to read:

> *I will sing of mercy and judgment: unto Thee, O LORD, will I sing. I will behave myself wisely in a perfect way. O when wilt Thou come unto me? I will walk within my house with a perfect heart. I will set no wicked thing before mine eyes: I hate the work of them that turn aside; it shall not cleave to me* (Psalm 101:1-3 KJV).

There it was, one word, one healing word, "cleave." As soon as I read that one word, I knew I had been instantly healed and healed through and through. As soon as I read that one word, it was as if my Lord said to me, "I do not allow anything wicked to cleave to me—to become one with me—and neither did David, and neither will you." Somehow I knew that all the pain and suffering I had been exposed to in my work as a psychologist had "cleaved to me," rendering me sick and utterly useless to help others. With that one word, He set me free from all the wickedness that I had allowed to settle into my spirit. I felt clean. I felt whole. I felt well. The breath of God had moved through my spirit, clearing out everything and anything that wasn't of Him and His goodness. Praise be to the One and Only Living God.

The miracle did not stop with me. As I entered the hospital room, the woman in need could instantly feel our Lord's healing presence. She, too, experienced a type of healing that she had never known before…all this from just One Word.

But wait. That is not all. The miracle of His Word continues.

My husband and I were going through an incredible time reading our Lord's Word together at night before we went to bed. It wasn't one of those "time to do our duty and read the Bible" kinds of things.

It was so much more than that. We couldn't wait to read the Bible. Every passage was coming to life for us. It was making sense like never before, and we were starting to "get it" historically, symbolically, and meaningfully. Then, we ran headlong into a brick wall.

I was reading out of Second Kings 19 and 20 where good King Hezekiah receives a letter from the bad king of Assyria. That was all I could understand about the entire message. I just couldn't understand what was going on. My mind had become clouded and confused. The more I read and re-read, the more frustrated I became. I remember that I just had to stop reading right then and there. I didn't want to; I had to. I rolled over and tried to go to sleep, wondering why in the world I couldn't grasp the message my Lord had for me that night.

The next day, I went to work as usual. Since I have about an hour commute, I almost always listen to worship music—loudly. I can't listen to the radio for most of my commute because it goes in and out of frequencies more times than I can count. Rarely, if ever, can I tune into a radio station and listen to it for more than a few minutes at a time. When my workday is done, well, that is a different story. More often than not, I am silent in my car. No music. No cell phone. No radio. Silence. I am tired and need a break.

The very next day after not being able to understand the Bible passage, something miraculous happened. I was on my way home from work, and once again, I was having quiet time with my Lord. A semi in the lane next to me began to crowd over onto my side of the highway. He just wouldn't let up. He was really harassing me. My first thought was to give him the "what for," but I decided to act as if I didn't even notice him. I began to rummage in my purse, put on lipstick, and then I did something I almost never do on my way home from work.

*I turned on my radio.*

*The station was as clear as can be.*

I began to hear a *pastor preaching* on the Word of God.

The pastor began preaching about *the prophets during the time of King Hezekiah.*

The pastor began preaching about *King Hezekiah.*

The pastor noted that we could go to *Second Kings 19 and 20* ourselves if we wanted to find out more about King Hezekiah.

The pastor began preaching on the specifics of Second Kings chapters 19 and 20—after *stating specifically that he had not intended to preach from this passage.*

The pastor began preaching on the *king of Assyria.*

The pastor began preaching on *the letter* the king of Assyria sent to King Hezekiah.

The pastor began preaching on *details of the meaning of the letter* and its importance in biblical history.

*The frequency of the radio station was clear* and never wavered, not once during the entire message.

I was laughing all the way home. I could almost see my Lord smiling down on me, head thrown back with delight saying, "My Word is alive. I am alive. I am with you always. I am with you when you are reading and in My Living Word."

The Word, He is Scripture of Scriptures, the Lord of lords, the King of kings, the Word, He is the Miracle of miracles.

## ABOUT THE CONTRIBUTOR

After searching for God for 40 years in almost every world religion, Dr. Theresa Veach finally met the One True God, Jesus, in one miraculous moment on February 22, 2002, at 8:05 in the morning. She shares her journey home to Jesus with other seekers in her book, *The Force of My Yeshua.* She has been interviewed on radio programs across the United States and has shared her testimony on "The Harvest Show," which is viewed around the world. Interviewing other believers who are passionate about sharing their love for Jesus, Theresa reported their miracle messages on her webtalkradio.net program, "All About Miracles." Currently, she is working with veterans from wars, past and present, as they heal from the trauma of combat.

# CHAPTER 21

# "Remember This"—Heaven Is Real

## *Ron and Glenda Pettey*

*Jesus answered, "I am the way and the truth and the life. No one comes to the Father except through me"* (John 14:6).

"What do you mean, my name's not there?" I asked, for I knew that I stood at the very gates of Heaven. Seeing I was determined to enter, the bookkeeper angel carefully searched the pages of a massive book once again. Yet my name wasn't there.

"But I've done everything necessary to enter Heaven. I've accepted Jesus as my Lord and Savior. Have I been deceived?"

Suddenly, a second angel stepped forward and asked, "Can I be of service?" After the keeper of the book explained my dilemma, he offered to go in and double check.

I began to feel better, expecting this delay would soon be over. As I waited, a low hum of voices became audible, as if coming from an auditorium filled with people. Able to hear the hum but not able to distinguish the words, I asked, "What's all that noise?"

"Don't you know?" replied the keeper of the book. "These are the intercessory prayers coming up on your behalf."

Though I deeply appreciated their concern for me, I felt a bit quarrelsome. The truth was, I didn't *want* their prayers answered. I *wanted* to enter Heaven and be with Jesus and worship Him.

Then the sound changed. I heard a host of little ones at play in a bubbling stream of water just beyond the gates of Heaven. As I listened, I recognized the unmistakable voice of my son, Jason, who would have been three years old, had he lived. I stepped forward to find him, but a powerful angel blocked my way.

"That's far enough," he said. "Your son is fine and well taken care of."

Then, a new scene unfolded before me. A vast flow of people of all ages, including a multitude of quiet, orderly children, moved toward the source of the ethereal light all around me.

It was the Lord! Light radiated from and through Him. In my human experience and limited vocabulary, I can't fully describe the magnificent beauty and stunning radiance of His countenance.

Aware that I was watching as He welcomed each person, the Savior raised His arms to receive a particular young man. As He embraced this child, whom I didn't recognize, Jesus looked directly into my eyes and said: "Remember this."

Overwhelmed that He would speak to me, I paid close attention. As the young man came near to Jesus, the lad glanced at me and smiled. Then he disappeared, engulfed in the flowing sleeve of Jesus' glowing garment. Suddenly, I realized the boy had literally passed *through* Jesus into Heaven.

The truth of John 14:6 suddenly became clear. *"No one comes to the Father but through Me"* (NASB). Could it be that the scriptural references to Jesus being the door and the gate into Heaven were not figurative as I had thought? My mind could scarcely contain what I had witnessed.

Years later, the Lord helped me understand the wonder and power of the two words. Just as He spoke our world into existence, "Let there be light," He commissioned me to "Remember this," though my natural memory would remain severely impaired for years to come.

I'll also never forget His eyes. Dark and crystal clear, they overflowed with a love beyond my comprehension. Although He knew my heart and my thoughts, He accepted me as I was: transformed in His sight, without faults or blemishes.

Though I was keenly aware of His majesty as King of kings and Lord of lords, the relationship He imparted to me was Abba, Father. Daddy. I felt accepted as part of His *family*. Love was in the form of a person.

His eyes also revealed a deep sadness, yet deep compassion, for the people who refuse to accept His free gift of life and love.

Suddenly, the second angel returned. With sympathetic firmness, he said, "It is not yet your time; your mission is not complete. You're being sent back, and I'm going with you." (I would realize later that my name was certainly in the Lamb's Book of Life, and would appear in the registry when the right time came.)

Desperate for an excuse to stay, I demanded to see my wife, whom I actually had no memory of at that moment.

Immediately, I found myself back in the operating room where I'd left the Earth and gone to Heaven. I could see the surgical staff working furiously to bring me back. One of the doctors had straddled my body and was pounding my chest in an effort to revive me.

"You must go back to your body now," said my escort.

"That body...so full of pain and grief...you want me to get back in there?" I asked.

"Yes," he answered. I obeyed, entering my body at the head.

After some time in recovery, I awakened. The angel told me I would see my wife, but he didn't tell me how I would react. I had absolutely no memory of our life together, so when I saw her, I was amazed and awed with the wife God had provided.

I'd soon learn her name was Glenda. We'd met on a blind date nine years before, fallen madly in love, and shared the birth of two beautiful daughters. She'd kept faithful vigil at my side for the past several weeks, praying for me, as her mother watched our children at our home.

I would also learn my severe headaches had been caused by spinal fluid collecting in my brain, a condition called hydrocephalus. Though urgent surgery to drain the spinal fluid had helped, relief was short-lived, as I was back in the hospital within three years for additional shunt revisions. Less than a year after that, an internal infection meant the shunt had to be replaced. Glenda reminded me how we'd both hoped this brain surgery would finally solve the problem, but neither of us could have imagined what challenges still lay ahead.

Inadvertently, the neurosurgeons had implanted the new shunt into a massive blood clot not visible on X-rays. It was from this operating table that my spirit had taken its incredible journey into the realms of Heaven.

Thankfully, my escort back to Earth, whom I later realized was my guardian angel, stayed at my bedside. What a constant source of encouragement and comfort he was during the remaining weeks in the ICU, though visible only to me. His ear-to-ear smile was like no other: Heavenly, full of the Father's love...and Jesus Christ, Himself.

As my health improved, my angel spoke to me, saying, "Ron, be slow in sharing your testimony."

"*Slow.*" I thought, "How can I be slow? I want to climb atop the highest building in Houston with a megaphone and shout '*Heaven is real. Put your life in order.*'"

But the word *slow* would also describe my recovery, a trial the Holy Spirit used to teach me extraordinary patience. Despite my severely impaired memory and constant headaches, my judgment remained intact. Glenda and I made lifelong decisions, including allowing the Lord to bless us with more children.

Simultaneously, God opened the door for Glenda and I to share our miraculous story. Whether a deacon's business meeting, a Saturday morning men's breakfast, or a one-on-one encounter with people in offices or restaurants, God was glorified each time, as we kept our central focus on Jesus: the Way, the Truth, and the Life.

Soon, the Lord prompted us to move back to Lufkin, Texas, my hometown, to honor my parents while also relinquishing our debt. By May of 1992, we joined a friendly little church where a catfish dinner was planned on a Saturday afternoon.

I awoke that day with a terrible headache, but Glenda insisted we attend the outdoor gathering. Encouraged by Glenda to find something on the buffet table to eat, I struggled to choose wisely, as the multiple brain surgeries had made me diabetic. As I scanned the table, I caught a glimpse of a single fried founder. Staring at the small fish, I subconsciously muttered, "That's a flounder; I've been floundering."

In that instant, my headache left, and my memory returned. I beamed across the table at my wife, barely able to control my excitement.

"Glenda...it's back," I said. "My memory's been fully restored."

By the mid-'90s, a college professor invited us to speak to his psychology class with time reserved for students' comments. We honed our skills in spontaneity as we answered all concerns from this nonreligious crowd. A second offer soon came from another professor across the campus, reinforcing our reputation of the "dead man" coming to class. For many glorious years, we openly declared, from *personal experience*, that Jesus is the only way into Heaven—none other but *Him*.

Our autobiography, *Heaven Is Real*, became reality in 1998, putting into print the glorious details of my out-of-body encounter, miraculous healing, and the supernatural ministry that's come from these life-changing events.

Not long after, we found a new home in a local, Spirit-filled church. Scriptures we'd read many times before in the Bible came alive to us, helping us realize the power of Jesus, through the Holy Spirit, remains just as available to us today as it was to Jesus and to His disciples more than 2,000 years ago.

Prophetic guest speakers to our congregation were quick to recognize a gift of healing Jesus had given to my hands. Though this was a new concept to us, we trusted the Lord to show us the way in His new ministry. Frequently, people asked us to pray for their physical needs after hearing our testimony. First friends, then complete strangers, began to call us for prayer appointments.

Miraculously, Jesus' healing gift began to manifest as an ability to "see" the need. Many times we were asked to pray for someone, the Lord graciously provided a heightened sense of discernment, illuminating the actual organ or body part in need of prayer.

Glenda and I also quickly learned to ask the Lord *how* to pray, for the Holy Spirit to specifically give us the right words, to help us always be attentive to His voice and fully submit to Him.

Eventually, the Lord began to show me emotional scars and unhealed inner wounds that people carry. How marvelous to see the Lord mend a broken heart.

In 2008, Sid Roth invited us to an interview on his program, "It's Supernatural." With the radio, television, and Internet interviews broadcast throughout the United States and the world, our book, *Heaven Is Real,* went into its third and fourth printing.

We love to celebrate the Lord with the power of His testimony, the touch of Jesus on a life. And because it *is* the touch of Jesus, those miracles are made available in the lives of all those who listen and believe. We learned long ago that "a man with an argument is no match for a man with an experience."

We publish testimonies on our Website to praise *Him*, and encourage people. These gifts the Father so generously gives us are not about us, but rather all about *Him* and His purposes. All Glory belongs to Him alone. May you find yourself drawing closer to *Him* as you progress in the destiny He's planned just for you.

## ABOUT THE CONTRIBUTORS

The Petteys' powerful prayer ministry, which incorporates specific, God-given insights into individual physical, emotional, and spiritual needs, has helped hundreds of people over the years. To learn more about their ministry or to order their book, available in English and Spanish, visit their Website: www.rgministries.org.

# CHAPTER 22

# FACE TO FACE WITH JESUS

## *Dr. Sherry Anne Lints*

*And He died for all, that those who live should live no longer for themselves, but for Him who died for them and rose again* (2 Corinthians 5:15 NKJV).

The question has been asked of me many times, "When did Jesus Christ become more than just a name to you?"

Truthfully, I don't remember Him ever being *just a name* to me. My mother has vivid memories of me loving Jesus as a child. When I was a mere six years old, I wrote a poem about Jesus in school and would talk about Him and would even talk *to* Him. As far as I knew, I always loved Him, always knew Him—surely, I must have known Him, right? After all, didn't I do all the right things? I went to religious education classes. I attended church regularly. I wore my pretty Sunday dress, with white bobby socks and black patent leather shoes. I sat, bowed, and kneeled. I prayed, confessed, and communed. Yet, sadly, I was soon to learn that I knew *of* Him, but, no, I didn't really *know* Him—until one painful day, when I met Him face to face.

To understand the circumstances leading me to this pivotal moment, allow me to first explain what my growing-up experience was like. Between my two parents, there were six divorces. Out of that came nine half-brothers and sisters, five step-brothers and sisters, as well as my brother and myself. Therefore, my upbringing was, shall we say, tumultuous at best. Love meant intense discipline, followed by vicious cycles of tearing down and building back up, only there was no time to build back up before the next storm would hit again. Self-worth did not exist, and family members all needed to search for various ways to make meaning out of chaos. Some chose alcohol, some chose sex, some chose violence and rage, but all played the game—all were actors in this drama that repeated itself daily; all wore masks.

For some reason, and maybe it is because of His sovereign hand on my life, I did not turn to these "bad vices." I was going to be a "good girl." I would go to church and pray that I would "do right by God." I decided I would not smoke or drink, and I vowed that I would not have sex outside of marriage. This, I figured, would make God very happy with me, and then at least one person would love me and not be angry with me, so I thought.

Unable to please or change my alcoholic, abusive parents at home, I became an extreme over-achiever in school—striving my way to the top. This was in spite of the fact that, at the age of five, it was discovered by the school nurse that I had a hearing and speech impairment. Little did I know that I was becoming addicted to man's accolades and to my drug of choice, pride. I had trophies in everything from fishing to bowling to pageants, complete with tiaras and sashes, full scholarships, and a whole lot of newspaper publicity. I couldn't get enough. I was the poster child for perfectionism—not that I even knew what that meant at the time. I was gloating with success, and I seemed to have it all.

Sure enough, this standard of excellence drove me right into a nervous breakdown during my first trimester of chiropractic college. I couldn't achieve the grades that I was used to in high school and undergraduate college. I was overwhelmed by the poor acoustics of the large auditoriums, and the school was not set up for the disabled. I was so used to being a big fish in a little pond, and now I was nothing but a little fish in a very large pond. I was scared and confused, and my ego was becoming bruised.

Shortly after, I lost my first and only serious relationship—a man I loved and who I thought loved me. At that point, I was convinced that I was unlovable and began to believe all those lies I heard as a child (that I was no good, that I was a mistake, etc.). I wondered how I could be worth anything if my parents didn't love me, my family didn't love me, my boyfriend didn't love me, my school didn't love me—if I didn't love me?

I felt there was no purpose for my existence, and therefore no hope for me. I wanted to throw in the towel. I threatened the Lord that I was going to end it all unless He could give me one good reason not to. I lay on the floor kicking and screaming, begging Him for help, asking Him for any sign that He was real or even heard my prayer. It was at that moment that I literally saw the bloodstained face of Christ as He hung on a cross with a crown of thorns piercing His brow, lift His battered head to say, "I *died* for you; will you *live* for Me?"

I cannot even begin to express what a freeing moment that was for me. I immediately got up from the floor and onto my knees and began to thank God for saving my life, for dying that I might have life and have it more abundantly (see John 10:10). I did not need to do *anything* to please Him; He already loved me and chose to die for me to pay the price for any sin that I ever could and ever would commit. He paid the price for all the times I would fall short of His perfect will for my life, even when I thought I was doing everything right and didn't know that I wasn't. He gave His life as a sacrifice for me so that I could be reconciled to the Heavenly Father. I could never make right all the wrong things that I've done, but Jesus covered it once and for all by His death, by the giving of His life for mine. The Bible says, *"For the wages of sin is death; but the gift of God is eternal life through Jesus Christ our Lord"* (Rom. 6:23). Jesus paid that price for me—and you. Thanks be to God.

From this point on, I began to internalize the concept that Christ died to give *me* life and that I needed to die to *myself* and the sin of pride; I needed to turn it all over to Him and live for Him, not me. Through the workbook, *Search for Significance,* I realized that I did not need to earn Christ's love and that He already loved me even before

I ever got a single A+ or trophy in school. According to Ephesians 1:4-6, God chose me before the foundation of the world, and He accepted and adopted me before I ever knew Him or loved Him.

For the first time, I had a deep spiritual awakening in Christ. I saw the depths of my own sin and how very much I, in all my perfectionism, needed a Savior; I was not God, but He was. I now *knew* who He was and who I was not. I began to pick up the pieces of my broken, torn life and asked God to show me how I could best be used to show His glory and goodness to others who are lost and hurting and still trying to do it by themselves, for themselves. Christ never commanded us to "go it alone," but rather, through Him, we can achieve all things to reveal His image and bring glory to His name—to build His kingdom and not ours, for the betterment of mankind.

In the ten years that followed, I've been awe-struck watching God unfold a number of lifelong dreams before my eyes. You see, I have always wanted to be a singer, and I have also always wanted to be in a movie. I used to sing into a little one-dollar hairbrush as a young girl pretending that I was Whitney Houston and told myself that one day I would be on a tour bus. When I started attending a Pentecostal church as a teenager, a spiritual mother recognized a gift of music in me and introduced me to Christian music, specifically, Gospel and more specifically, the Gaithers. At 17, I did my first church solo and have been singing for churches and other events ever since.

As I watched the singing desire start to become fulfilled, I began to pray more earnestly for an opportunity to be in a movie, specifically a Christian movie. Through a series of God-orchestrated events, I made contact with Kelly's Filmworks, and in 2008, the same year I made my first CD, I appeared in my first movie. I have also seen the fulfillment of my longing to be on tour buses as I have enjoyed visiting a number of artist's tour buses in the last few years, either as a friend or to pay a doctor visit. I have since appeared in another film as well as a music video. I have written and continue to write community passion plays and have seen the salvation of unsaved family members and friends.

My prayer is that I would continue to grow daily in relationship with the Heavenly Father, the Son, and the Holy Spirit and in the knowledge of His Word. I ask that He would use my abilities, disabilities, and challenges to inspire hope among all people of all walks of life. I share my life story to tell you that God *does* have a plan, even when you don't see it or you didn't come from the best of circumstances. I've heard it said, "When you are at the end of your rope, you are not at the end of your hope." God hears you and He loves you. He has not forsaken you and will not leave you. Turn to Him, lean on Him, and trust in Him—*and Him Alone.*

I conclude this testimony with one of my favorite Scripture verses, encouraging us that God truly knows our heart's desires and is certain to bring His will to pass in His way and in His time, for His word says, *"He has made everything beautiful in its time"* (Eccles. 3:11a).

## About the Contributor

A native of Utica, New York, Sherry Anne Lints achieved a Doctorate of Chiropractic degree at the age of 24 and is certified as a fitness trainer. She currently owns and operates Better Health Chiropractic in upstate New York. Born with a bilateral hearing and speech impairment, Sherry Anne has a special love and ministry for individuals with disabilities. Frequently lecturing at elementary schools, vocational schools, and colleges, Sherry Anne shares the message of hope and instructs in abstinence, modesty, and self-respect.

Sherry Anne's greatest passion, however, is sharing her love of music and drama in churches, coffeehouses, conferences, events, seminars, and other venues. In the fall of 2008, Sherry released her debut CD, *Thank You,* produced by Woody Wright and recorded at Gaither Studios in Indiana. Sherry Anne's music can be heard on many radio and Internet stations across the globe. Additionally, Sherry Anne had the opportunity to play the role of a news reporter in the film *Clancy,* and also appeared in *The Perfect Gift.*

Her testimony can be seen on "100 Huntley Street" (Crossroads TV), where she made a guest appearance in Ontario, Canada. It is Sherry Anne's true desire to minister, worldwide, the message of God's unconditional love to the brokenhearted.

> *"Therefore, whether you eat or drink, or whatever you do, do all to the glory of God"* (1 Corinthians 10:31 KJV).

For booking information, contact: Sherry Anne Ministries, 2044 Genesee Street, Utica, NY, 13502, 315-735-1947. You can also visit www.SherryAnne.com, or email at office@SherryAnne.com or at drsalin@juno.com.

# CHAPTER 23

# JEWELS FROM HEAVEN

## *Daphyne Reiff*

*Do not store up for yourselves treasures on earth, where moth*
*and rust destroy, and where thieves break in and steal. But*
*store up for yourselves* treasures in Heaven, *where moth and*
*rust do not destroy, and where thieves do not break in and*
*steal. For where your treasure is, there your heart will be also*
(Matthew 6:19-21).

Our pastor laid hands on our baby, Lauryn, and we prayed for her life and for guidance for her surgeon. With tears and a certain amount of fear, we let them wheel her away to what turned out to be an eight-and-a-half-hour surgery.

Lauryn was only a year old then, and like many babies, she was born with a hole in her heart that was expected to close within the first year. But Lauryn had been different. The hole in her heart didn't close, and unlike most babies, she spent her first two months in the intensive care unit at Children's Hospital. She had been born three months premature, weighing two pounds, ten ounces, with a broken arm and underdeveloped lungs.

The operation seemed to go as planned: a few surprises here and there, but nothing out of the ordinary. We thanked God, thinking our prayers had been answered with the successful outcome—that is, until two years later during a bedtime prayer, she told us something about her surgery we couldn't have known.

Our tradition for Lauryn was to begin bedtime with the prayer, "Now I lay me down to sleep…and if I die before I wake."

When we got to that point, Lauryn said to us, "Do you remember when I died?"

My husband and I looked at each other as chills ran down our spines. We both said, "No, we don't remember a time when you died."

She said with a smile, "Yes, I did, during my heart surgery." She then continued to tell this amazing story.

"I saw you and Daddy playing that game you always play." (Lauryn's dad and I played backgammon to pass the time, and still play it today.) We asked her where she was when she saw this. She said she was above us looking down and watching. Then she went immediately to Heaven.

Lauryn continued, "I was in Heaven, and I saw Jesus standing there. I ran into His arms and He said 'Oh Lauryn, I have waited for you for so long.'"

She told how Jesus sat her down and gave her a hand full of jewels and a beautiful gown that sparkled. They walked and talked for a while, and Jesus let her sit on a cloud. And then He introduced her to her sister, Lisa. Lauryn had never been told that she had a sister in Heaven, nor did she know about receiving jewels for a crown.

"I saw angels. They were so beautiful," Lauryn said with a huge grin.

We asked if they had wings and if they looked like us.

"Yes, some of them did have wings and some did not," she said. "And no, they look nothing like us, but they are so beautiful." (She had never been told that many angels don't have wings.) Lauryn also mentioned that the colors in Heaven are more beautiful than here, and there are colors that are not in the rainbow.

We asked her if there were any toys in Heaven, thinking that if she were making up a story, like most kids at this age, she would include the best toys in the world. She thought for a moment and said there weren't any toys, but there was beautiful music and that she and Jesus danced.

Then she got very sad and tears came into her eyes. She said that Jesus told her it was time to go, that she must return to her parents, who needed her. She really started to cry, I told her it was OK. I knew what she was going to say and understood she didn't want to hurt our feelings.

She looked up into my eyes, tears shining on her cheeks, and said, "I didn't want to leave Jesus and Heaven." I hugged her and told her I wouldn't want to leave, either. Then she wiped her eyes and with her forehead wrinkled up she said, "Then He wanted to take my pretty jewels. I didn't want to give them back." Jesus assured her that He would take care of them and that there would even be more when she came back. So she let Jesus take the jewels for safekeeping.

In the weeks that followed, any time Lauryn would see a picture of Jesus, she would walk up and say, "That's not what He looks like." People would be curious, and once we asked her to draw a picture of Jesus, and as only a child could, Lauryn proceeded to draw the most beautiful, amazing stick figure of our Lord Jesus Christ.

As for Lauryn's sister in Heaven, I had an abortion when I was eighteen. I was encouraged to go through with it, being told that it was not alive. But afterward for several years, until Lauryn told me about her sister, I had always felt sick about it, like I had destroyed my own child. But when I heard that Lauryn had seen Lisa in Heaven, that heaviness was lifted. And I praise God for His matchless wisdom, answering a prayer I had never voiced. I never cease to be amazed by His Grace.

Jesus said to His disciples, "You must come to Me as a child, for such is the kingdom of God." We could clearly see His Kingdom in the tears of our little princess.

## ABOUT THE CONTRIBUTOR

Daphyne Reiff lives in Greenwood Village, Colorado, with her husband, Rick, daughter, Lauryn, and son, Jared. Daphyne is currently writing a book on the rapture, as well as a book on her own testimonies. In addition, she writes Christian songs, but her central passion is fundraising for abused children. She believes deeply in the power of sharing testimonies with others to further the Kingdom of the Lord.

This testimony is used by permission from story contributor Daphyne Reiff, and also by Jack Olson of www.OlsonHouse.org, where this testimony has been posted.

# PART III

# SUPERNATURAL HEALING STORIES

*Praise the LORD, O my soul; all my inmost being, praise His holy name. Praise the LORD, O my soul, and forget not all His benefits—who forgives all your sins and heals all your diseases, who redeems your life from the pit and crowns you with love and compassion, who satisfies your desires with good things so that your youth is renewed like the eagle's* (Psalm 103:1-5).

# CHAPTER 24

# FROM DEATH TO LIFE

## *Russell VerMulm*

*Then the angel showed me the river of the water of life, as clear
as crystal flowing from the throne of God and of the Lamb
down the middle of the great street of the city. On each side of
the river stood the tree of life, bearing twelve crops of fruit,
yielding its fruit every month. And the leaves of the tree are for
the healing of the nation* (Revelation 22: 1-2).

Every life is a story, each day another page being written. To a
certain extent, we each get to choose how our stories will read by the
choices we make each day. My story starts in a small town in South
Dakota. I was born in a large family of eight, with the youngest dying
during birth. We were poor, and at the time I resented it, but as the
years have gone by, and the people I have met and shared Christ with,
I have come to realize how fortunate I was growing up in a poor
Christian home, instead of a non-Christian home.

My father and mother could not always provide for us, but we
never lacked love. They always saw to it that we went to church,
Sunday school, and Wednesday night services. In my senior year
of high school, it was the year that the pastor made his last play for
the senior class souls prior to each child going off to college, the
military, or trade school. I was no exception, as he met with me one
Wednesday evening, asking if I was ready to make a commitment

for Christ. I was probably like most people believing the lie of satan, thinking I was coming up with some grand new scheme to dodge the bullet. Being a Christian would be living a life without fun, so I, the fool, thought.

I informed the pastor that I would be going into the military, and that before I made that commitment, I wanted to be sure and not just go through the motions. I'm sure he had never heard that story before. I was not a bad kid; I wasn't doing drugs, drinking, or anything wild. My respect for my father would have never allowed that. I would have never wanted to disappoint him. It was not that he forced that; it was an unspoken love by my mother and him that keep me from that highway in life.

So I left for the military free from the perceived bars of the Christian life, finally on my own. I went to basic training at Great Lakes in Chicago. I got my bunk assignment, and who do you think I got to sleep next to? A Christian sharing the Gospel. I spent nine weeks bunked next to this guy, wow, but it went fast, and I was finally off to San Diego, California, for Radioman (A) School. I get to the barracks and checked in, and guess what? My roommates were Christians sharing the Gospel. Can you get away from these people or what?

I spent two months in San Diego and finally was off to my duty station, Norfolk, Virginia, at the naval communications station. I get to the barracks where I will be living and get my room assignment, so I drag my duffle bag with all my gear to the second floor. I find my room and open the door; there in the corner on his knees is Ken.

Now Ken is not your normal Christian. No, Ken is on his knees speaking in some kind of language I have never heard. Later I would discover he was speaking in tongues. I learned one of the verses in the Bible is true. Where can I go where the Lord is not? If I go into the depths He is there. If I go into the heavens He is there (see Ps. 137:9). If He's not, believe me, He has someone else there doing His work. Ken started right in on me to give my life to the Lord. A short time later, at my new home, I would ask Christ into my life. That was June 1975. Little did I know that in October of this year I would be in the fight for my life. The fight for my spiritual life was now behind me, as it had been given to Christ.

In October of 1975, I would suffer a ruptured appendix, but not in any type of normal way. I started getting sick and throwing up, but that was normal for me. I thought I had the stomach flu, which for me was always bad. I did not think too much of it at first. But after about three days, I went to the dispensary for care. The first day they told me I had gastritis and told me to go back to work. I did not go back to work; I went back to bed. The next day I went back for care and was again sent back to work. On the third day, they ran some tests and sent me back to work. However, I did not go back to work, as my chief told me to stay in the barracks until I felt better. I was only getting sicker and weaker with each passing day.

Then it hit me, as if the weight of the world had been placed on my back, and I could not move. I was lying in my bed the entire evening until early the next morning when one of my roommates came off shift. I was lying there only able to move my eyes, unable to speak, and in tremendous pain. My roommate must have felt that death was in the air. All I remember is he came into the room, he came right to my bed, and he looked at me. He asked if I needed an ambulance. All I could do was move my eyes up and down.

The ambulance came and hauled me to the hospital. I remember it was a horrible ride, extremely rough, and with my abdomen so tender, every bump was excruciating. When I finally arrived in the emergency room I laid there for about an hour before I was looked at. The staff was taking care of an alcoholic in the next bed. He was throwing up blood, which I could hear them talking about.

Finally they drew some blood from me, and when the results came back, immediate action began to happen. They quickly prepped me for surgery and took me to radiology for an X-ray. They had to strap me to the X-ray table because I could not stand on my own. From radiology, they took me to surgery for exploratory surgery. Fear began to consume me like a cancer; I was weak, sick, and 2,000 miles from home in a place filled with strangers. At least I had the Lord Jesus Christ.

When I came out of surgery, I was in a strange place and a strange world, with my health being taken care of by a people I did not know. I remember wondering, *What is wrong with me? Where am I? Will I ever see my family and friends again?* I asked the staff what was wrong with me and if I would be all right. Each day I was told I was getting better, but I had no real idea what was even wrong, nor was I being told. This went on for six days. On day seven I was told I would have to have another operation. Each day I had thought I was getting better, only to be told on day seven I was going back into surgery. That was heart-wrenching. I didn't have the strength to call my family; I couldn't speak anyway. I was told that the Red Cross would contact them. I found out later that the Red Cross told my family that I had a ruptured gut, so they thought I had been drinking. I was a sailor, you know.

When they finally got me ready for surgery, they had a priest come in and give me my last rites; they didn't figure I would make it through the surgery. I don't know why it was a priest. I was not Catholic. Late on a Sunday night, that may have been the only clergy in the hospital. As they were getting me ready, giving me the last rites, I was wondering if I would ever see my family again. For some reason, I was at peace. Whenever I began to lose it, I would look at my left arm. I had a tattoo of Christ on that arm. That reminded me that He was with me.

By this time, they put a tube down my throat so I could be hooked up to a respirator, as they already knew I would not be able to breathe on my own after the surgery. It's funny what you remember, what you think of when you don't know if it may be your last hour or day. All I remember is being able to see faces and smiles, as if they had come from the negative of a picture deep within my memory. Oh, how good it is to draw on those when the ones you love are not there.

When I came out of surgery, I was not sure of what day or week it was. I was back in intensive care. After the first surgery, I had a girdle-like contraption on me. This allowed them to unhook it each day. They would take out all of the gauze packing, so I could look right into the wound to the stomach lining. This was so the infection could work its way out. After the second surgery I had that, as well as five irrigation tubes, coming from my abdomen, the respirator, stomach tube, and a line coming out of both arms, as well as arterial line. Shortly after coming out of surgery, I started to have multiple complications. I was running a very high fever, so they put me on a cooling blanket. This helped keep the temperature down. I developed pneumonia, so I had to have respiratory treatments twice a day. I kept getting worse. They then had to give me blood transfusions. Immediately I got jaundice. They were doing everything they could to keep me alive. I was continuing my way downhill, fighting hard to stay alive.

The worst thing about being in an intensive care unit is you are totally at the mercy of those around you. They then brought in a patient next to me. He came out of anesthesia and had the strength of ten men. That put the fear of God into me immediately. It wasn't bad enough that I was sick and helpless. Now I had someone next to me who was ripping out his tubes and IVs and lifting people off the floor. I was scared he was coming for me, with no one who could stop him. I thanked God they did.

During my second week, my parents came to see me, I remember not being able to speak. Somehow they knew I was thrilled to see them. Tears came to my eyes. God, what a blessing to see someone who you know loves you. It was just what I needed. A few days later, my sister and her husband came to see me, and once again my spirit soared when I saw them. But they had to go back home, and I was still very sick, weak; I never got to talk with them, but their presence gave me hope.

Again my condition got worse, and one night I remember bells going off and staff calling a code. The next thing I remember was being above water. It was so clear, as if it were 200 hundred feet deep. I could see the bottom, as if it were right in front of my face. It appeared to magnify everything below it. I remember seeing a blue sky above me with beautiful trees on each side of the stream. I felt the stream was moving, but there were no ripples to be seen. I was being drawn into a bright, warm, beautiful light, and I felt at peace. For the first time in weeks, I had no pain, no fear, just peace.

The most significant part of this experience was the fact I could see down in the water and see every rock and pebble as if I were looking through a microscope. I saw each object individually, only I saw them all at once. I could see each leaf on the trees. I saw every detail, up to the life moving through them. This was to the left, right, up, down, all at once, everything in detail. It is hard to explain, but I can still see it in my mind's eye as if it were burned there for eternity. Then, just like being dropped from a building, I came back into my sick, hurting body, and the pain and sickness returned.

After a month in the hospital, I was finally discharged home for 30 days of convalescence leave. I went in the hospital at 185 pounds; I came out at 128 pounds. I had pneumonia, jaundice, a 105 fever, two surgeries, and the physical scars to prove everything to those who might doubt. For years I had wondered where I had been when I left my body.

I also wondered after only six months as a Christian why I ended up in that hospital. But as I have lived out more of my life, God has revealed to me both. First, in 2000, my wife and I felt we were to move, yet I kept wrestling with God. He kept telling us to move. Finally we started to look for a home. We could not find one, so we started to build and put our house on the market. When it came about time to move into the new home, ours was still not sold. I remember praying and praying our home would sell, to no avail.

Then one Friday, a couple who had been in our home several times went through it again. But late that Friday, we got a call from our Realtor that they just could not afford our home. I remember driving home that night listening to Christian Calvary Broadcasting, the program "To Every Man an Answer." I was wrestling with God why He wanted us to move, yet now our house would not sell. Then a man came on the radio asking a question about the river of life. As he asked that question, God spoke to me as clearly as if someone was sitting in that truck next to me.

This is what God said: "I breathed life back into you on the river of life, and you question whether I can sell your house." Needless to say, I felt pretty foolish questioning the King of kings. I got home; the weight was off my shoulders. I realized God could do what He wants when He wants. The weekend passed, and Monday came. That Monday morning, our Realtor called and said that the people who were in our home Friday had put in an offer on our home. The man had gone to work on Friday afternoon after looking at our home in the morning, and then his boss gave him a raise that qualified them for our home. Is God big or what?

Why was I in the hospital? I wrestled with that for a long time, and God spoke to me again and said, "Do you remember the nurses who read your cards to you while you were in the hospital?" I did. He said "Do you remember when you were lying there unable to talk and they were reading those loving get well cards to you? You for all practical purposes were dying, and through tear-filled eyes they said they wished they had what you had. Today they do." Did you hear what I said? While I was dying, they wanted what they saw from this dying young man. Even while standing by the fragrance of the dying, you can smell the victory of life. I had a life eternal, and they wanted that.

By the part I played, just lying in that hospital, a good work was done. I give praise and glory to God. The time was well spent. That was my best witnessing to date; I couldn't talk or move, so God did what God needed to be done with no interference from me.

The physicians told me that I had a one in a million chance of surviving. They also said I would probably need further surgeries because of adhesions. What I have learned is statistics don't mean anything to God. I have not had one surgery for adhesions, and the surgery was over 34 years ago. Glory be to God. I pray what I have been through gives you hope.

I know our God is not blind to our needs; He is not too slow or too fast but always right on time. I know this: had I not given my life to the Lord and died in that hospital, I would be in eternal hell. Do not wait; ask Him into your heart today. I thought I would live forever at 19 years old. Little did I know I was only one heartbeat away from eternity. Satan says to you, your sins are too big. Do you believe that? If you do, that is saying that Jesus on the cross was a waste of time. Don't believe satan. Know where you are going today, for eternity. He forgave me; He will forgive you.

I was a little part of His story; you are a part of His story, too (history). It is His story. There is no greater story than the Bible. Read the word and pray. God wants to do a miracle in your life today. They are not limited to a sinner like me. I know I was given more time on this earth because of the prayers of some great prayer warriors. I also know He has used me since that time. What a feeling to have been used by the King of kings. Can you think of anyone else in the universe who you want to hold you in his or her hands? I can't. Give your life to Him today, and be used by the Master Carpenter Jesus Christ to change the world.

## ABOUT THE CONTRIBUTOR

Russell VerMulm, and his wife, Pam, reside in Sioux Falls, South Dakota. They have two grown daughters. Their eldest is a registered nurse, and their younger daughter is presently completing a business/marketing degree. Russell has a passion for rescuing marriages and runs a men's group outside of his time employed in the computer field. Along with his wife, Pam, they have run several group courses and events, including couples groups, and they have also assisted with coordinating several Truth Project events. They are avid supporters of groups such as Promise Keepers and Women of Faith, and yet they still manage to find the time to go biking, camping, and to spend time enjoying their two Yorkies named Faith Hill and Willie Nelson.

# CHAPTER 25

# BAM! THE MIRACLE OF LIFE AFTER TRAUMATIC BRAIN INJURY

## The story of Patti G. Foster as written by Dr. Theresa Veach

*I waited patiently for the LORD; He turned to me and heard my cry. He lifted me out of the slimy pit, out of the mud and mire; He set my feet on a rock and gave me a firm place to stand. He put a new song in my mouth, a hymn of praise to our God. Many will see and fear and put their trust in the LORD* (Psalm 40:1-3).

It happened at 6:45 in the evening during rush-hour traffic. This is when my life was changed forever. I was with three other women in a red Tahoe, on our way to our last Bible study meeting before taking a summer break. Envision this with me.

I was sitting in the backseat behind the driver. We were all talking with one of the front seat passengers, Heather, a wonderful young lady who had just graduated from high school. She had just come from her senior trip to New York City.

I had bought flowers for all the ladies in the Bible study. As we stopped at the intersection, I took off my seatbelt so I could turn and check on the flowers behind me. At that exact point, *bam!* The impact happened. A semi pulling a trailer full of cars going full-speed down the highway (70 mph, to be exact) rear-ended us with no warning. That's when life changed.

I was ejected out of the back—opposite side—of the Tahoe and thrown into the air. An eyewitness later told me, "When your body flew out of the vehicle, it was as if the hand of God came down to suspend you in the air right above the very SUV you had been thrown out of." The eyewitness remembered seeing the Tahoe spinning beneath me.

When it had stopped spinning and had gone out from beneath me, my body went down to the ground and across the highway. I was told by an RN, who had just finished her shift, that my body looked like a piece of laundry floating in the air.

Cars and trucks were still zooming by us on the highway. And thankfully, one of the trucks pulled in front of my body to keep other vehicles from running over me. From what I've been told, I could have been run over time and time again.

My body went into a coma as they air-flighted me to the nearest hospital. I remained in the coma for the next six weeks.

Everything I have learned about what happened to me during those few weeks is from doctors, nurses, family, and friends. I was told that the doctors had to prepare my friends and family for the worst. They expected me to die. The doctors said, "Bodies can't endure this kind of trauma. If she does live, she will be a persistent vegetable. She will never see out of her right eye again. She will never walk again. She will never have the use of her right arm. She will never be able to speak in complete sentences. Her personality will not be anything like it was before the wreck. She will barely be able to exist."

When I began to wake up from the coma, I was at Baylor Institute for Rehabilitation in downtown Dallas. Because of the continued severity of my condition, the staff secured me in one of the beds in room 307, "The Gwen Goddard Ward," where the worst of the traumatic brain injury patients are admitted. All of us required 24-hour nursing care.

At that time, I could not make any sort of connection with my own thoughts and emotions, let alone make a connection with others. But the Lord gave me a wonderful caretaker, a nurse I called "Mama Joan." I began to trust her and to connect with her, something I was not supposed to be able to do because of the trauma. This connection was one of countless things I had to re-learn about myself, about others, about life.

After some days and weeks had gone by, I began to learn how to connect with others by using nonverbal communication. This was the first language I learned after I began to wake up from my coma. I didn't have any other way of communicating with others or the outside world. I had to learn how to communicate by reading the look in someone's eyes, watching facial expressions, paying attention to the slightest of gestures, responding to tone of voice, and sensing the touch from another human being.

I became like a toddler. I had to re-learn the ABCs, how to identify them, write them, and read them. I even had to learn how to walk again. I had to wear a "gait belt" that was woven into a vest that I wore over my t-shirt. I had to learn how to put one foot in front of the other and to keep going. There is one thing I never had to relearn, and that is the truth of Jesus. At one point, I did get to go to Heaven. I remember seeing the beautiful blues. It was gorgeous. Most of all, I remember the presence of Jesus coming up beside me and touching me. I never turned to look at Him. I never saw His face, but I remember His Presence. I knew He was with me every step of the way. *"Never will I leave you, never will I forsake you"* (Heb. 13:5).

I continue to make miraculous progress along my journey of recovery; however, there are still moments of darkness when the stressors of life become overwhelming. I know I will never be the same, but I am learning to *cope* with my new life. That is what you have to do after suffering from a traumatic brain injury—*cope*.

When I get discouraged, I *cope* by talking to God and giving it to Him. He gives me passages of His Word to hold onto and not give up. Deuteronomy 31:6 from The Message Bible has helped me many a time when struggles have weighed me down: *"Be strong. Take courage. Don't be intimidated. Don't give them a second thought because God, your God, is striding ahead of you. He is right there with you. He won't let you down; He won't leave you."* Hallelujah, I proclaim.

God has blessed me as I learn to live again. I am walking again and talking again. I am now able to speak to others all around the world about that fateful night at 6:45 in the evening when my life was changed forever. I am able to tell others about the miracle of life and about how the Lord brought me through a deep, deep pit.

Each day the Lord Jesus helps me and brings encouragement to my heart in some way through someone at some time. It's very much like He showers my insides with, what I often refer to as *Vitamin B-12...it gives strength to the heart*. Sometimes it's a smile or a phone call or even a note of encouragement. No matter how it's *packaged*, I've learned that, oftentimes, the *small* things in life make the *biggest* difference. As I'm writing this paragraph, I'm remembering a deep truth that the apostle Paul taught us: *"Praise be to the God and Father of our Lord Jesus Christ, the Father of compassion and the God of all comfort, who comforts us in all our troubles, so that we can comfort those in any trouble with the comfort we ourselves have received from God"* (2 Cor. 1:3-4).

Though the evil one meant the wreck for evil and to harm me, God meant it for good, so that many lives would be saved (see Gen. 50:20). As long as I live, this miracle that started on June 18, 2002, lives on to my Father's Glory.

## ABOUT THE CONTRIBUTOR

Patti Foster's life is a testament to the intense love she feels for others. Her joy and laughter refreshes those around her, and she welcomes opportunities to influence lives and make a difference.

Originally from Jacksonville, Texas, Patti comes from a supportive family who encouraged her to take risks, to try hard and learn from mistakes. As a college student majoring in music education, Patti traveled with a fine arts team to Australia, toured with the university choir to the British Isles, and spent a week in the heart of Mexico with a mission group. Performances with the Fort Worth Chamber Orchestra and the Sam Houston State University Orchestra further broadened her scope of music and expression. She graduated from Sam Houston State University (Huntsville, Texas) in 1989, and shortly after, traveled abroad to Eastern Europe providing music for crusades and teaching conversational English through music.

Since 1990, Patti's focus has been radio. She was the morning show host at WFRN, an inspirational Christian radio station in South Bend/Elkhart, Indiana. Before that, she fulfilled a variety of positions for KVNE, a non-commercial Christian music station in Tyler, Texas. Patti's radio career provided opportunities that led her into becoming a full-time speaker. She traveled nationwide speaking to church and corporate organizations of all sizes.

On June 18, 2002, Patti was severely injured in a horrific traffic accident. She suffered severe head trauma and was in a coma for six weeks. Her life hung in the balance. She has had to learn to live again. And now, as her restoration process continues, Patti's desire is still to inspire, encourage, and motivate so many through her speaking. You may contact Patti by going to her Website: www.pattifoster.com or by emailing her at patti@pattifoster.com.

# CHAPTER 26

# My Miracle Marine

## *Connie McClellan*

*Again, I tell you that if two of you on earth agree about anything you ask for, it will be done for you by my Father in Heaven. For where two or three come together in my name, there am I with them* (Matthew 18:19-20; 2 Corinthians 12:9).

My son, Marine Cpl. John McClellan, is living proof that prayer really works and that God is still in the miracle-working business.

John joined the Marines immediately after graduating from high school in June 2004. Immediately I began an email prayer chain, leading my address book in prayer for John's future in the Marines, knowing that he would ultimately be deployed to Afghanistan or Iraq.

While serving as a machine gunner in Afghanistan in 2005, at the age of 19, John was shot twice in the same arm, in the same week. The injuries he sustained were viewed as miraculously minor. The first, an AK-47 bullet, ricocheted off John's Humvee and embedded in his right wrist. Within three days, he was back in the turret. Three days later, he earned his second purple heart when he was shot a second time, again an enemy AK-47 bullet that, this time, penetrated the front of his right shoulder and exited the back, and again neither hit nor hurt anything.

Within two weeks, he returned to his position in the turret. In the *Stars & Stripes* publication for Wednesday, October 27, 2005, a five inch by ten inch picture of John's picture adorned the front page with the headline, *"Marine Shot Twice, Same Week, Same Arm, Answers to...Lucky."*

I attributed this entire chain of events to God answering the prayers of my prayer network. Yes, he was shot twice, but he was not *hurt*.

On September 11, 2006, John deployed to Haditha, Iraq, where 15 days later, on September 26, while on patrol, he was shot through the head by a sniper. The bullet penetrated in front of his left ear and exited the back of the lower left side of his head. My husband, Carl, and I received the "every parent's worst nightmare" phone call at 12:15 A.M. CST on September 27. The phone call revealed that John was in a hospital in Balad, Iraq, where he had just endured five hours of surgery in which bone fragments and brain tissue were removed. We were told, "If he survives the brain swelling, he will never be the same, and will probably be in a vegetative state."

Immediately after the phone call, I sent an email to my address book, which by this time was around 80 in number. I relayed what had happened and led them in prayer, asking God for the desperately needed miracle for John to: (1) live and (2) fully recover.

That afternoon a candlelight vigil, with 120-plus people was held on our front lawn. Twenty-four hours later, the doctors called back to tell us that John's condition had done a "180." Even though he was unconscious, he was responding favorably to every test given to him. The doctor went so far to say, "I'll be honest; I don't see any reason he can't make a full recovery."

On September 28, John was flown to the military hospital in Land-stuhl, Germany, and on the 29th, he arrived at the Bethesda National

Naval Medical Center (NNMC) in Bethesda, Maryland. Carl, my stepdaughter, Jane, and I arrived at the NNMC September 30.

Two days later, we met with John's neurosurgeon at NNMC, Dr. Rocco Armonda, who informed us that 99 out of 100 people with this type of injury do not survive, and that the bullet missed John's carotid artery by a thickness of two sheets of paper. John was in the ICU for seven days, after which he was transferred to the fifth floor, the surgery floor, where he remained until October 25.

While at the NNMC, John McClellan was presented his third purple heart by General Michael Hagee, Commandant of the Marine Corps. It was also at NNMC that John was presented with his Quilt of Valor, which will be treasured forever. It is a quilt big enough for a full-size bed and is breathtakingly beautiful. Women from all over the United States make quilts and send them to the hospital to give to injured soldiers and Marines.

John was at NNMC until October 25, 2006, at which time he and I were flown to the James A. Haley Veterans Hospital in Tampa, Florida, where John endured three and one-half weeks of intensive physical, occupational, and speech therapy. John's left facial nerve was severed, so the left side of his face had no activity, which gave him a very "saggy" appearance. In addition, the facial nerve controls the closing of the eyelid, so a gold weight was inserted in his eyelid to assist it in closing. When an EMG was performed at the V.A. in Tampa, the doctor's prognosis for the recovery of the facial nerve was very poor. The doctor told us, "This nerve is so badly damaged, it will take years for it to recover...if ever."

On November 21, 2006, John and I returned home to Columbia, Missouri, where we were greeted by Carl and approximately 150 friends, family, and well-wishers. The next week, John began occupational, speech, and physical therapy at Rusk Rehabilitation Center in Columbia, Missouri.

Within four months of his return from Tampa in November 2006, John's face was totally restored, and the gold weight had been removed (and added as a charm to John's necklace). Because his eyelid closed perfectly, the weight was no longer needed.

The miracles that God has done in this situation are many. Following is a list of the most dramatic. Each one of these miracles was a major concern at some point. Each concern was expressed as a prayer request via email to the hundreds of people plugged into this story. One by one, God answered the prayers of the people:

1. He lived. (His buds in Iraq prayed for him when they put him on the helicopter.)

2. He's not a vegetable.

3. He can see. (Originally there was a fear that he would be blind.)

4. He can hear. (His left ear is deaf, but his right ear is perfect.)

5. He can talk. (Sometimes brain injuries can cause a problem talking, so this was a serious concern.)

6. He can talk with both vocal cords. (For a month and a half, John had only one functional vocal cord, so he had that "Marlon Brando, *Godfather*" thing going on.)

7. He can swallow. (For one day, after removing the breathing tube, he couldn't swallow.)

8. He has no headaches or pain of any kind. (For two months, this was a problem.)

9. He has no dizziness. (For over a month he was extremely dizzy.)

10. He laughs a lot. (It took a month and a half for him to get his "joy" back; now, it's 100 percent restored—and then some.)

11. His left hand and left side work again. (This was a problem that was 100 percent restored around February of 2007.)

12. He can walk. (He had to totally relearn walking.)

13. He can run. (With his imbalance created by the injury, this was almost impossible after his injury.)

14. He is not mentally impaired.

15. His personality is exactly the same. (This is a major concern with traumatic brain injury victims.)

16. His left dimple was restored. (His left dimple was lost with the loss of the facial nerve.)

17. His left eyebrow movement was restored. (This was also lost with the loss of the facial nerve.)

18. His left eyelid closes.

19. He had his forehead wrinkles restored. (These were lost with the left facial nerve.)

20. He has a full smile. (With the loss of the left facial nerve, his smile was only half.)

21. He can read.

22. He can write.

23. No cranioplasty was needed. (In March 2007, we returned to NNMC for cranioplasty surgery, but the surgery was canceled because the muscle had grown over the brain sufficiently to protect it.)

24. The vision in his left eye was deemed 20/20 by the eye doctor in May 2007.

Following are the two remaining deficiencies for which we continue to believe God:

1. He still has short-term memory loss issues.

2. He is still deaf in his left ear.

John has made amazing progress in improvements to his short-term memory in the past few years. In fact, while attending Florida State College at Jacksonville, for the 2009–10 academic year, he attained an overall 3.75 grade-point average. In his college algebra class at Florida State College, he earned a 98 percent.

In October of 2009, John ran—and finished—the Marine Corps Marathon in Washington, DC; not bad for someone who couldn't walk just three years ago.

John's story is a story of hope, not only for our soldiers and Marines, but also for every living human being going through a difficult time. I truly and sincerely believe that God is there for us every step of the way, but in most cases, prayer is critical for inviting God's intervention.

This story is relayed in its entirety in the recently released book, *My Miracle Marine.* A pictorial account can be viewed at mymiraclemarine.com.

## ABOUT THE CONTRIBUTOR

Connie McClellan, author of the 2008 book, *My Miracle Marine,* is an independent insurance agent and resides with her husband, Carl, in Columbia, Missouri. She looked forward to her son John's return from Florida in August 2010 to resume his college career at the University of Missouri, Columbia, to work toward a major in nutrition and fitness.

Connie invites anyone and everyone to visit her Website, mymiraclemarine.com, or to contact her directly via email: phil46me@gmail.com. (That would be for Philippians 4:6, her favorite Bible verse.) Also, she is available to speak to organizations and/or churches to relay her story of hope. She does not charge a fee for speaking.

# CHAPTER 27

# MIRACLE IN THE OR

## *James Rennie, M.D.*

*For Thou, Lord, art good, and ready to forgive; and plenteous
in mercy unto all them that call upon Thee* (Psalm 86:5 KJV).

Chitokoloki is a 110-bed mission hospital in the northwest prov-
ince of Zambia, on the banks of the Zambezi River. My wife, Kathy,
and I went there as medical missionaries in 1973 from Mississauga
in Canada. For the first two and a half years, I was working under a
30-year veteran missionary doctor who helped teach me the ropes of
medical care in an isolated setting.

I had only nine months of surgical assisting in a Toronto hospital to prepare me for the surgical challenges. Surgery came easily
to me, and soon I was doing a variety of major procedures. When
this doctor left to return to England in 1977 (due to a family-related
decision), my heart was full of fear that I would not be successful in
doing the work alone. But after prayer and seeking God's grace, I
was fortified for the task. Indeed, there were many episodes where
God gave grace and skills both in medical and surgical treatments.
Many patients were helped. However, one day in 1983, I was faced
with a life and death dilemma that superseded any ability or wisdom
that I possessed.

A young girl, perhaps 16 years old, had been out in the cassava fields working with her mother when suddenly she developed intense abdominal pain. Her relatives carried her several miles to the hospital. By the time she arrived, she was in a weakened and desperate condition. When I examined her, it was plain that she had an acute abdominal emergency. She would require immediate surgery.

The operating room was quickly prepared and the patient made ready for surgery. Because we lacked an anesthetist, the girl was given a spinal anesthetic, which allowed several hours of abdominal surgery. When the abdomen was opened, I was not prepared at all for what I found. There was loop after loop of swollen small bowel and even some of the large bowel that was blackened and dying. I felt for a pulse on the artery that supplied the bowel with blood. There was none.

How could it be? This young and otherwise healthy girl was suffering from a totally unexplainable arterial blockage. Zambians living in the bush have perfectly wonderful arteries because they are physically active and don't ruin their blood vessels with Western foods. I could not explain this girl's tragic condition, and even worse, I felt I could do nothing about it.

A fellow missionary and operating room nurse saw the confusion and helplessness in my eyes. There were no answers. We couldn't even suture up the wound because the bowel was too distended.

"We need to pray," was all I could say.

We stepped back from the operating table. The operating room nurse assistant and I prayed together. We called on the Lord to save this young girl. We prayed that He would help us to do what would be best for this girl.

After praying, we looked back at the bowel, and to our amazement, there seemed to be a pinking up of the bowel wall. Sure enough, a pulse was detected in the artery. Within minutes the bowel took on a normal color. It also began to function normally. The distention decreased, and we were able to close the wound. I checked on the girl several times that night because I feared that she could have a recurrence of the blood vessel obstruction. But all remained well.

The next morning on my rounds I spoke to the girl in Lunda, her native tongue. "You almost died yesterday, but God had great mercy on you and wonderfully healed the disease. Were you ready to die?"

"No, I was not ready," she answered. "My parents are Christians but I have resisted believing in Jesus up until yesterday. When you all prayed in the operating room I heard it and I realized that my time was short. I called on Jesus to save me, and He did."

As a witness to this physical miracle, I thank the Lord for such an encouraging experience. I firmly believe God can do anything He wants. But the greater miracle is that the Lord changed this young girl's heart and brought her into the family of God.

This miracle will have an eternal benefit.

## ABOUT THE CONTRIBUTOR

Dr. James Rennie is a general practitioner in private practice in Ontario, Canada. For 20 years he has specialized in Bible-based and faith-based counseling and psychotherapy. He maintains a busy schedule of Bible teaching in various churches and has conducted numerous seminars on counseling-related topics.

Prior to this, Jim and his wife Kathy, an RN, spent 14 years in medical missionary and church work in Zambia, Africa. They are the parents of three children and the grandparents of nine grandchildren. To contact Dr. Rennie, or to purchase CDs of seminar recordings on a variety of counseling subjects, please go to www.pursuingwisdom.com.

# CHAPTER 28

# WONDERFULLY GUIDED

## *Siegfried Tepper*

*And the Lord shall guide thee continually*
(Isaiah 58:11a KJV).

The following is the translation of an article, used by permission, that appeared in *Voice Magazine* in March 2005. This is a monthly magazine distributed in Germany by *Christen-im-Beruf*, Christians-in-Business, and was written by Siegfried Tepper.

I often ask myself, *How do I recognize God's leadership, His will, and His direction for my life?* More precisely, I ask about not just His will in general. I would like to hear His voice specifically and recognize His directions even in the smallest detail. This brings me to the realization that our journey through life requires smaller and sometimes larger steps of faith, and often only in looking back do we see God's path for us. Within our family experiences we have often observed God's leadership in this way.

## The Accident

My career as a concert pianist, composer, and conductor provided my wife and me with opportunities to visit many countries. After returning to Canada from Germany over 25 years ago, I was successfully engaged as a university lecturer, composer, pianist, and conductor of the Mozart Chamber Orchestra of Burlington, Ontario, Canada.

In January 1990, I accidentally crushed two fingers of my left hand in a rolling garage door. The injuries were so severe that it appeared my career as a pianist had ended. The ligaments of my fourth finger were chronically inflamed and were reinjured every time I attempted to perform. Therapy and treatments were of no help, and I had to come to terms with the reality that my piano performing days were over.

## The Crisis

God uses different ways and means to guide us. Sometimes it is a simple word or certain individuals, sicknesses, a crisis, or supernatural and unusual events and miracles. For my family and me, August 1993 proved to be just such a time.

## The Surprise

For over three and a half years, many friends and acquaintances prayed for the healing of my hand. When God suddenly healed my hand in August 1993, I did not want to believe it at first. It wasn't until three days later, and after several lengthy attempts to fully engage my left hand at the piano, that we realized God had performed a miracle. Up until today, my hand is fully restored, healed, and functional. Since the summer of 1993, our family has performed and taken part in hundreds of concerts and services worldwide. However, several steps of obedience were necessary for God's miraculous healing power to become evident.

## In Partnership With God

This is the most important point, upon which everything else in contingent. The leading of God in our lives is evident not because we are inherently good, have an abundance of faith, or because we deserve it. No, it is simply because of His mercy and because of His desire to reveal His grace to us. Even though we have not earned this grace, God still uses our cooperation to reveal His will to the world at large. We have the wonderful privilege and opportunity to work and live as partners with God.

## Our Ministry

Since that time, our family has experienced many miracles of healing and provision, not just in our own lives, but in the lives of many people in different parts of the world. Our son, Christer, is a highly skilled violinist and has played with us and alone in well over 700 concerts worldwide. In 1993, we incorporated as a registered Canadian charity under the name of Tepper Ministries of Music. Our goal and mission is to glorify God by sharing the Gospel of Jesus Christ through an inspired presentation of music of the highest standards, testimony, and the preaching of the Word. God has guided us in such a way that we gladly serve Him with everything He has invested in us.

## God Is Working Worldwide

We have performed concerts in very poor countries, such as India, and also in more well-to-do countries, such as Germany and Japan and in North America. However, the same questions are asked everywhere: if God exists, how do I recognize His voice and His leadership? The answer is the same everywhere: we can never find God within ourselves. Jesus Christ is the way, the truth, and the life. Whoever submits himself to Christ in genuine humility will hear His voice and recognize His leadership. It is up to us. Whoever seeks Him sincerely will find and experience Him. We can confirm this with absolute conviction, not just in our lives, but in the lives and experiences of many other people throughout the world. God's leadership is like a book that has long been completed, yet unfolds itself in a new way every day of our lives. There is probably nothing more exciting than to be a partner with God.

## ABOUT THE CONTRIBUTOR

Siegfried Tepper is married to his wife, Linda. They have one daughter, Nadine, and a son named Christer, a daughter-in-law, Gwen, and one grandson named Jacob. He lives in Burlington, Ontario, Canada. As a pianist, conductor, and composer, he has traveled throughout the world. The ministry Website is: www.tepperministries.com.

# CHAPTER 29

# THE GIFT OF HEALING

## *As notated on November 1, 1971, by Mrs. Margaret Maffey*

*But they that wait upon the LORD shall renew their
strength; they shall mount up with wings as eagles; they shall
run, and not be weary; and they shall walk, and not faint*
(Isaiah 40:31 KJV).

I am writing these facts down now, while they are still fresh in my mind, so that nothing will be added to the story, nor indeed that anything will be left out.

On September 7 of this year—a beautiful, sunny day—I drove Russ to the office and then drove myself to the hospital for X-rays of my kidneys. As the technician X-rayed me, she said, "Just lie still until I read your X-rays." She kept the X-ray plate in her hand until it had been read and marked. This she did each time she X-rayed me (five times in all). This is to prevent the X-rays of one patient getting mixed up with another patient, as has happened in the past.

I had been sent to a urologist and surgeon of high repute by my own GP because, as he said, I had had inflammation of the bladder too long. This surgeon to whom I was referred, in turn, sent me for X-rays.

On September 9, my surgeon phoned me to say that I had a very large stone in my right kidney (large for a kidney stone; he said that it was the size of his thumbnail), and he made an appointment for me to see the X-rays in his office the next day.

I was shaken to know that I would have to have an operation, as the doctor said that would be the only way to relieve me of that trouble-causing stone. He added that it was like sitting on a volcano, and that it might cause great pain and trouble at any moment, so I said to Russ, "Now first please let us ask God to give me peace, and release from the fear and shock that I am suffering," and within 24 hours, I had that peace. I rested in God's love, knowing that He was allowing me to have this experience for a purpose—His purpose. I became willing (never eager, but willing) to accept His will, whatever it might be.

The next day, I kept my appointment with the surgeon and saw my X-rays. I saw the large stone pointed out to me by the doctor (like a big button in my right kidney), and there was another smaller particle that the doctor said might be a small stone or calcium bits.

I had read of medication for dissolving stones so I asked the doctor about this. He said that some stones will dissolve, but that this one would not dissolve—that it was a hard stone and so very large, and in such a position in the kidney (lodged in the kidney, he said) that the stone would not move, and to try to dissolve it would dissolve my kidney.

"Well, I can't have that," I said. Then I asked, "Will the stone not pass if we give it a little time, and I drink lots of fluids?"

He sat for a minute, and then he said, "No one is going to force you to have an operation, Mrs. Maffey, but it would be very foolish not to have this stone removed. It will only grow larger and larger, and it has already damaged one quarter of your right kidney. As for its passing, there is not a tube in your body large enough to let that stone pass."

So it was settled. I was to have this operation, and I said, "The sooner, the better. But I cannot go into the hospital until after my sister's 25th wedding anniversary dinner that Russ and I are giving in their honor."

So he agreed to operate anytime after September 19.

With my God-given peace of mind, I continued on with life. I phoned our rector and asked him for prayer. I went to a mid-week Communion, and he prayed there for my special need. He prayed that God's love would surround and protect me, that God would continue to give me peace and joy, and that God would use all my experiences in all of my life, including this experience, for my spiritual good. He prayed in Jesus' name.

At this time, our prayer circle took my name for prayer, and many square dance friends who knew of my upcoming surgery phoned to say they were praying for me. For this, I was most grateful, and I continued to float on the cushion of God's love and mercy.

I have a good friend who said, "You should have gone to Kathryn Kuhlman when she was in Toronto."

I replied, "She is indeed a wonderful person, and God uses her in a wonderful way, but God could heal me right now. He made me; He can re-make me. But I keep remembering that Jesus, God's own Son, said, 'Father, if Thou art willing, remove this cup from Me; nevertheless, not My will, but Thine, be done.'"

And in the days that followed, I often said, "Dear God, I know You could remove this stone; nevertheless, not my will, but Thine, be done." And for the first time in my life, I really meant it, even knowing that on rare occasions surgery can be fatal, despite the efforts of the best of our good doctors. I knew that God had something to teach me in this experience, something spiritual, and I was willing to learn.

There were times when I thought of the pain, the incision (Russ' incision for the removal of his kidney stone is 12 inches long), and the slow recovery, and I was plain scared. But I just turned and looked into the face of Jesus and said, "Lord Jesus, I'm scared. Please give me Your peace."

He never failed me. I received peace and was able to talk about my possibly stepping through that doorway into the next world with my sisters and Russ calmly. But I never dwelt on that. I only said that through Jesus Christ, my Savior, I will never die. I may have to lay my body aside now, or at least I will certainly do so sometime, but I will live in His light. I will love you always and wait for you there, and I will be with Mother and Daddy and Jim. In Jesus I am at peace and have joy.

So three weeks passed. I entertained, I danced, I laughed, and I prayed. And I thanked God for all His wonderful mercies, and on September 27, I entered the hospital. Blood tests were taken; a chest X-ray was taken; and an ordinary kidney X-ray was taken.

My surgeon came that evening. Russ was with me. The doctor said, "I've reviewed your X-rays taken on September 7. The stone is large, hard, and lodged in your right kidney, so we will do the surgery to remove it on Wednesday at 1:00 P.M."

I said, "Fine, doctor. I'll be glad to have it over with." And then I added, "Oh, doctor, did you see the kidney X-ray they took this afternoon?"

He said, "No, but that is only an ordinary X-ray; it wouldn't show us any more than the X-rays we took on September 7."

I said, "Fine, thank you, doctor." And he left.

On September 28, the next day, at 11:00 A.M., my doctor came to me where I was sitting by a window in the hospital corridor, reading a book on healing. He looked perplexed, and he put a hand on the back of my chair and said nothing for a moment. Then he said, "I don't know whether this is good news or bad news. It is very uncertain, but we can't find the stone on your latest X-ray. So we'll prepare you for surgery and give you the full anesthetic, and you will sign for surgery, and also for a cystoscopy. We will also do special X-rays while we are doing that examination, and if we can't reach your stone with our cystoscope, we'll have to remove it surgically."

I said, "It would be a shame if you operated and the stone was gone." As soon as the doctor had gone, I raced to the phone and called Russ and said, "They've lost my stone."

All that day, they prepared me for surgery—shaving my side, telling me about deep breathing, moving and my feet after surgery, and finally, no food and no fluids.

Then September 29 at 12:30 P.M., they gave me a pill to quiet me, and I didn't think I needed that, but they said I must take it, that it was pre-surgery medication. Then later they gave me Pentothal, and then when I was floating into unconsciousness, I committed myself and my loved ones into God's care and keeping for now and for eternity. Then I felt myself moving, and I heard a voice saying, "Mrs. Maffey, Mrs. Maffey." I opened my eyes, and answered, as a kindly face was bending over me, telling me, "I will be giving you the anesthetic."

I thanked the doctor and remembered no more.

Russ tells me that it was 7:45 P.M. before I stirred. He had been at the hospital since 4:00 P.M. waiting for me to be brought back into my room and then to regain consciousness. I remember seeing Russ' beloved face (as though I was seeing him through a long tunnel). He was smiling at me and patting my face to arouse me. I heard him say, "Are you going to wake up now, dear?

"You have no stone. It is gone. You had no operation."

Understanding this wonderful news, I spoke through cracked lips with difficulty and said, "We know who took that away, don't we? I am so very thankful."

My surgeon came in the next day and told me he had no explanation. The stone was gone. His diagnosis had been correct. He had X-rays to prove it, well documented. He said that my damaged kidney showed no damage. It was fine. Everything was fine. I told him that I had many people praying for me, and he said, "Good, good," and he continued that since there was nothing wrong with me, I could go home that very day. I went home thankfully.

All those who prayed for me know that prayer works—that God does heal.

Some skeptics have said (only two so far, but there may be others), "Oh it just dissolved, that's all."

Why, of course it dissolved, but how? Who dissolved it?

My surgeon was an excellent urologist, a specialist, with years of experience behind him, and he was still a comparatively young man at this time (around 35). He really knew his business and did not misread his X-ray plates, and even if he had made a mistake, my own GP and other doctors read the X-rays and concurred with the diagnosis.

Russ and I and many others know that God dissolved that stone. Then the question is asked, why for Margaret Maffey?

He didn't dissolve it for me, although I know He loves and forgives me and does answer prayer. He dissolved it for His own glory, so that all may know that He does indeed love all men, and that He does heal, that He heals even a very ordinary sinner like me. I am most grateful and will be forever, not only for His gift of healing, but most of all because He touched me, forgave me, and now I can tell others, "I know God heals, because He healed even me."

## ABOUT THE CONTRIBUTOR

Mrs. Margaret Maffey is retired and currently resides in Hamilton, Ontario, Canada. She is a well-respected and much-loved past volunteer with such organizations as 100 Huntley Street and the Salvation Army's Prison Ministry, among other ministries. She is a member of the 1st Church of the Nazarene, in Hamilton, Ontario, Canada, and is 91 years old.

# CHAPTER 30

# TURNING IT OVER

## *Hal Weeks*

*Let us hold fast the profession of our faith without wavering;*
*for he is faithful that promised* (Hebrews 10:23 KJV).

My name is Hal Weeks. I discovered I had cancer of the lymphatic system when I was 58 years old. The prognosis was a 35 percent chance of survival for five years. But God had other plans. I was 96 last January 20. This is the story of this miracle that occurred without any medical intervention other than diagnosis. Although it was originally treated with cobalt for a period of 21 days, as it turned out, it did not heal me.

As time went on, I discovered several nodes in my neck and under my right armpit that seemed to be growing. In August 1977, at the age of 64, a large node was removed from my right armpit. It was diagnosed as a poorly differentiated nodular lymphoma, which meant my cancer had metastasized. I was then referred to an oncologist for treatment.

However, he agreed to defer any treatment on the basis of my belief that I would be divinely healed. I was scheduled to return in three months. Over the three-month period, the tumors kept getting smaller until they were gone. When I returned, the doctor could find no evidence of the cancer. He said, "If I were examining you for the first time, I would have diagnosed you as not having the disease."

I continued having periodic checkups until August 1982, at age 69, at which time he transferred me back to my family doctor. Then in 1995, I discovered two large lumps over the right collarbone. It was determined to be lymphoma that had apparently returned. I did not have a biopsy, since I did not plan to have medical intervention and the surgeon said there would therefore be no point in it.

Again, I turned it over to the Lord. Over the next six months, the tumors increased in size and number. I began to have second thoughts about not having medical treatment. As clear as I have ever heard the Lord speak, He said, "I thought you had turned it over to Me." I repented of my concerns and again trusted God for a healing. It stopped getting worse for two months, at which time the Lord said it would be gone in three months, and it was. Since then I have had many other conditions healed, again without medical intervention. There has been no further reoccurrence of the cancer.

This is not to say we should not seek medical help. I have and do use the resources of medical science. In fact, in June 2001, my heart went into fibrillation. I called my doctor and was told to go to the hospital emergency room. They kept me in the hospital for ten days until they had determined what medication I needed. Although the side effects of the medication are a downside, I am still able to function, and the Lord still ministers to me in many, many ways.

## The Spiritual Corollary

Having always believed in prayer, I had been asking God to heal me all during the course of this disease. However, since I had not revealed my condition to more than a couple of friends, I had not received much—if any—general prayer. For several years, I did believe I had been healed, and I did receive what the doctors called a marvelous remission. But with the recurrence in August 1977, and a diagnosis that the condition was now more advanced, I became deeply troubled.

At that time, a friend of mine invited me to attend a Full Gospel Businessmen's Fellowship dinner. Since I was not "charismatic," their emotional behavior turned me off. So I decided to "lay a fleece" before the Lord. I said, "Lord, if this is something You want me to get involved in, heal my back." (I had a back problem that had been causing me pain for some time.)

Immediately the pain left, and my back was healed. I now believe this was the deciding factor in my seeking the experience known in charismatic and Pentecostal circles as the baptism in the Holy Spirit. I was prayed to receive this at a Full Gospel Businessmen's Fellowship meeting on August 18, 1977, at the age of 64. Nothing seemed to happen at the time, but I was assured I had received this baptism, and I thanked God for His gift.

At about 10:30 the following Saturday evening, while in bed reading some charismatic testimonies and reflecting on them, my attention was drawn to a strange tingling sensation in my right arm. This subsided, but shortly I noticed the same sensation on the side of my face. As I began to rub my face and neck, where the tumors were, I felt a sort of electrifying of my right arm. I remember exclaiming, "Lord, Your hand is holding my hand."

Immediately, waves of an indescribable sense of the power of God began to sweep through my entire body. I have had similar sensations since but never again with that intensity or duration. For several days afterward, the power of God was so strong on me that I finally had to ask God to "lead me beside the still waters."

I did then experience some abatement for a time of rest, but this was the beginning of a whole new way of life and the beginning of a new relationship with Jesus that I had never known before. At the time, it was impressed on my mind that I had received three prizes. The third prize was the healing of cancer; the second prize was the deliverance from spirits of fear and doubt; and the first prize was going from knowing about Jesus to knowing Jesus in a personal way as my Lord.

As to speaking in tongues, although I had had no objections to doing so, I was not actively seeking to do so. About a month later, I woke up in the middle of the night and felt the power of God come over me. An inaudible voice said to me, "Speak." When I did, I began to speak in tongues. For a time I found myself speaking in a different tongue. Now I speak in many different tongues, although I do not have the gift of interpretation of tongues. I have been told that one time I spoke German by someone who knows German.

Although medical science classifies this as a spontaneous remission, I claim it as a divine healing. I continue to see others healed through my prayers, as well as through those who have followed our teaching on how to heal the sick. I have told the Lord I am more than satisfied with the lifespan He has already given me, but He says this is not my time and I am to continue in ministry several more years. My leaving this "vale of tears" will be peaceful and without trauma. Who could ask for any more than that?

## About the Contributor

While at 96 years of age Hal Weeks no longer teaches classes on healing, he still readily welcomes people in need of healing to contact him for an appointment for prayer at his home. He may be reached to make an appointment for prayer at 619-435-7556, and his informative Website on healing may be found at: www.howtoheal.org.

# CHAPTER 31

# Tuned in to God's Frequency

## Collin Stoddard

*Give thanks to the Lord of lords: His love endures forever. To Him who along does great wonders, His love endures forever* (Psalm 136:3-4).

I grew up in a tight-knit Christian home with parents who daily taught me how to pray and seek the Lord, but along with my great family came unexpected complications with my ears.

When I was three, ear tubes were surgically inserted. For the next couple of years, everything went as planned. My ear infections became less frequent, but then prematurely, my eardrums pushed out the little rubber tubes that had saved me from so many painful infections.

My eardrums were the only things that didn't react according to plan—I think they were reacting to The Master's plan. My eardrums, instead of growing back to their original shape, did just the reverse; they completely deteriorated. I remember monthly vists to the doctors and time after time the prodding of metal instruments being stuck in my ears as doctors checked for changes in the eardrums.

There was no possible way I could hear without my ear's ability to feel vibrations for my brain to translate into sound. I also remember the shocked look on my doctor's face, after he informed my parents that I was an excellent lip reader (I think that he thought that I couldn't hear, but my hearing was just fine—which was a miracle in and of itself!). My wonderful parents, wanting their six-year-old to lead a normal life, made me wear the bright blue and red earplugs the doctor molded of my ear, to keep out unwanted water in the shower or the swimming pool. Able to hear well (despite the deterioration of my ear drums and continual pain, pressure, and repeat ear infections), and recognizing that I had an ear and affinity for music, my parents enrolled me in piano lessons. I don't consider it a coincidence that I played by ear rather than actually obeying my piano teacher and reading the notes.

I couldn't go through life forever without a vital part of my ear, and simply wear earplugs every time I even looked at water, so soon enough it came time to prepare for reconstructive surgery. I spent my summer as a seven-year-old eating milkshakes and pudding after having a tonsillectomy/adenoidectomy to prepare for ear surgery. Saying I was scared would be an understatement.

I continued my doctors visits preparing for my next reconstructive ear surgery. Night after night my Mom climbed the stairs to the upstairs room I shared with my older brother and she sat on the edge of my bed, placing her hands over my ears. As if she was talking to an old friend, she would pray passionately for the Lord to make my ears healthy again that I might not go through the tedious procedure of rebuilding the sensitive tissue of my deteriorated eardrums. I think she felt the musical calling the Lord had on my life and knew the only way for it to happen was for a miracle to happen in my ears. Some nights that she prayed for me holding my head in her hands I opened my eyes to look at her face but I don't think she ever noticed. The look of urgency and struggle of giving her son's future to the Great Physician will stay with me for the rest of my life.

On the day of the operation, my doctor changed the subject and asked me to hop up on the examination table, his gigantic "audio scope" looming dangerously over one end of the cold table. I compliantly laid down like every other time and tried not to flinch as he gently lowered the microscopic camera into my ear canal. "This is odd," he said in the same preoccupied, skeptical voice. My dad leaned closer to the giant microscope and asked him what he saw. "Collin has eardrums. All the scar tissue is gone," my doctor pronounced. My doctor then immediately brought me to the audiologist's lab and asked for a thorough hearing test. The results came back with data comparable to a newborn baby's hearing.

All I remember was hearing my parents gasp as I laid there on the table that had gradually become acclimated to my body temperature. My mom grasped my white-knuckled hand (you should try laying still with a metal probe in your ear as still as possible for longer than five minutes), and I could tell that she was beaming. Sensing the magnitude of what had just happened, I blurted out, "Well, we prayed!" I'm not sure if my doctor is still an unbeliever today, but he said, "Well you sure did something because I've never seen anything like this before." If he doesn't believe that the Lord heals and answers prayers and is intimately involved in every aspect of His children's lives, then He may be one of the only people who witnessed a supernatural intervention right before his eyes and chose not to believe.

I praise the Lord that I'm old enough to remember what the Lord did that day. He changed my life. He chose to show me that He exists—that He cares and that He needs me on this earth for a reason. He showed my parents that their love and prayers for their son didn't go unheard—that He has a greater plan for my life, greater than they could even desire for me. He confirmed in their hearts and minds that the Lord does have a specific calling on their son's life.

So here I am many years later, still healed by the power and presence of the living God. What the Lord did in my parents' lives through this journey is their story for them to tell, one that the Lord deepened their faith through. I believe I did have a calling on my life—and I'm still discovering the depth of that every day. For years I competed in numerous piano competitions taking home large trophies and winning several music scholarships to music colleges. Asked to help start 33Miles, in January 2006, we received a Dove nomination and had four successful radio singles on Christian radio. I attended over 150 dates a year playing music, listening to the reminder that my future and my life are governed by a gracious and loving God. The joy and success of my music career pales in comparison to the realization that I would not be where I am today if it weren't for the Lord giving me this totally priceless gift on September 8, 1993. Each time my ears get plugged in the car or an airplane on the way to the next place the Lord would have me go, I'm reminded that I have eardrums because of God. Every time I hear a beautiful song or play a beautiful grand piano I know that God exists, or else I wouldn't even be able to hear it.

Our God can do miracles. I promise you.

## About the Contributor

Originally from Colorado Springs, Colorado, Collin's musical education began at an early age as a child with extensive classical and theory training. Collin quickly developed a love and passion for worship music and wanting to pursue worship music and music performance, Collin ventured to Nashville, Tennessee, to pursue a commercial music degree with an emphasis in piano performance from Belmont University.

While in Nashville, Collin joined and co-founded the Pop/Rock Contemporary Christian Music trio, 33Miles in 2005 and began touring and recording professionally receiving a Dove-Nomination and releasing numerous chart-topping singles on Christian radio.

Collin is married to his high-school sweetheart, Jenna, and they recently had their first child, Gabriella.

Collin currently works as the worship pastor of Grace Church, Granger, Indiana. Collin draws encouragement and inspiration from Colossians 3:16, *"Let the word of Christ dwell in you richly as you teach and admonish one another with all wisdom, and as you sing psalms, hymns and spiritual songs with gratitude in your hearts to God."*

# CHAPTER 32

# To Do the Impossible

## *The testimony of Ellen Stevenson-Harkema as written by Carolyn Curran-Fyckes*

*Jesus looked at them and said, "With man this is impossible, but not with God; all things are possible with God"*
(Mark 10:27).

As a pastor's wife and as a Christian, I knew that God was able to do the impossible, but would He do the impossible for our seven-year-old son, Tim? Experience had shown me that not every prayer for healing is answered.

Tim had awakened with a swollen ankle. Gerald, my husband, had been digging a footing for a set of steps under the carport that he had recently built. We suspected that Tim had sprained his ankle by jumping into the hole, even though he was forbidden to do so. "Boys will be boys," we said. The neighborhood kids loved to jump into the hole. Our doctor was also of the opinion that his ankle was sprained and that given time and rest, the ankle would be better soon.

Three days later, Tim's pain had spread. He couldn't even open the bathroom door because his hand was swollen almost up his elbow. Back to the doctor we went. The doctor examined him carefully and ordered tests to be run. The laboratory results confirmed the pre-liminary diagnosis of rheumatoid arthritis. Tim would have to see a specialist in Halifax. The first available appointment wasn't for a few weeks. In the meantime, the arthritis took a firm hold on his young body. It was so difficult to watch our little boy suffering.

Finally, the appointment date with the specialist came. The spe-cialist confirmed our fears that the arthritis was all through him, even in his ears. Now we knew why he was such a restless sleeper. He was in a lot of pain, but he didn't express it as pain. He was unable to relax his body comfortably. I had thought that he was just a hyper child. Aspirin and hot wax treatments were prescribed. Tim was encour-aged to play with a ball or putty in order to free up his hands. On the way home, after the visit with the rheumatologist, Tim shocked us both by informing us that on the next trip he would take, he would be seeing Jesus.

That startling revelation that Tim was thinking that he might die soon was almost more than we could bear. He usually had so much life in him. Gerald instructed me that at the very next communion service, I was to bring Tim forward to the altar for prayer. The elders of the church were called upon to anoint him and to pray over him. That night, Gerald said that he believed that Tim was healed.

Well, Tim didn't notice any difference, and neither did I. We continued to follow the doctor's orders to apply hot wax treatments and to give him aspirin regularly. Six weeks passed until the follow-up visit with the specialist, in Yarmouth, Nova Scotia. The doctor studiously checked his old notes from the last consultation. He was dumbfounded to discover that Tim no longer had any arthritis. He said that if he had not written the notes himself, he would not have believed that Tim had suffered with such limiting arthritis because he was completely free of it now. We didn't have to continue with treatments anymore. We knew that the Lord had delivered him from the clutches of this horrible disease. The doctor warned us that blood tests, at some point, might show the presence of arthritis, since he had definitely had juvenile diabetes.

Tim is now 53 years old. He is totally free, full of energy, and completely healed of arthritis. There has been no recurrence. Praise the Lord. The memory of that miraculous healing is still fresh in Tim's mind, even after the passing of 46 years. Today, he works, along with his wife, Colleen, as a missionary in Africa. I am so grateful to the Lord for doing the impossible for our son.

My husband and I saw firsthand God accomplishing the impossible on other occasions. If you have the time, I will tell you of a few.

When we were pastoring Central Pentecostal Church in Elora/Fergus, there was a young girl in our congregation who had cancer the size of a loonie (a Canadian dollar) in her throat. We often prayed for her healing during the ladies' meeting and also in the Bible meetings. Although she did not come from a Christian background, she was born-again and had accepted Jesus as her Lord. She accompanied me to many Christian meetings, which often involved a time set aside for prayer. Everyone would pray for her. On one particular Sunday, Rev. McKnight, our superintendent, and his lovely wife visited our church. We had an altar service, which was our usual custom. Mrs. McKnight prayed earnestly for this young lady. Many among us felt that she definitely was going to receive the healing prayed for. Something very unusual happened one morning when she was at home. Her vision was cloudy, and she was having trouble breathing. She made her way to the bathroom, where she was astonished to realize that she was coughing up what appeared to be a cancerous growth. Quickly, she made an appointment with her doctor, who confirmed that there was no longer any sign of cancer. All he could see was a little bit of scar tissue. This sudden healing was an answer to prayer. Today she is still alive and resides in Elora, Ontario, Canada.

On another occasion, while ministering in Africa, we passed through a village. Visitors, especially visitors who owned a car, were a great novelty there. The evangelist who was traveling with us stopped the car in order to greet the crowd that had gathered. He had recognized some of the Christians who attended the local church. I noted that the people were beautiful, with fine features and a small build. One child in particular caught my attention. He was quite large and appeared to be about four or five years of age. His mother was holding him, protectively, on her hip. Unlike the other children, he wasn't running around.

Through the evangelist, as interpreter, the people asked us to pray for this child. These people were people of faith. When they prayed, they expected God to answer them. Unaware of what the child's problem was, we began to sing some choruses and prayed. The mother set the child down on the ground. He immediately started to run around like the other children. The villagers were "beyond themselves" with excitement. We were bewildered until it was explained to us that this child had never even walked before. He had been given an instant healing.

Our God is the God of the impossible. Many, many times throughout our lives, He would again prove this to us.

## ABOUT THE CONTRIBUTOR

Mrs. Ellen Stevenson-Harkema was the wonderful wife of many years to former missionary/pastor Rev. Gerald Stevenson, a pastor with the Pentecostal Association of Canada, as well as a former senior pastor of Glad Tidings' Church in Burlington, and founding pastor of Living Waters' Church, in Burlington, Ontario, Canada. During Mrs. Stevenson's missionary days, she journeyed with her husband to places such as Mombasa, Kenya, and Lilongwe, Malawi.

At present, Mrs. Stevenson is retired and makes her home in Paris, Ontario, Canada. She is the mother of two wonderful children, Tim and Heather, who are both serving the Lord. She is also a grandmother to six, and a great-grandmother to one.

Tim is married to Colleen. They have two boys and two girls. He is currently serving with his family on the mission field in Kampala, Uganda. Heather is a high school principal in Ontario. She is married to Brent. They have two children.

# PART IV

# MIRACLES OF ENCOURAGEMENT AND MOMENTS FOR THE HEART

*Not to us, O LORD, not to us but to Your name be the glory, because of Your love and faithfulness* (Psalm 115:1).

# CHAPTER 33

# THE WONDERFUL CHRISTMAS

## *Captain Irvin L. Rozier*

*And thine ears shall hear a word behind thee, saying, This is the way, walk ye in it, when ye turn to the right hand, and when ye turn to the left (Isaiah 30:21 KJV).*

*"And he lifted up his eyes, and saw the woman and children, and said, who are those with thee? And he said, the children which God has graciously given thy servant"* (Gen. 33:5 KJV). Children are a gift from God. He blessed me with two wonderful daughters and a good son. When their mother left in 1986, I became a single parent to 6-, 8-, and 1-year-old children.

My heart grieved for them as they missed their mother. After the Lord saved me, I began to pray for them. One of my prayers in December 1989 was that they would be blessed to have a wonderful Christmas, including spending some precious time with their mother. Shortly thereafter, my children's mother called and asked if she could have the children a few days. She would get them about four or five days before Christmas and bring them back Christmas day.

I readily agreed. She asked if I would drive them halfway. She lived in Atlanta, so Dublin was the agreed meeting point. The children were all excited about this rare visit with their mother. They had not spent much time with her since our separation. I scraped together a few dollars to give to them to spend. We loaded up and headed out.

Well, you should have seen the look of happiness on their faces as they hugged and greeted their mom. She had been such a wonderful mom to our children before. She always made sure they were well fed, clothed, clean, and hugged and loved. She roller-skated with them and read to them; they were her life. Tragically, the devil can destroy and take away a mother's concern and love for her children, whether it's through drugs or other methods.

As they drove away, I sat in the car and cried. My tears were a mixture of joy for their happiness of being with their mom and sadness and grief for the losses they had experienced. I loved these children that God had given me, and when they hurt, I did too. What I didn't tell the children was that I had given them all the money I had. My car's gas needle showed empty, and it was 110 miles back home.

It was Sunday morning about 10:30 A.M. as I began to drive back home. I said, "Lord, I guess I'll run out of gas within a few miles, but I'm trusting You in this situation." About three miles down the road, I saw a small sign displaying an arrow pointing left to a small country church. The Lord suddenly spoke to me and said, "Go to that church." I said, "OK, but I'm not dressed very well." (I had on old blue jeans, a T-shirt, and tennis shoes.) The Lord replied, "Go just like you are and don't even concern yourself about what others may think about your clothing. I know what is in your heart."

I drove up to that church, got out of my beat-up old Pontiac, and went inside. Services had already started, and several heads turned to stare as a badly dressed stranger entered. I sat down on a seat, and after a few songs, the preacher preached on the famous faith chapter in the Bible, Hebrews 11.

The Lord anointed this pastor as he preached. It seemed as if most of the words he spoke were directed at me. I needed that encouragement at that particular moment. Thank You, Jesus. After service, the preacher was led to ask for testimonies. A few dear saints stood up and testified. Their testimonies were very uplifting.

Suddenly the Lord spoke and said, "Irvin, get up and testify." As I stood, I wiped some of the wrinkles from my blue jeans and began to speak. As the Spirit of the Lord anointed me, every eye in the congregation was on me, and every ear was attentive. I told how the Lord has directed my footsteps to that church, how the sermon and testimonies had encouraged me, and how happy I was that my children would be spending a few days with their mom. I asked for prayer. At this request, the godly pastor asked his little flock to gather around the altar and especially pray that not only my children but also that other children from broken homes would have a happy Christmas.

After the service, I slowly walked to my car. An elderly woman came up to me, shook my hand, and told me my testimony had touched her heart in a special way. After I withdrew my hand, I looked in my palm and saw the folded five-dollar bill she had given me—gas money to get home. God will provide.

When I got home that Sunday evening, a friend of mine called and asked if I would drive him to a city about 50 miles away. His truck had quit, and it was too cold to drive his motorcycle. I said, "OK, I've got to pick up a few pecans to sell to get a few dollars. My children aren't here, so I'm free to go." He was a nurse and was going to work two 16-hour shifts during Christmas. He said he was renting a hotel room and I could stay there while he was working.

It snowed hard the night before we left. Not only had it snowed, but the temperature had also dropped and black ice had formed on the roads. As I slowly drove that old Pontiac down those icy roads, we saw many vehicles in the ditch. People in south Georgia are not equipped to drive in these conditions. As I pulled up to an intersection, I applied my brakes to stop. I hit a patch of black ice, and said to my unsaved friend, "Brace yourself, we are going to crash." Sure enough, we did, but the Lord protected us both. There was only a small dent in the car. We were stuck in the ditch, so we went looking for a kindhearted farmer to pull us out.

Shortly we found one. We asked for help. He pulled on his brogans, walked to the shelter, cranked up his John Deere, and quickly pulled us out. We tried to pay him, but he refused. Thank God for people like this kind farmer.

We arrived safely at the hotel, checked in, and then went and got a bite to eat. This was two days before Christmas. I then drove my friend to the nursing home and went back to the hotel and went to sleep.

I woke up early Christmas Eve and said, "Lord, I sure would like to go to church this morning. Show me where to go." I picked up the paper and saw where a church was having an early morning service.

The Lord spoke and said, "Go there." So I went, and although only about 30 people were there, it was a sweet service. I was blessed by the words spoken about our Savior's birth. After this was over, I said, "Lord, I sure would like to go to Sunday school. Please show me where to go." Well, the Lord led me on a road out of town and in the country. It surely was beautiful scenery: gently rolling, snow-covered hills, the whiteness and brightness of everything. As I was driving, I thought about Christmas coming up. My friend was going to pay me $50 for driving him. That was not much to buy Christmas for my children. While I was thinking about things, the Lord interrupted my thoughts with a command, "Turn left here on this dirt road." I did, and about two miles down that road, I came up to a beautiful little country church sitting on a little hill surrounded by snow-covered pine trees. The Lord said, "Here is where I want you to go for Sunday school."

The parking lot was full of cars, and I felt a warm and peaceful presence about this little place. As I walked in, I was warmly greeted and directed to the right Sunday school class. The people there were friendly and warm-hearted. They made me welcome, and they were genuine, not fake like some places I've been. I thought to myself, *This is a praying church that God loves.*

I didn't stay for church services because the Lord directed me to go on back to the hotel. I did as He directed. After I had eaten dinner, I went back to the room and laid down to take a nap. Around 2:30 p.m., the Lord awoke me and said, "Go on over to the nursing home." I obeyed.

I found my friend and talked with him a few minutes. While we were talking, I heard the sound of singing. I told my friend I was going on down there to listen, as they were not only singing Christmas carols but also singing old hymns.

As I entered the area where the service was being held, I recognized many of the folks conducting the service. They were the ones I had Sunday school with that morning. Nothing was mentioned in the Sunday school class about a nursing home service. They recognized me and invited me to join them. I did as I enjoyed the presence of the Lord.

After the service, I said my good-byes and walked down the hall to the nurse's station. In a few minutes, the preacher came up and said, "The Lord told me to give you this check." It was for $150. I had only asked the Lord for some money so I could buy my children something for Christmas. He tested my faith by ordering my steps. I passed; thank God.

We came back home, and my friend paid me. My children came home late Christmas day. I was so glad to see them. I had missed them so. I told them I didn't have much for them for Christmas, but we were together. Thank you, Lord, for this wonderful Christmas memory.

*For as the Heavens are higher than the earth, so are My ways higher than your ways, and My thoughts than your thoughts* (Isaiah 55:9 KJV).

*My Walk With the Lord*, Irvin L. Rozier ©Copyright 2003, www. selahbooks.com.

## ABOUT THE CONTRIBUTOR

Irvin L. Rozier is a retired army captain, chaplain at the local American Legion, and minister at a local nursing home. He has written a book, *My Walk With the Lord*, and many articles and poems that he shares on the Internet.

His address is 3124 Spatola Loop, Blackshear, GA 31516, and his email is iwcroga@aol.com.

# CHAPTER 34

# A MARRIAGE MADE IN HEAVEN

## *Dr. Trudy Veerman*

*...O you afflicted one, tossed with tempest, and not comforted.
Behold, I will lay your stones with colorful gems, and lay your
foundations with sapphires...* (Isaiah 54:11 KJV).

In my early twenties, while living in the Netherlands, I was bearing the consequences of a sinful life. My past sins had become very obvious, and they could not be swept underneath the carpet. I became very desperate. I did not know what to do, or where to turn. I had been deceived. I walked around with a very heavy burden on my shoulders. At times, I thought I would go out of my mind, and I contemplated suicide.

I started to call upon a God I did not know. I said my childhood prayer. That was all I knew, and I added, "God, if You just would help me this time, I am so desperate." My simple prayer came from deep down in my heart. Through an instant miracle, as described in my testimony, the Lord reached down and grabbed me right in time, while the waters already had come to my nostrils. He saved me by the Blood of His Son Jesus Christ and set me free. I clung unto His hand, never to let go again.

*"But I trust in the Lord, I will be glad and rejoice in Your mercy,
for You have considered my trouble: You have known my soul in*

*adversities, and have not shut me up into the hand of the enemy;*
*You have set my feet in a wide place"* (Psalm 31:7-8 KJV).

My new walk with my Savior Jesus Christ had begun. *"Therefore,*
*if anyone is in Christ, he is a new creation; old things have passed away;*
*behold, all things have become new"* (2 Cor. 5:17 KJV).

I will concentrate further on how the Lord provided me with a
husband.

I often wondered if I ever would meet a decent man who would
marry me.

My lady pastor, Neeltje Bouw, said to me, "Trudy, just let the
Lord find you a husband. He can do a much better job in finding you
one than you ever can." I just had seen the Lord heal my mentally ill
sister, so…was there anything impossible with God?

Of course not. But waiting for almost two years seemed like an
eternity to me.

This particular time in August I went to Luxemburg for a one-
week vacation with a Christian youth group. We camped out in a
small field surrounded by woods and hills.

The second day, I noticed a tall, dark-haired young man, and right
away my heart started pounding. I thought, *Perhaps he will be my hus-*
*band-to-be.* I did not want to give in to my feelings, because I really
wanted the Lord to give me the "right" one. So, I prayed to the Lord
and said, "Lord, You have to take this 'in-love' feeling away from me
if this young man is not going to be my husband, because that does
not make sense." I didn't think this was any problem for the Lord to
answer this prayer. I gave even my feelings to the Lord. I meant business, and so did the Lord. Praise His wonderful name.

The next morning, when these feelings were still there, I knew
that I was going to marry this young man. This poor man (now my
husband) did not know what was hanging above his head; he never
had noticed me and neither did he know that I was in love with him.
No way did I want to show anything either.

I went off the camp a few times, prayed, and fasted while I was sitting near a little brook. I could hear the water rushing by, and its sound outdid my praying and crying unto the Lord. While I was at the brook, the Lord gave me the following Scriptures. *"Fear not, for you will not be ashamed; be not confounded, for you will not be put to shame; for you will forget the shame of your youth, and the reproach of your widowhood you will remember no more"* (Isaiah 54:4 KJV) *"And you shall be called by a new name, which the mouth of the Lord will give"* (Isaiah 62:2b KJV).

How *amazing* is His loving-kindness. Of course, I knew that the Lord will give us a new name, once with Him. But this Scripture was for *now*. This meant for me a new last name, as through marriage. That was all OK with me, but who was going to explain this to that young man, Casey? I said to the Lord that He had to do the work for me, because I was not going to tell this man anything, period. No way was I going to make a fool out of myself. I really thought he was too good looking for me anyway.

It's wonderful, how the Lord even must have known my taste—tall, slim, dark…

A few days went by, and I reminded the Lord that there were only three days left before we all were going home and asked if He would please move on my behalf. I thought the Lord was wasting some precious time.

That Thursday we had the afternoon for ourselves, and some of us walked through the countryside to the nearby village while talking to each other about what the Lord had done in our lives. Then I noticed that Casey came closer by and started to mingle in our conversation. Before I realized it, the others had left us and here we were, just the two of us. We shared Jesus Christ and Him crucified and how He had saved us. By now, I had become a little tense. I knew something that he did not know yet. Casey mentioned that he had asked the Lord for a wife, but so far had not met the "one."

I nearly burst when I heard this. He then looked at me and said, "Could it be you, perhaps?"

I didn't say a thing. Casey carried on with the conversation. After awhile, I said, "Do you think that the Lord plays cat and mouse and that He brings us together without a purpose?"

"No," Casey said, "I don't think the Lord would do that." We talked a little more and he said, "Let's ask the Lord for confirmation, that one of the young people will tell us the Lord's purpose for us two."

He hardly had finished his sentence and lo and behold, Jannie, the preacher's daughter, came running up to us and hollered, "I know you two are getting married. Trudy, I am glad for you but sorry for myself, because I am going to lose you." She then cried. A fellow from the camp came rushing by with a big box in his hands with a cake in it.

"I bought it not realizing what for, but I know now that this is your wedding cake," He said. He handed everybody a piece. The marvelous thing about it all is that another person took a movie from this, which later was shown at our wedding. I even have the picture of me eating that cake.

This was *far* better than any movie from Hollywood; this was the *real* thing.

I had found a husband, handpicked by the Lord. How could it get any better than that?

*"Many, O Lord my God, are Your wonderful works which You have done; and Your thoughts toward us cannot be recounted to You in order. If I would declare and speak of them, they are more than can be numbered"* (Ps. 40:5 KJV). When we arrived at the camp, somebody else threw rice over us, which is the tradition at a wedding of people from Indonesia. Well, we had enough confirmation and were engaged one month later and married a few months after, on November 15 of that same year. We had lots of time ahead of us to come to know each other better.

*"In the multitude of my anxieties within me, Your comforts delight my soul. But the Lord has been my defense, and my God the rock of my*

*refuge*" (Ps. 94:19,22 KJV). By now, we have been married for over 44 years and have four children, and four grandchildren. As you can understand, many things have happened between then and now. I can honestly say that the Lord Jesus Christ has been so faithful to us. He always has been my only hope, even in difficulties in our marriage and family life.

Even though our marriage was made in Heaven, it was our chore to keep it there. It took a lot of effort on our part. Together, we went over hills and through valleys. If it had not been for the Lord, I couldn't tell you where we would be today. We have learned to appreciate each other in the love of Christ. Our love for the Lord and each other has become as strong as a three-ply cord. I can only give Him *all* the glory.

> *Whom have I in Heaven but YOU? And there is none upon the earth that I desire besides You. My flesh and my heart fail; But God is the strength of my heart and my portion forever* (Psalm 73:25-26 NKJV).

> *But it is good for me to draw near to God: I have put my trust in the Lord God, that I may declare all Your works* (Psalm 73:28 NKJV).

Please come and see our wedding picture and our 40th wedding anniversary picture on our site: http://achristiancounselor.com/wedding.html.

## ABOUT THE CONTRIBUTOR

Minister Dr. Trudy Veerman, her husband, Casey, and their four children came to Canada in 1966 from the Netherlands. In her early twenties, she was confronted with major problems. Through the instant healing of her mentally challenged sister, she accepted Christ as her Savior.

She has been involved in God's service most of her adult life, in different capacities. Since 1997, she has provided counseling through her Website and has written many helpful writings and poetic pages on her Website: http://achristiancounselor.com.

Dr. Veerman is a Licensed Clinical Christian Therapist, a Certified Christian Counselor, and a published author.

# CHAPTER 35

# DIAMONDS DROPPED FROM HEAVEN

## *Dusty May Taylor*

*If you, then, though you are evil, know how to give good gifts to your children, how much more will your Father in heaven give good gifts to those who ask him!* (Matthew 7:11)

"Congratulations to such-and-such and so-and-so on their engagement!" my pastor announced. The congregation cheered and hollered and hooted and clapped, while another pair in a steady stream of couples stood up with beaming smiles to share their joy with the world.

I'm going to be completely honest with you: It took me some effort to clap along. It wasn't that I wasn't happy for them, because I most definitely was. Such-and-such and so-and-so were great. The problem was the man sitting next to me, whom I loved with an adoration bordering on ridiculous, and the giant void in both our bank accounts.

My Marc and I had been dating for over a year. I knew he was the man I would marry the first time we had a real conversation, just a couple weeks after we met. We were spending a day alone together, with a good excuse for doing so that managed to cover up any romantic interest very nicely. We talked non-stop, and by the time I went home at the end of the day I felt happy and nauseous and angry and scared all at once, and felt God whisper cheerfully, "Ta-daa! Told you he existed."

I was not amused.

We were best friends for about a year before he finally asked me out. When he did, he asked on one condition: "If I'm going to date you, you better be ready to marry me, because you could destroy me, and I am not going to get my heart broken."

I think I raised an eyebrow at him on principle, but readily agreed.

It is worth mentioning that as an unmarried Christian couple dedicated to obeying God's Word, physical intimacy is almost entirely off limits. Like a couple from a classic novel, our status as "officially dating" meant we held hands and hugged and snuck kisses on the cheek.

Now, fast-forward. A year had passed. We were more in love than ever, and every time we turned around another young couple was getting engaged. We both knew that the only reason we weren't was because my Marc couldn't save up for a ring while paying his rent, and helping me with mine, and helping me with food. There is a story in that, too.

For a very long time, I felt like I was receiving odd instructions from God that caused me to go against common sense. I was to stop working in cafes and retail stores, and begin cultivating my gifts and abilities by teaching singing, volunteering in ministries, and working as a freelance writer. This resulted in me not making enough to pay my rent, let alone eat. I cried on Marc's shoulder about this many times, and all he would say was, "But Hunny, look at all the great things God is doing with your life. If you think this is what He wants you doing, it's OK if you don't have a lot of money. That's what I'm for."

And so our devotion to one another increased, while our bank balances wavered. For a while I pestered Marc to just get me a nice little pawnshop ring, but he was very saddened by this and I felt God tell me to knock it off, so I did.

One day I felt like God spoke again. In my heart, I felt Him challenge my trust by asking me to pledge a thousand dollars to help our church build a new facility to reach the people of our city. Sitting next to me, my Marc felt challenged to give even more. We discussed the issue, and hugged, and agreed that obeying God was more important than us getting married. And so the money that would have allowed us to get engaged was given to God. A short while later, I felt God ask me to give away a month's wages on top of my original pledge. I talked to my Marc, and again, we agreed that God came first. Shortly thereafter, my Marc felt challenged to give away a comic book collection he'd been collecting since childhood, which had substantial monetary and emotional value. He let it go.

I'm going to be real here: It was fun in a way, but in a way it was also terrible. We fully believed that God would provide for us, but we also couldn't help but wonder why other couples in love were being allowed to marry, and we weren't. It hurt my feelings a bit, even though I knew rationally that God was incapable of being anything but good and loving toward us. I prayed for a miracle. My Marc would encourage me by talking about all the great things God had for our future, and I would pour and say, "But I do not want all that right now. I want to marry my Marc." He'd sigh, then smile, and kiss me on the forehead. "I know," he'd say. "Me too."

Three weeks passed. Caught up in our church's little season of engagements, people kept innocently approaching and asking us when it would be our turn. I'm telling you, you haven't lived till you've had an eye twitch in church. After the service, I went home, but Marc stayed behind, because somebody asked to talk to him.

A week later, he filled me in on their meeting.

The man approached holding a plastic bag. He wasn't somebody Marc was close to, or who knew about what God had been doing in our lives, or anything else like that. While Marc wondered what was up, the man said something like, "Here. God told me to give you this."

Marc took the bag, looked inside, and promptly started to weep. It contained a large diamond solitaire engagement ring, a ladies wedding band with 12 diamonds, a wedding band for him, and a diamond necklace. The solitaire came with papers and receipts that indicated that it was a Canadian diamond (which means "Not a Blood Diamond" in my language), and that it had a retail value of $6,000 but had been purchased on sale for $4,000. An official appraisal from a couple years earlier demanded that it be insured for $8,500.

A week later, on his birthday, my Marc planned a beautiful romantic picnic date for us with all my favorite things, and took me to my favorite spot. We sat on a bench beside an old church, in the shade of a maple tree, and he handed me a pretty antique teacup. It was upside down on a saucer. He knelt down in front of me with a thermos of my favorite kind of tea, and asked me to pick up the cup so he could pour. I did so, and there on the little gilded saucer was the ring, sparkling up at me. Handwritten in gold on the saucer were the words, 'Will you marry me?'

I wish I could say I reacted sweetly and romantically, but my first instinct was shock. I exclaimed, "What is this?! How did you get this?!"

"Well, will you marry me?" he asked, laughing nervously.

"Of course I will!" My heart pounded a million miles a minute as he explained to me the mysterious circumstances surrounding the ring. We hugged, and thanked God, and ate chocolate, and everything was beautiful.

When he slipped the ring on my finger, it was a perfect fit.

## ABOUT THE CONTRIBUTOR

Dusty May Taylor is a vocal instructor, visual artist, and freelance writer living in Hamilton, Ontario. She has been in a love affair with Jesus Christ since she was three years old, and in the past four years has learned to follow Him with her whole heart. This has resulted in blessings such as script writing, ministry collaboration, appearances on the Canadian daily talk show *100 Huntley Street*, and meeting the love of her life. More is undoubtedly on the way, and she fully expects to have a beautiful wedding with zero debt.

Dusty on the Web:

http://dustmay.tumblr.com/

twitter.com/dustymaytaylor

http://www.facebook.com/pages/Dusty-May-Taylors-Writing-and-Such/311571330425

# CHAPTER 36

# THE GREEN CARD STORY

## *Jeannie M. Berry*

*And I will do whatever you ask in my name, so that the Son
may bring glory to the Father* (John 14:13).

My name is Jeanne Berry, or as my friends and family call me,
Deanie. I am a retired postal employee who, while working for the
post office, used to regularly deliver mail to large apartment com-
plexes. I have found that quite a few people living in an apartment
were single, divorced, lonely, and wanted friendships. I seemed at
times to fill a void in my customers' lives. I wasn't just a mail lady; I
also became my customers' friend. They seemed to look forward to
picking up their mail and having conversation with me as I put mail
into the slots of the mailboxes. At times I felt as if I was not only their
mail lady but also their therapist. I would hear a lot about abuse from
a spouse, or how they couldn't find the right person, or they would
talk about their problems in the work place.

On one occasion, I noticed a man who had come by to talk and
pick up his mail. He seemed very down in the dumps, and I quickly
picked up on it. I asked him why he seemed so sad. I was comfortable
in asking him this question because I had been delivering his mail
for over a year and we became friends. We were not close but had a
closeness that you would have with your hairdresser or barber.

He began his story, trying hard not to choke up with tears, saying, "I am a married man, but I have only spent my honeymoon with my bride and one other visit in over a five-year period. You see, my wife is not an American citizen, and I haven't been able to get a green card for her. And you know that is not the worst part of the story, not being able to be with my wife; the worst part is my homeland culture. In my home country, my wife is considered a bad or loose woman because she is not with her husband. She is under so much pressure from her community because of her situation. And sadly, she is almost a prisoner in her own home. She is not able to leave her home without a male escort."

He said, "It would be so hard for you to understand what it is like for a woman who is not with her spouse."

I felt such pity for the man. He was in so much pain and was missing the woman he loved but could not be with her and was about to give up hope of getting the green card in the mail for his wife. After all, he had been waiting for over five years, and he was so discouraged.

I talked to him about the love of God and told him that in the times when you are feeling hopeless and feel things are impossible, pray to Him. Tell Him all of your troubles, and He will be there for you. I told him that I would say a prayer on his behalf, and to expect to have an answer. I said, "When you receive that green card, and you will, all that I ask in return is that you acknowledge that God did this for you, and acknowledge He is the one and only true God."

I went home so full of hope for the answered prayer that God would soon answer for my friend. I told God that I took such a leap of faith with my words to the man, telling him the green card would come in. I said, "Please answer this prayer. Have it come true, not for my sake but for his sake. It doesn't matter how people feel about me. It only matters that the man knows of Your love and power and for him to know You are the one and only true God." I really surprised myself by making such a promise. I had never done that before. But at that time in my life, I had such a strong faith. I had seen so much evidence of His presence in my life that I knew He heard me and would come through.

Two days later, that green card came through. I was so excited and praised God for my answered prayer. As soon as I received the card and left for my route, I went straight to his mailbox. The following day, he waited for me to arrive in the mailroom; I can't tell you how thrilled he was to get the card. He came with a present for me; it was a very expensive perfume set of lotion, perfume, and cologne. He thanked me over and over again as he handed me the gift. I said, "I'm so happy for you, but please do not thank me." I had only said a prayer for him. I then conveyed that it was God who had sent that card to him. I'm not sure if I hurt his feelings, but I wouldn't accept the gift. I told him to save it for his long-awaited wife.

## ABOUT THE CONTRIBUTOR

Deanie M. Berry was raised in Hurst, Texas, and currently resides in Fort Worth, Texas, along with her husband. She has two beautiful grown daughters, and with great love, remembers a wonderful son who passed away tragically from an automobile accident in 2008. She has five grandchildren, who are the "light of her life," and add much joy to her life.

When she is not actively running around after these precious little grandchildren, she may be found tending her beautiful garden and pruning her stunning rose bushes.

# CHAPTER 37

# A SCOTTISH WEDDING

## *Janette Webster*

*Do not be anxious about anything, but in everything, by prayer and petition, with thanksgiving, present your requests to God* (Philippians 4:6).

This is the story of an ordinary family, their daughter and son-in-law's engagement and wedding, and the faithfulness of God. I know the story well because it happened to my family.

My family lives on the east coast of Scotland, in a fishing town called Arbroath, noted for its smoked haddock, the Arbroath Smokie, and for the Arbroath Abbey, where the Scottish Declaration of Independence was signed in 1310. Our home was a maisonette, three stories up, overlooking the main roundabout of the town. The view from the living room window faced the main dual carriageway toward the town's harbor, which at that time still landed fish, though tourism was its primary industry. If you stuck your head out of my son's window, you could catch a glimpse of the sea.

At that time, I was working as a registered child minder, looking after preschool and school-age children on a full-time and part-time basis. My husband, Alan, was unemployed but was kept busy with re-training and volunteer work. He had been laid off three times in thirteen months, first after being a deputy officer in charge of a children's home for 13 years, then from working as a factory worker, and finally from being employed as a store man. My son, Steven, was being prepared for a position with Youth for Christ, near Kidderminister, in England. My daughter, Jillian, was attending college and taking courses in order to become a nursery nurse. Mark, my son-in-law to be, was employed as a fitter with a double glazing company. Upon graduation, Jillian eventually found employment in Dundee with the City Council Child Care Services. No contract was offered, so the job was not secure.

In the meantime, the friendship between Jillian and Mark began to blossom into a serious relationship. Soon they were dreaming of the future and discussing engagement. A beautiful ring was chosen of twisted gold with a Ceylon blue sapphire set in a cluster of diamonds. They didn't know how they were going to pay for it, though. Mark had been laid off from work. Fortunately, they discovered the same ring in a mail-order catalog. The cost was much more reasonable and was now affordable.

After a rollercoaster ride of emotions and prayer, their engagement was happily announced. We joyfully celebrated, along with Mark's parents, his brother, and his brother's fiancée. During a conversation with Mark's Mum, Muriel, I was reminded of a time, many years before when Alan and I had been discussing our wedding plans and our future together. I had thought that I would like to have four children. I even chose their names: Steven, Jillian, Mark, and Jenny. Instantly, I was jolted out of my reverie. No one knew about this wish. *Oh my goodness, Jillian is engaged to Mark. His name is Mark. Oh God, that was one of the names. Wow, this is something else. This wedding is meant to be,* I thought silently to myself.

If God wanted this wedding to take place, He would have to arrange it. During this uncertain time of unemployment, we could not take on such a debt. As was my habit, I asked God for a verse of Scripture to hold onto. That duly came in the shape of Philippians 4:6, *"Be anxious about nothing, but in prayer and supplication make your requests known to the God, and the peace of God that passes all understanding will guard your heart and mind."* This verse was to be the anchor and the answer to every part of the wedding plans and to the future that was ahead of us.

Tentatively, the first small steps of faith were taken. A venue for the reception was searched for. I already had a location in mind. Not wanting to interfere I didn't voice my opinion. The Windmill Hotel, with its straight staircase and beautiful stained glass window of bright greens, blues, and reds, was chosen. The dining room, with practically floor-to-ceiling windows overlooking the ever-changing North Sea, was magnificent. All looked promising—until, that is, we were shown where the meal would actually be served. The room was large enough, but the wood panelling made it so dark. The windows were very high up and allowed no view. My heart sank. Surely this was not the place. Everyone else seemed pleased with it. Again, I kept my uneasiness to myself. I simply prayed that the Lord would make the decision.

With the business concluded and the deposit of £120 paid by Mark and Jillian, the choice of reception hall was one less thing to think about before the 16th of September the following year, or so we thought. Bookings for the photographer, video man, and the DJ quickly followed. With the permission of the minister, the church service would take place in St. Andrews Church of Scotland. The minister did not take the granting of this permission to marry lightly. He arranged for Jillian and Mark to take a pre-marriage course with him before he would give his blessing on the marriage. I thanked God for this input. The course was completed successfully, and the decision to marry them was affirmed by Martin Fair.

Across from the church were council-owned gardens, the backdrop to which was the Abbey. The photographer suggested that the wedding photographs be taken there. Arrangements for the council's approval were made. Approval was granted. So much was fitting into place, but how would all of these bills be paid for? I continued to pray, "Lord, You said, 'Don't be anxious about anything.'" With still no sign of jobs, Alan and I checked into cashing our insurance policies, but our efforts bore no fruit.

At least Mark had another job as a store man/forklift driver. Jillian was still employed but without a contract. They hadn't even found an apartment to rent or buy yet. "When, Lord, will things turn around?" I asked. "When will this miracle of seeing Your word realized take place?"

Still we moved on with the wedding plans and just kept trusting. It was decided that the men of the wedding party should wear kilts. There was a kilt rental shop in town, near the church and Abbey. In went Mark, Alan, Mark's brother, Mike, the best man, and Mark's father, Angus, for their first fitting. There were so many styles to choose from. At last, they settled on plain white shirts with black bow ties, smart-looking black waistcoats, and jaunty Bonnie Prince Charlie jackets with shiny silver buttons, skin-covered sporrans, thick wool socks with skean dhus (ornamental daggers) tucked in, and soft leather shoes. The tartans selected were Flower of Scotland for Mark, Mike, Alan, and Angus, and the Robinson Tartan of greens and off-white for the two ushers, Steven, and Mark's friend, Lyall. Angus remarked that he thought I had fallen in love with Alan all over again when I saw how splendid he looked in the kilt. I have to admit that my heart did flutter at the sight of him. Even Ross, the 5-year-old page boy, decked in his kilt, was quite taken with himself when he viewed his reflection in the mirror. He spontaneously gave the shop assistant a big hug and exclaimed in an excited voice, "I love you." These were special moments indeed.

Jillian decided she too would rent her dress and those of her flower girl and bridesmaid at a little boutique in Stirling. Clare, the brides-maid, was a quiet, shy girl. I prayed, beforehand, that God would give her the very special experience of feeling like a joyful child wearing her first party dress. Clare's eyes sparkled as she swished her bronze, taffeta dress, with off-white sash belt. Fiona, Ross' sister, wore a matching off-white taffeta dress with a bronze sash belt. On the day of the wedding, the two young girls would have their golden hair arranged in ringlets, complimented with silk roses and posies in hues of autumn gold and pale orange with silk ribbons trailing.

A radiant bride emerged from the fitting room. I held my breath. My beloved daughter, Jillian, looked stunning in the simplicity of her white off-the-shoulder dress, fitted at the waist and then falling gracefully over a hoop to the ground like a cascading waterfall. The bow on the back of her dress was covered with delicate embroidered flowers, symbolizing a promise of a future with hope. Her autumn bouquet of dried flowers and pods would be a harvest reminder of so much to be thankful for. Her veil could barely hide her shining eyes. "Lord, please gift each woman who attends the wedding with an outfit that will make her feel as special as the wedding party feels. Let them all have a story to tell about Your gift to them," I prayed.

It was now May, and events were about to begin moving fast. The DJ called with some disturbing news. He had attended a wedding at the Windmill Hotel. The wedding had been a disaster. Not only had the service been poor, but the hotel had also run out of food. He had felt a nudging to call us with this information. As soon as possible, we arranged a meeting to discuss this unsettling revelation. When we spoke with the hotel's management, we were not given adequate assurance that this disaster wouldn't be repeated. There was only one sensible choice. The reception was cancelled and the deposit lost.

Prayer, prayer, and more prayer ensued. Later that same week, the Meadowbank Restaurant, with its many windows and welcoming atmosphere, was contacted. The wedding date in September was free. By the end of the week, the whole reception had been rearranged. "Thank You, Lord." And yes, it was the very location God had put upon my heart. I hadn't shared this secret with anyone.

A traditional bride's night out with friends, called a "Hen Night," recouped the money lost in the previous deposit. This was followed by a phone call inquiring how the wedding was to be paid for. A check was given to cover the expense. "Thank You, Lord."

The Lord wasn't finished tying up all the loose ends yet. Two checks arrived in the nick of time, just two weeks prior to the wedding, to pay for my mother-of-the bride outfit. I was so very pleased with the elegant two-piece suit of fern green, with long jacket and mandarin collar. The ensemble was topped with a lovely hat in a soft mango shade, trimmed with cream, and completed with cream accessories, including a silk scarf in mango, pink, and green.

Jillian was at last given a contract of employment. This promise of a more permanent employment helped to secure a mortgage on a one-bedroom flat in the center of town. "Thank You, Lord."

The rain that had poured down each Saturday for weeks never materialized on the 16th of September. The weather stayed dry, with only a light covering of clouds. Leaving Jillian with her dad, I made my way to the waiting taxi. My legs were shaking beneath me. *Don't be anxious. Don't be anxious about anything.*

Disembarking from the taxi, I was welcomed and hugged by Steven—oh, I needed that. Once Jillian arrived, I could not trust my emotions and quickly made my way into the church to be with my friends and other family members. Inside the church, standing nervously at the front, were Mark and Mike. The watery sunlight streaming through the windows threw a haze over the purple and creams and light rusts of the altar flowers.

Music burst forth to announce the bride's entry. Mark tried valiantly to compose himself...*don't be anxious about anything*. The wedding the Lord had planned commenced with Jillian and Mark's vows, their signing of the register, and the music to accompany them back down the aisle as husband and wife. The photographer commented that it was a good day for taking photographs, as there were no streaks of light and fewer shadows. The crowd was outside cheering, and confetti was being thrown. There was a warm welcome at the Meadowbank with the crisp, white tablecloths, blue drapes, and posies of chrysanthemums. *Don't be anxious. Don't be anxious.* There was a delicious meal, infectious laughter during the speeches, and time to relax before the dancing commenced. There were stories from women about their gifts of outfits for the wedding. "Thank You, Lord." There was Scottish dancing, the Birdie song for Aunt Cathy, and the restaurant staff commenting on the enjoyment of the guests.

The manager said that they had never experienced such an orderly day. Nothing had gone wrong.

Jillian and Mark departed to use their final gift, an overnight stay in a Dundee hotel. With the singing of "Auld Lang Syne," completely satisfied, we ended this memorable day. "Wow, Lord, You did it. You were faithful to Your word and worked a miracle."

NOTE: In May 2003, our son Steven married Jenny. I now have the four children I prayed for: Steven, Jillian, Mark, and Jenny.

Thank You, Lord, for Your faithfulness.

## ABOUT THE CONTRIBUTOR

Janette Webster resides in Arbroath, Scotland, with her husband, Alan, who works as a debt counselor. They have two grown children: Jillian and Steven.

Jillian is currently employed with a child and family center and, along with her husband, Mark, of 14 years, has been blessed with twins, Georgia and Jacob. Jillian recovered from an operation and radiotherapy treatment for a pituitary gland tumor. The twins are now 5 years old, and their family currently resides in Arbroath, Scotland.

Steven and his wife, Jenny, whom he married six years ago, are the proud parents of a 15-month-old son, Rory. They reside in Manchester, England.

# CHAPTER 38

# GOD'S GOT YOUR NUMBER

## *Dr. Rev. Ken Gaub*

*When thou passeth through the waters, I will be with thee; and
through the rivers, they shall not overflow thee: when thou
walketh through the fire, thou shalt not be burned; neither shall
the flame kindle upon thee* (Isaiah 43:2 KJV).

*God, sometimes I wonder if You really know where I am*, I thought. A
melancholy cloud of self-pity enshrouded my mind. My hands tensed
their grip on the steering wheel, and I stared through the windshield
of our bus. The endless ribbon of superhighway stretched before me
as I recalled the last few days of our fast-paced existence. I seemed
to have used up all my faith in ministering to others. Even my sense
of humor was hollow. *God, even a preacher needs to know that You are
aware of him once in a while*, I pleaded inside.

"Hey, Dad. Let's get some pizza." The voice of my younger son,
Dan, stirred me out of my self-induced cocoon of despondency. My
wife, Barbara, and daughter, Becki, agreed with Dan. It had been
a long day, and it was way past time to eat. "OK," I yelled back. A
large, green sign loomed ahead. I flipped on my right turn signal and
picked up the CB microphone to inform my oldest son, Nathan, of
our plans to pull off the highway. He and his wife followed closely in
another bus.

We exited from I-75 and turned onto Route 741 just south of Dayton, Ohio. Bright, colorful signs advertising a wide variety of fast food restaurants were a welcome sight. Satisfied murmurs arose behind me as we sighted the local pizza parlor.

As I maneuvered the big Silver Eagle bus into the parking lot, Dan and Becki were already clamoring to get out and go into the restaurant. Even examining menus offered a diversion from the limited activities available inside our "home on wheels."

Barbara stood at the bottom step and turned to wait for me. I sat staring into space. "Aren't you coming, Ken?" she asked.

"Naw, I'm not really hungry," I replied. "You go ahead with the kids. I need to stretch out and unwind a bit."

"OK, we'll be back soon," her voice trailed off.

I moved back into the living room area to the sofa, folded my arms behind my head, leaned back, and sighed. *It really is a beautiful day*, I thought as I glanced out the window. *Maybe I should get some fresh air.* I stepped outside, closed the bus doors, and looked around. Noticing a Dairy Queen down the street, I thought, *Maybe I'm thirsty.*

After purchasing a Coke, I strolled in the direction of the bus, still musing about my feelings of God's apathy toward me. The impatient ringing of a telephone somewhere up the street jarred me out of my doldrums. It was coming from a phone booth at a service station on the corner. As I approached, I heard the phone continuing its unanswered ring. Ring. Ring. I paused and looked to see if anyone was going to answer the phone. Noise from the traffic flowing through the busy intersection must have drowned out the sound, because the service station attendant continued looking after his customers, oblivious to the incessant ringing.

*Why doesn't someone answer that phone?* I wondered. The ringing continued. I began reasoning, *It may be important. What if it's an emergency?*

I started to walk away, but curiosity overcame my indifference. I stepped inside the booth and picked up the phone. "Hello," I said casually and took a big sip of Coke.

The operator whined, "Long distance call for Ken Gaub."

My eyes widened, and I almost choked on a chunk of ice from my Coke. Swallowing hard, I said, "You're crazy." Realizing I shouldn't speak to an operator like that, I added, "This can't be. I was just walking down the street, not bothering anyone, and the phone was ringing…"

The operator ignored my crude explanation and asked once more, "Is Ken Gaub there? I have a long distance call for him." It took a moment to gain control of my babblings, but I finally replied, "Yes, he is," searching for a possible explanation, I suddenly had the answer. "I know what this is. I'm on *Candid Camera*."

While trying to locate the hidden camera, I reached up and tried to smooth my hair. I wanted to look my best for all those millions of television viewers. Stepping outside the phone booth and looking quickly in every direction, the telephone cord nearly broke as I stretched it to its limit. I couldn't find a camera anywhere. Impatiently, the operator interrupted again.

"I have a long distance call for Ken Gaub, sir. Is he there?"

Still shaken, as well as perplexed, I asked, "How in the world can this be? How did you reach me here? I was walking down the street, not bothering anyone, the pay phone started ringing, and I decided to answer it." My voice grew louder in the excitement. "I just answered it on chance. You can't mean me. This is impossible."

"Well," the operator asked, "is Mr. Gaub there or isn't he?" The tone of her voice convinced me the call was real and that her patience was at its limit.

I then replied, "Yes, he is. I'm he."

She was not convinced. "Are you sure?" she asked.

Flustered, I, half-laughing, replied, "As far as I know at this point, I am."

To avoid any further disasters, I sat my Coke down as I heard another voice say, "Yes, that's him, operator. I believe that's him."

I listened dumbfounded to a strange voice identify herself. The caller blurted, "Ken Gaub, I'm Millie from Harrisburg, Pennsylvania. You don't know me, but I'm desperate. Please help me."

"What can I do for you?" I responded.

She began weeping. I waited until she regained control, and then she continued, "I'm about to commit suicide, and I just finished writing a note. While writing it, I began to pray and tell God I really didn't want to do this. I suddenly remembered seeing you on television and thought if I could just talk to you, you could help me. I knew that was impossible because I didn't know how to reach you, and I didn't know anyone who could help me find you. I continued writing my suicide note because I could see no way out of my situation. As I wrote, numbers came to my mind, and I scribbled them down."

At this point she began weeping again, and I prayed silently for wisdom to help her.

She continued, "I looked at the numbers and thought, *Wouldn't it be wonderful if I had a miracle from God, and He has given me Ken's phone number?* I decided to try calling it. I figured it was worth the chance. It really was. I can't believe I'm talking to you. Are you in your office in California?"

I replied, "Lady, I don't have an office in California. My office is in Yakima, Washington."

Surprised, she asked, "Oh, really. Then where are you?"

"Don't you know?" I responded. "You made the call."

She explained, "But I don't even know what area I'm calling. I just dialed the number that I had on this paper."

I told her, "Ma'am, you won't believe this, but I'm in a phone booth in Dayton, Ohio."

"Really?" she exclaimed. "Well, what are you doing there?"

I kidded her gently, "Well, I'm answering the phone. It was ringing as I walked by, so I answered it."

Knowing this encounter could only have been arranged by God, I began to counsel the woman. As she told me of her despair and frustration, the presence of the Holy Spirit flooded the phone booth, giving me words of wisdom beyond my ability. In a matter of moments, she prayed the sinner's prayer and met the One who would lead her out of her situation into a new life.

I walked away from that telephone booth with an electrifying sense of our Heavenly Father's concern for each of His children. I was astounded as I thought of the astronomical odds of this happening. With all the millions of phones and innumerable combinations of numbers, only an all-knowing God could have caused that woman to call that number in the phone booth at that moment in time.

Forgetting my Coke and nearly bursting with exhilaration, I bounded up the steps and into the bus. I wondered if my family would believe my story. *Maybe I better not tell this*, I thought; but I couldn't contain it. "Barb, you won't believe this. God knows where I am."

God also knows where you are. No one is immune to life's many problems, but God knows about them and acts according to your faith. He knows where you are. The Bible says, *"When thou passeth through the waters, I will be with thee; and through the rivers, they shall not overflow thee: when thou walketh through the fire, thou shall not be burned; neither shall the flame kindle upon thee"* (Isaiah 43:2 KJV).

Place yourself in your Heavenly Father's hands. Concentrate on knowing His will for your life, and He will never forsake or forget you. He knows what you face spiritually, physically, emotionally, and financially. Because God cares, you can cast all your cares on Him.

## ABOUT THE CONTRIBUTOR

Dr. Rev. Ken Gaub has been in involved in ministry for most of his adult life. He began his ministry by pastoring at a mountain church in Kentucky and then traveled the country, taking his musical family across America. Rev. Gaub has now been in ministries over 50 years, traveled over eight million miles to over 115 countries, and has taken 120 trips to Israel. He has spoken everywhere from colleges and universities, to churches, conventions, prisons, and even the Pentagon.

Ken is also the founding president of Y.O.U., a multi-faceted organization dedicated to helping troubled youth, and he is a current member and trustee of the Presidential Task Force. Through his years of well-respected service, he has earned numerous governmental awards, both abroad and at home. Ken has written numerous books, including the book *God's Got Your Number*, from which this story has been excerpted. Ken's organization is currently headquartered in Yakima, Washington. He may be reached at: Ken Gaub World Wide Ministries, P.O. Box 1, Yakima, WA 98907.

# CHAPTER 39

# Does God Hear Me?

## *Carolyn Curran-Fyckes*

*I tell you the truth, anyone who will not receive the kingdom of God like a little child will never enter it* (Mark 10:15).

Have you ever wondered if God even listens to your prayers—never mind if He will answer them? I have. My secret prayer just seemed so, so impossible to be answered. You see, I was raised in a home in which the existence of God was firmly believed in but in which Spiritualism was also believed in and practiced faithfully.

My mother had a very strong influence on me while I was growing up. My parents emigrated from Scotland to Montreal, Canada, when I was 18 months old. My father, who couldn't speak French, was unable to find work as a licensed carpenter in the Montreal area. Consequently, he was forced to seek employment in remote areas, such as the arctic. He spent a number of years in Fort Churchill, Manitoba, where he was in charge of construction for Defense Research Northern Laboratories, under the Canadian government. He came home for extended visits once or twice a year. So, I lived virtually in a single-parent household, along with my two older brothers.

Despite the heavy workload, Mum managed to create a welcoming, impeccable home for us. She had a sense of style that was evident both inside and outside our home. In the summertime, strangers would often stop to admire and ask questions about her beautiful garden. The intermingling colors and perfumes of honeysuckles and lilacs beckoned passersby. In the wintertime, shivering, snow-covered, pedestrians were encouraged with the hope of summer when, through our picture window, they saw bright red, blooming geraniums vying for space to stare out at them.

Our home was always open for friends in need, and the kettle was soon whistling. I frequently had to give up my upstairs bedroom for unexpected guests, who would arrive with suitcase in hand and tears in their eyes. After unloading their worries, their tears dried, and they gradually started to perk up with Mum's infectious sense of humor. Mum willingly helped others.

Mum saw herself as a Christian. She tried to live a Christian life of doing good deeds. Although she hadn't attended a church since her teen years, she encouraged me to go. Once in a while, from about the age of 9, I would venture out to a church by myself. My mother recognized no conflict between being a practicing Spiritualist and being a true follower of God. She would never even eat food without saying grace. A few close friends knew that she had intuition, but they didn't know that she was a medium. Somehow we knew that this information would not be socially acceptable. Many of our acquaintances, even if they attended church, were quite comfortable with the occult practice of having their palms or tea leaves read, though.

Needless to say, our family séances were not announced. The séances were opened with Christian hymns and prayers to God. How ignorant we were of God's abhorrence of attempting to contact the dead (see Lev. 20:27; Isa. 9:19-20). Our motives were to seek guidance in order to walk with wisdom through this life and to help others along the way. Little did we know that we were walking with the devil. I was so proud of my mother for her many abilities, which included being a medium.

On one particular occasion, a very close family friend had referred a desperate, young doctor to my mother for psychic advice. He had failed his practical exam to become a surgeon. The examiner was not permitted to reveal the cause of his failure. To the doctor's aston-ishment, my mother, who had no medical background, described accurately and in detail the instruments that were placed before him on that fateful day. After describing to him which instruments he had picked up, she confirmed that he had chosen the correct instruments and in the right order but because he had wanted to be extra careful, he had hesitated in his choice for a few seconds. His hesitation earned him a failure. During his retest, he acted instinctively, without hesi-tation, and passed his exam to become a surgeon.

I never thought that one day I would be ashamed of the fact that I was born into a Spiritualist family and that I would not even be on speaking terms with my mother. Although Mum would demonstrate, in sincere, practical ways, concern for others, she could also disown, without a prick of conscience, an old friend who had offended her. She had a very stubborn, complicated personality. In my forties, I was to learn that she could disown me as easily as she could her friends. Up until that time, we were very close.

The rift in the relationship between my mother and I developed about a year after my husband became a born-again Christian. Doug, my husband, had been very enthusiastic when I informed him that I was a Spiritualist. He had a strong interest in learning about different religions. Raised as an active Anglican, he was not made aware that palm reading and such was not an acceptable pursuit for a Christian (see Deut. 18:10-12). The Lord knew Doug's heart. He was aware that Doug was an explorer, who was earnestly seeking a closer relation-ship with Him. The Lord nudged him forward on his quest. Many born-again Christians would be placed in his way on this journey. They would impact him with their amazing testimonies. One such encounter occurred over Doug's CB car radio. Doug, who is very outgoing and enjoys conversing with people, had started to talk with a stranger, whose CB handle, his CB nickname, in other words, was "Sky Pilot." Doug thought that he was probably a pilot. He was, but not the kind of pilot one would assume. He was a pastor the Lord used to help direct Doug to his spiritual runway. The Lord continued to mark his course.

Doug now enthusiastically sought to change my spiritual direction. I would have no part of his sudden need to evangelize me. Many arguments about religion ensued. Exasperated, Doug finally asked the Lord what to do in order to convince me that Spiritualism was wrong. The answer that flowed into his heart was, *"Be still, and know that I am God"* (Ps. 46:10 KJV). He was to step aside and let the Lord do His work. With relief, I noticed that Doug had stopped harassing me about my religious views. I didn't know why there was this sudden change, and I wasn't about to ask why. I was just happy to have peace between us.

About one year passed, and then the Lord intervened in my life. I became aware of the fact that I was being fed lies mixed with truth at séances. Attending church, by myself, as a child had provided me with some basic knowledge of the Bible. I knew that God was incapable of telling lies (see Prov. 8:7). I also knew about the importance of Jesus in Christianity. Why was Jesus never mentioned? Even though I had been raised since childhood as a Spiritualist, I now was forced to take a good hard look at some of the niggling doubts I had collected over the years about our form of religion. From early on, I had been uncomfortable with the fact that the spirit guides wanted to be addressed as "friend." I used to think of how ironic it would be if they weren't "friends." The power displayed by an unknown voice that filled our house during those meetings was sometimes even scary. The spirit guides proudly took credit for all good that occurred in our lives. Without them, we were told we would be nothing, just bums lying in a gutter. What kind of "friends" were these who would delight in pointing out their superiority to us? Didn't God, not spirits, deserve all praise for blessings (see Matt. 7:11)?

I felt like my world was turned upside down when I realized that central religious beliefs I had been taught since childhood were completely wrong. I felt very insecure. I wanted to tread very carefully. Reluctantly, I started to pose religious questions to my husband, while cautioning him that I didn't want to hear a sermon from him. He was prone to elaborating extensively on religious topics when any interest was shown. I didn't even want to reveal to him the turmoil I was going through. I wanted to come to my own decision regarding which form of religion was right for me. The more mainstream a denomination was, the more comfortable I felt. I didn't want or need any more surprises. Consequently, my spiritual growth was taken at a slow and cautious speed. I wasn't willing to pay for a wrong decision again.

When I became a "born-again Christian," my mother was not impressed. In her eyes, my husband and I had become "Holy Rollers." Why, we didn't even allow social drinking in our home anymore! My husband was obviously the bad influence on me. A slight rift between my mother and I had emerged. She would not permit me to discuss religion with her. This rift would widen when Mum was in her eighties. As was her habit, my mother had called us from her home in Montreal and had asked if it would be all right for her to spend a few weeks with us in our home in Burlington, Ontario. We gladly agreed and drove down to Montreal to pick her up. We were in for quite a surprise. Mum was planning to live with us permanently. Furthermore, she instructed us to arrange for the sale of her house. My father had passed away several years before.

The first few months of living together were peaceful, but the peace was not to last. Mum suffered a slight stroke but seemed to make a full recovery. We did notice that she had grown moody, though. For example, if we had Christian friends over and had quiet Christian music playing in the background, Mum would emerge from her bedroom, which was located at the farthest end of the house, to complain about the loudness of our music. But actually Mum was a little hard of hearing.

On one particular evening, my husband, Doug, and I arranged to dine with friends about a half an hour away from where we lived. Our two eldest children, both teenagers, were to have dinner at home with my mother. Dinner had already been prepared. The plan was that our daughters would leave home right after dinner to attend a swim party. We had provided them with the restaurant's telephone number to be used if there was an emergency. This was before cell phones became so popular. When we reached our destination, there were two emergency telephone messages directing us to call home. With anxious and empty stomachs, we picked up the telephone. Through heaving sobs, our eldest daughter, Allison, began to describe an argument over a minor issue that had broken out between my mother and her. Bonnie, our middle child, was also distraught as she took over the telephone from Allison. She had always been close to my mother and thought that she could diffuse the situation. Instead, my mother's anger escalated and she glowered, with hatred in her eyes, at Bonnie. Bonnie was in total shock. Then my mother launched a renewed attack on Allison and threatened to hit her. With a typical teenager's reaction, Allison countered with, "You have no authority over me." Allison did not realize the spiritual significance of this reply (see Rom. 13:1-5). Instantly, my mother lost all self-control and let out a terrifying scream. Needless to say, both girls were extremely upset. We advised them to leave the house immediately, and we raced home.

Upon our return, we found my mother alone in the house. She appeared to be quite calm and didn't try to address the argument that had erupted. Instead, her strategy was to pit Doug and I against each other by reminding me of an unrelated, long-past argument Doug and I had engaged in. I honestly couldn't remember what incident she was referring to. Immediately, a strong thought came into my mind that she was using a divide and conquer battle strategy. When I replied that I didn't recall what argument she was referring to, her apparent calmness vanished. Empty-handed, except for her cane, Mum barged out of the house into the warm summer night.

I followed her outside and tried to convince her to come indoors so that we could discuss the situation. Between sobs, she shouted that she was leaving for good and that I was no longer her daughter. That evening she would publically disown me twice more. Panic stricken, I phoned the doctor on call and told him that I suspected that she was ill. Her behavior wasn't normal. The doctor told me that we could not force her to go to the hospital. She had to go of her own volition. I knew that was impossible. I was at my wit's end. What was I to do with a pathetic-looking mother who was hobbling with her cane down the street while crying loudly and exclaiming that she no longer had a daughter and that it was cruelty at work on our part? Desperately, I dialed 911 and told the dispatcher that my mother was acting irrationally, maybe as the result of a stroke. I requested that only an ambulance, not a police car, be sent. If a police car came, I reasoned that my mother would become more distraught. Of course, both a police car and an ambulance arrived. Fortunately, the paramedic was very soothing with my mother. He gently convinced her to accompany him to the hospital.

Mum was admitted to the hospital for a few days, in order to conduct tests. During this period, I came to visit her several times. Each time the nurse would announce my arrival, my mother would break down into uncontrollable sobbing. Needless to say, I retreated to the elevator. On one of these occasions, while both I and my mother's very taciturn gerontologist were waiting for the down elevator, the doctor started to converse with me. I had never had a conversation with him since my mother's change in behavior. He very kindly told me not to take to heart everything that my mother said, since her CT brain scan had shown brain damage from multiple mini strokes.

With my mother's hospital tests finished, the discharge planner notified me that I was responsible to find accommodations for Mum within a few short days. Mum was still not speaking to me. I was reluctant to inform her that we didn't want her to live with us anymore. Fortunately, I was relieved of that task when Mum made her wishes known to the staff that she didn't plan to live with us. However, I still had to locate a new place for her to live. This task was made more difficult since we were still not communicating. One of my relatives suggested that I "wash my hands of her." For a short time, that was a tempting resolution, but the Lord spoke to my heart. There was only one way to rebuild our relationship, and that was to ignore the past tumultuous episodes and just to carry on as if nothing negative had transpired. It took approximately three visits together before Mum was again talking with me as if she too had forgotten the upsets.

She moved into a lovely retirement home where she resided contentedly only for a few months. She couldn't get along with the staff. Finally, I moved her into a brand-new, assisted-living apartment, where she was quite happy until she had an unfortunate fall in the bathroom. As a result of this fall, she injured her back and had to be hospitalized. Eventually, she had to be placed in a nursing home where she would receive more care. Since the accident, she had become bedridden. Her mental status had deteriorated as well. She would drift in and out of reality. Sometimes she would think that she was in her own home in Montreal and she would offer me tea. Other times, she was absolutely sure that I was her mother.

The upside of this sad mental decline was that Mum had become childlike. I could now talk freely with her regarding Jesus and His gift of salvation for all people. I explained to her about the sinner's prayer and asked if she was willing to repeat the prayer after me. During the prayer, Mum interjected with her addition of words that were very appropriate to the prayer. I knew then that she clearly understood the meaning of what she was saying. I had the answer to my secret prayer.

My secret prayer, made years before my mother's death, was that she would be saved and that I would know of it. Before my mother even came to live with us, I had attended a dinner, with my husband, put on by the Oakville Full Gospel Business Men's Fellowship. After giving an inspiring testimony, the guest speaker asked if anyone wanted to come forward for one-on-one prayer with her. I remember, very clearly, going forward and requesting prayers for several concerns, including my mother's salvation. The speaker, to whom I was a stranger and who knew absolutely nothing about my mother or my family, began to pray. When she reached the part about my mother's salvation, she used the exact words of my secret prayer: "that she would be saved and that I would know of it." I was stunned and very encouraged. The Lord had heard my special prayer. Now the prayer had been wonderfully answered.

Months later, Mum developed pneumonia and passed away. The funeral service was intimate and lovely. God had performed a great miracle. He is faithful to the end. He does hear our prayers, and He does answer them. Never cease praying for those who seem impossible to save. Remember, nothing is impossible for the Lord. The Lord knew that Mum had to become childlike to be saved. *"Assuredly, I say to you, whoever does not receive the kingdom of God as a little child will by no means enter it"* (Mark 10:15 KJV).

## ABOUT THE CONTRIBUTOR

Carolyn Curran-Fyckes holds a BA (English Literature, class of 1972) from Concordia University (formerly Sir George Williams University) in Montreal, Canada.

She currently resides in Burlington, Ontario, Canada, with her husband, Doug, and their youngest daughter, Susan. Carolyn has two older daughters, both married, and as well she has one young grandson. Professionally, Carolyn is responsible for running a busy doctors' office. In her spare time, she enjoys reading and cooking.

Carolyn attends Bethel Gospel Tabernacle, on Upper Wellington Street, in Hamilton, Ontario, Canada.

# CHAPTER 40

# IT ALL STARTED WITH A WOMAN AND A COW. WHAT A CHRISTMAS.

## *Lynn Donovan*

*...If ye have faith as a grain of mustard seed...nothing shall be impossible unto you* (Matthew 17:20 KJV).

*In everything I did, I showed you that by this kind of hard work we must help the weak, remembering the words the Lord Jesus himself said: 'It is more blessed to give than to receive'* (Acts 20:35).

The prayer request popped up on my computer screen:

When you all have a minute, please read my blog or see my post of about an hour ago on FB. Girls, we need to pray for rain on the plains of Kenya. It is serious. Lynn, the woman in this post, Nanyu, received gifts from you all in November. Lynn, your $1 Kingdom assignment/challenge from your Website started the snowball rolling, and we gave, which bought Nanyu and their family's first cow. The status of that cow right now, we're not certain.

Seeking Him,
Marsha

*Lynn, your $1 Kingdom assignment/challenge from your Website started the snowball rolling and we gave, which bought Nanyu and their family's first cow.* These words resonate in my mind. I read the email again. *Sigh.*

I slumped as I sat at my desk. "Oh Lord, my heart is moved almost on a daily basis by the needs of this world. I desperately want to give money away. But Lord, we have been unemployed for eight months now. There isn't any money to give."

"Lynn, do you remember months ago you paid for a registration for a conference? Do you remember the administrator told you they had already paid your registration? Do you remember that seventy-five is still sitting there waiting for you to tell them how to disperse it?" God will often speak directly to my heart.

"Yes, Lord, but I was thinking I might need that money to pay for travel."

"You could give this money to the woman with the cow."

I sat there truly in a quandary.

Right then, $75 was a lot of money. On top of that, my unbelieving husband would likely be annoyed with me if I handed over money to a woman with a cow when we needed to pay bills.

My head hung as the battle raged over my heart and mind. These very moments are the quiet and unsuspecting decision points in which the spiritual realm is desperately fighting over our heads.

"Keep that money. No one will know."

"You need that money. It is yours. Why give it away to a woman and a cow?"

And then I prayed, "OK, Lord. I will trust You. It is Yours. I will give it to the woman and the cow." Finally, the Holy Spirit triumphed over earthly logic.

I lifted my head. The word "faithfulness" floated gently about in my mind. I resigned to let go of that $75 and believe the Lord would handle my finances.

I emailed my friend at the conference and instructed her to use the money for the woman with the cow or for the conference, whichever she deemed best. I knew she could make the right decision because she knew the financial needs of both very well. Either way, I released my claim and gave it to Jesus.

I smiled, knowing that I did the right thing.

The next morning: Ring, Ring.

"Hello."

"Merry Christmas." I heard a giggle. My mother's enthusiastic greeting sang through the phone.

"What?"

"Today is Christmas," she repeated.

"Um, Mom, it's September. What are you up to?"

"Well, I came into some unexpected money, and I was planning to give you and your sister a portion this Christmas. But your sister wants hers now. So, do you want yours now or do you want to wait to Christmas?"

"What?" I repeated.

You can hear the broad smile in her voice. She likely was picturing my dumbfounded look from three states away.

"Mom, what?" I stammered. "Who, where, what, tell me everything. How much are you talking about?"

"A lot."

She spoke a figure.

I started to tremble. "Oh, Mom, just yesterday the Lord told me to be faithful. He said I was to trust Him and to believe He would provide for us. Mom, He sent you."

My measly $75 was dwarfed more than 100 times over by the Lord's faithfulness.

Gulp.

Tears rise now as I reflect on this encounter with God. Still today, I am barely able to believe. Why is it after all these years of walking with God, I'm continually amazed by His faithfulness? Then I'm amazed that I'm amazed. How utterly patient He remains with me. He gently pushes me along to bigger trusts and faithfulness.

I had been praying for a miracle. I planned to use this money to serve the people of His Kingdom.

To surprise and delight me further, my husband, my unbelieving husband, later said to me, "Use it for your ministry."

God has provided much more than I can dream or desire. Time and again, I have experienced the faithfulness of God. And for those things in which I still wait, I can wait patiently. Our God knows what He is doing. More than anything, He wants us to experience Him in profound and life-altering ways.

Does God always work like this in my life? Rarely.

Does He often tell me no more than yes? Frequently.

Will He on rare occasions surprise me beyond my vast imagination? Absolutely.

Sometimes I need only to trust Him when it doesn't always make sense.

God holds in His hands miracles. His deepest desire is to pour them into the lives of His followers. It is only a matter of faith and trust—trust as small as a mustard seed or even a woman and a cow.

## ABOUT THE CONTRIBUTOR

Lynn Donovan would likely hug your neck the first time you meet and skip the small talk to ask, "How are you today, down in your heart?"

As a writer and speaker, she shares from her heart the myths women believe about love and marriage and then points them to the freedom that is theirs through living in the truth and relationship with Christ. It is her passion to encourage women to thrive in their marriage and discover their purpose.

Married to her husband, Mike, for more than 17 years, they love, live, and now thrive in a spiritually mismatched home. They reside in Temecula, California, with their teen daughter, and neurotic but comical dog, Peanut. Lynn loves to laugh, a strong cup of coffee, and fantasy football, and not necessarily in that order.

To learn more about Lynn, visit her blog at www.spiritually-unequalmarriage.com, or follow her on Twitter @LynnDonovan. Look for her first book, *Winning Him Without Words: Ten Keys to Thriving in a Spiritually Mismatched Marriage.*

# CHAPTER 41

# A Voice So Bad Even God Couldn't Stand It

## Donna Martonfi

*Delight yourself in the LORD and He will give you the desires of your heart* (Psalm 37:4).

For 18 years, I have prayed to be able to sing on key. For those of you who can sing, this might not seem like an important request, but you see, I love to sing. I have yet to find anyone who loves to hear me. In church, I have had people turn around from two rows away, with pained looks on their faces, querying who was making the awful racket. I have had kids, with their noses all scrunched up, turn around and just stare at me till I stopped.

It's worse than that...this one time my husband and I went on a long drive with our friends, Fred and Carm. We were having such a glorious time that on the way home, I started to sing, "Praise God; praise God; praise God; praise God." Well that night Fred ended up in the hospital in intensive care. The doctor said it was digestive problems, but we all suspect it was my singing.

Another time, my pastor's little girl, whom I adopted as my grand-child-by-love, was about 2 and a half years old when I took her for a walk down by the intercoastal waterway. Naomi and I were walking hand in hand when my heart started to swell with appreciation for the beauty of the palm trees around us and the magnificence of the day. I was grateful to be in Florida and blessed to be loved by this darling child. Like a geyser that cannot be held back, I threw back my head and gushed, "Praise God; praise God; praise God; praise God." Naomi dropped my hand. She put both her hands in the air like she was pushing back an invisible wall and said, "Donna I love you, but just don't sing. OK? Just don't sing."

When a 2-and-a-half-year-old begs you to stop singing, that's bad—more than bad, actually. Only divine intervention could rectify my dilemma and grant my heart's desire. And wouldn't you know, God did just that.

One Sunday night in church, I was standing next to Judy, who was a gifted and strong vocalist and whose voice I knew would overshadow mine, so instead of just mouthing the words to my favorite song, I let loose and sang for real. I immediately noticed that something was very different. My voice had changed. I was not making a horrid noise. It sounded like I was singing on key. I leaned over and asked Judy, "Can you hear me singing?"

"Yes," she replied.

"Am I singing on key?"

"Yes, you are," was her astonishing reply.

I could not wait for the service to end so that I could report to Carolyn that God had just answered my prayer. She used to say, in that Southern drawl, "Honey, you just keep right on asking God, and one day He'll do it." Of course, she immediately wanted to hear me. Not wanting to make a fool of myself, in case I was mistaken and possibly still sounded like a barnyard animal, I decided I would validate this miracle outside in the driveway. "Praise God, praise God, praise God, praise God."

Carolyn gazed at me like a raccoon stares at headlights and then exclaimed, "Girl, you've got it." She actually stopped people as they were coming out of the church, pulled them by their sleeve, and declared, "You've just gotta hear this." Those who had previously heard me and knew the impossibility of any musical sound emanating from my lips were astounded. Oh the glory of being able to sing at the top of my lungs and know it is actually pleasurable to the listener.

As you can well imagine, I have almost become obnoxious. I sing everywhere, to everyone. I have no inhibitions. God has given me a most wondrous and marvelous gift, and I am going to make certain that anyone within earshot knows about it. I am also a walking, talking, singing billboard, advertising the fact that God answers prayer, as long as we don't give up and stop asking.

## ABOUT THE CONTRIBUTOR

Donna Martonfi has earned an associate's degree in biblical studies and a bachelor of arts degree in Christian ministry and is a qualified and trained Christian counselor. She has hosted live call-in television programs in both Canada and the United States and has also toured both countries as an evangelist since 1991, accompanied by her husband, Darko.

Donna is also a gifted writer and has written her autobiography, *Uphill Climb,* in which she details the troubled life she had before becoming a born-again Christian in 1980. During the past ten years, she has written more than 100 articles for a local newspaper in Florida. You can read these articles and *Uphill Climb* at www.donnamartonfi.com.

Because Donna and Darko have victoriously passed through the fire so many times in their many years together, her greatest desire is to serve God by sharing His wonderful message of hope through counseling people over the telephone and helping them turn their world right side up (941-485-5299).

# PART V

# DECLARATIONS OF GOD'S ABIDING FAITHFULNESS AND MIRACLES OF SALVATION

*Praise the LORD, all you nations; extol Him all you peoples. For great is His love toward us, and the faithfulness of the LORD endures forever. Praise the LORD (Psalm 117:1-2).*

# CHAPTER 42

# THE ROUNDABOUT

## The story of Evangelist Roger Whipp as written by Carolyn Curran-Fyckes

*But as for me and my household, we will serve the LORD*
(Joshua 24:15b).

Many of you will know what a roundabout is, but for those of you who don't, I shall explain. A roundabout, common here in the UK, is a traffic circle created in order to slow down traffic. Leading off from the roundabout, there are several other routes to choose from. The path of life is much like a roundabout. Some of us follow the wrong road and then wonder how we arrived at the end of this particular road. Others recognize the way they are to proceed and arrive safely at their intended destination on time. However, many will be confused while on this roundabout. They may even drive around the circle several times before deciding upon the route to follow. I was one of those drivers who kept going around the circle. My name is Roger Whipp. For over 20 years, I worked first as an ambulance attendant and then as a police constable in London, England. My journey in life was, *at times*, both confusing and irritating. Why was I plagued with stress? Why were others giving me attitude and cutting me off on the road? Didn't they realize that I just wanted to be left alone to enjoy the trip and to make my own decisions when I was ready to?

After 14 years of marriage to Maggie, we had both gone down different paths, doing our own thing and growing apart. Although Maggie was a Christian, she would be the first to admit that she had wandered far off God's route when the dramatic incident that was to change both our lives happened. The good news is that once invited into our lives, God never abandons us. He remains by our side whatever route or pathway we decide to take, ready to help us back on His route.

As a child, although my parents never attended, I was sent to church. I learned about Jesus and His sacrifice. I also knew what Jesus expected of a person. At the age of 13, as an act of independence, I decided not to attend church anymore. I wanted to have fun in life. I wasn't going to be bound by restrictive Christian rules. Did God really exist anyway? I didn't have time to think about such a heavy question. I would just put that unanswered question on the shelf, where it would remain for many years.

With my future unfolding, I was reminded of that haunting question frequently. During both of my careers as an ambulance attendant and finally as a police constable, I witnessed first-hand much intense suffering and tragedy. How would a loving God allow such sorrow? Why didn't He intervene? The answer to the question of whether a loving God existed or not was becoming clearer to me. I didn't need to trouble myself with such a philosophical question, though. Let someone else worry about solving it. I had to get on with my life.

On April 19, 1984, Easter weekend, my life came to an unexpected halt. Maggie had been on her way to visit her brother and had just taken her usual exit off of the roundabout. Without warning, another vehicle slammed violently into her car. The sound of metal crunching and ripping *must* have been terrifying. Blood poured from her mangled, glass-covered body. Ironically, the accident happened within a stone's throw of the City of London Cemetery.

The prognosis for Maggie was very grim. She was not expected to survive such a horrendous accident. Her parents and siblings, all

Christians, rushed to be at her bedside, in the intensive care unit of the hospital. Perplexed, I observed that they all seemed to have an inner peace and strength to draw upon even though they were saddened and shocked to see their unrecognizable, severely disfigured Maggie. I didn't have the comfort of that unexplainable peace within me.

The doctor informed us that if Maggie somehow, by some miracle, was restored to a modicum of health, she would probably exist in a vegetative state. I was asked to make a life choice decision. Did I want the doctor to discontinue life support or not? The doctor cautioned me to ponder this very serious answer, *and* if possible give an answer the following day. The sensible response seemed obvious—yes. Maggie wouldn't want to *be* left in such an unfortunate state. She would be at peace, and I would find peace, probably, with this decision also. In the morning, having decided to give permission to turn off the life support, I slipped out on to the hospital grounds to have a smoke while awaiting the doctor's arrival.

Isn't it strange that it can take a tragedy to make us aware of how much someone means to us? My world had come to a roadblock with the devastating news about Maggie. Although, just a week previous, we had agreed to divorce, the thought of losing Maggie was now nauseating. I quickly butted out the cigarette. There was no small enjoyment even in smoking now. The cold realization of my love for Maggie slapped me hard in the face. How could my mind have deceived me into thinking that I no longer loved or needed her in my life? The mind was simultaneously awesome and scary because it was an incomprehensible puzzle. Was there a creator who had designed this mind? Was there a creator who had tenderly painted each flower that graced the hospital grounds? I was now determined to find the answers.

My plan was that I would make a bargain with God for Maggie's life. What did I have to lose if He wasn't real? I sent up a simple prayer in the hope that God was listening. I would agree to investigate the reality of Christianity if God would heal Maggie. At least, I reasoned, I had not committed myself to becoming a Christian. Within an hour of saying this simple prayer, which even contained some strong expletives, God not only heard my prayer, but He also answered it. As the doctor turned off the life support, Maggie began to breathe again. For nearly one month, Maggie lay unconscious. No visitors other than family were permitted to see her for the first couple of months. The family was fearful that visitors would be so overcome by the sight of her that they would be unable to control their emotions in front of her. Maggie didn't need that to happen.

According to doctors involved in her care, Maggie's recovery, if it occurred, would be excruciatingly slow and racked with pain. The expectation was that she would require approximately two years of plastic surgery. Her right arm had been so extensively damaged that an orthopedic surgeon approached me and asked me in what position I wanted her arm to be set in. Puzzled, I questioned the surgeon as to why he would consult me regarding such a decision. After all, he was the one with expert medical knowledge, not I. The doctor explained to me that her arm, damaged beyond repair, would be totally useless, regardless of what position it was set in. There was nothing to attach screws or pins to.

The ophthalmological surgeon delivered dismal news also. Maggie's optic nerve could not be repaired either, but he could make her injured eye appear normal by implanting a contact lens and moving her eye upwards, in order to line it up with her good eye. However, he could not eliminate her double vision. The damage was permanent.

All of the doctors working on Maggie were in for a huge surprise. Within 13 weeks, Maggie was discharged from the hospital. Plastic surgery to fix her horrendous facial injuries was never needed. Her face no longer showed evidence of this near-fatal accident. Without physiotherapy, as the surgeon said, there was no point to therapy in her case; her useless arm became useful again. The orthopedic surgeon was beyond convincing that her arm was healed. He was a man who relied completely on the facts of a case. Only the clear proof of repeat X-rays would sway his opinion. After studying the repeat X-rays intensely, the surgeon, with a bewildered expression etched across his forehead, turned slowly toward me and said, "I do not understand this. This is a miracle."

The expressionless ophthalmological surgeon was equally stunned with Maggie's incredible progress. After Maggie's eye bandages were removed, he was stunned to discover that she no longer had double vision. This amazing change was impossible. The surgeon's cool, aloof countenance melted with this exciting discovery. Completely out of character, he broke out into a huge, contagious smile. At least ten churches were praying for Maggie's total healing by this time.

God clearly had His hand on Maggie and His hand on others who would be placed strategically in her life. The first car to come upon the scene was being driven by an off-duty ambulance attendant who managed to keep Maggie's airway open until a medical team arrived. One year after the accident, the same ambulance attendant contacted me to tell me that his cousin, who was a road sweeper, was dispatched to do cleanup work at the site. Coincidentally, this cousin happened to have a camera with him on that particular occasion. He offered to provide graphic pictures of the scene. These photos would give people proof of the devastation done to Maggie's car. It was nearly impossible to believe that anyone would even survive such an accident. I also learned that of the 12 physicians who rotated being on call to attend such emergencies, the only Christian among them was on duty that terrible night.

More fascinating information regarding early intervention for Maggie was provided by Maggie's own mother. Maggie's mother had canceled an appointment with her dentist when she rushed to be at Maggie's side. When she finally did return for a visit to the dentist, she recounted to her the details of what had necessitated the cancellation. She informed her that Maggie had suffered 28 fractures to her jaw alone. Astonished, the dentist instantly remembered that her father, who was a maxillofacial surgeon, had been flown in from Scotland to advise and assist with a woman who had 28 fractures to her jaw resulting from a motor vehicle accident. Yes, it was Maggie who was at the center of all of this attention.

The coincidences didn't end there. Two young off-duty constables, who just happened to come across the accident on their way home, had worked with me. Paul, a Christian, who had shared supper more than once at our home didn't even recognize Maggie. He told me that he had spent all of that Sunday at church praying for the Lord's intervention in Maggie's health. The doctor who cared for Maggie in the intensive care unit was a personal friend of one of my mates. The fireman who helped to free Maggie from the wreckage of her car was the brother of a former co-worker of mine. The night nurse was to become my cousin's future sister-in-law. Many lives, not just mine, were being interwoven and affected by Maggie's miracles. Also, the name of the hospital was Whipps Cross, and my surname, not a common name, is Whipp.

However, no life would be more changed than mine. Even though God had proven Himself by the miracles He had undertaken for Maggie, I had not decided to commit my life to Him. That was not a part of the agreement. I didn't feel ready to make that change yet. I was holding up my end of the bargain by attending church services, wasn't I?

In conversation with the minister, I was surprised to learn that God would forgive any sin if He was asked to do so at any time. Pleased with this information, I posed an interesting question to Him. Wouldn't it be reasonable to delay any confession and commitment to God until I was 70 years old? Very wisely, the minister said that he would like to conduct my funeral. Therefore, he inquired what date he should mark down for the service. I was very taken aback.

One Sunday, a guest speaker delivered the sermon. At the end of the sermon, the speaker gave the invitation, for those who wanted, to come forward for the prayer of salvation. In shock and against my own volition, I realized that my legs were taking me forward to the altar.

Finding myself now halfway up the aisle, I entertained the thought of returning to my seat, but I felt too embarrassed to do so. People in the congregation were smiling broadly at me and were whispering amongst themselves that it was about time for me to make this commitment. Not to lose face, I decided to continue forward. I would just repeat the prayer of salvation after the guest speaker, and then I would return quietly to my seat. That would be the best solution. I didn't expect that God would use this opportunity to speak directly to my heart during the prayer.

That powerful moment with God forever changed me and filled me with His peace and His love. Over time, through prayer and the studying of the Bible, I developed a close relationship with my awesome Creator. God clearly showed me the way off of the roundabout, miraculously healed Maggie's broken body and our broken marriage. I would never have even imagined that, on this exciting new journey, I would travel with my beloved wife, Maggie, at my side and that I, a former atheist, would work for God as an evangelist.

*But as for me and my house, we will serve the Lord* (Joshua 24:15 KJV).

## About the Contributor

Roger Whipp was born and raised in East London, UK, where he currently resides with his wife, Maggie. Professionally, he was first employed with London Ambulance service for seven years, and then as a police officer in London with the Metropolitan Police for a following 14 years of service.

Since giving his life to the Lord in 1984 at the age of 37 and establishing an itinerant ministry in 1985, Roger has recounted his testimony from Albania, Northern Ireland, through to and including 17 states in America, and much of the United Kingdom.

Roger has also obtained a certificate in Christian studies from St. John's Theological College in Nottingham.

The main thrust of Rogers' ministry is to encourage healing and deliverance through Christ and to provide an outreach to men. Roger is a recommended speaker for Christian Vision for Men, and currently heads up the men's ministry at his home church of St. Chad's, located in Chadwell Heath, Romford, UK. Roger may be contacted through writing at: Roger Whipp, 1 Clovelly Gardens, Romford, Essex, RM7 8NP. His Website is www.evangelist-rogerwhipp.org, or he can be reached by cell phone at: +4407952313544.

# CHAPTER 43

# GOD STILL SPEAKS

## *Anna DiGiacinto*

*For you created my inmost being; you knit me together in
my mother's womb. I praise you because I am fearfully and
wonderfully made; your works are wonderful, I know that full
well* (Psalm 139:13-14).

My name is Anna DiGiacinto, and I live in the city of Hamilton, Ontario, Canada, and what I am about to share is my real miracle story. It was the year 1970. I was expecting my fifth child but didn't know it then. Often I would have stomach pain, so I went to the doctor. I was sent for X-rays on my abdomen, but the results came back that everything was fine. I, however, was still experiencing pain. Again I went to the doctor, and this time he sent me for additional tests. This is when I learned that I was expecting my fifth child. We then discussed the X-rays, in light of any damage that may or may not have occurred to the baby. The doctor didn't really know what to say, but after a long pause, he suggested to be on the safe side that it was best to have an abortion. I remember that day well. That day I received two pieces of news. One good—that I was expecting a baby—and the other not good—that the doctor thought it best that I have an abortion.

I went home from the doctor's office crying. The next day I had an appointment booked with a specialist, my OB-gyn, and he too talked about me having an abortion. I was three months along, and I remember sitting outside on my veranda when I came home from that appointment. With my fourth child (who was 6 months old at the time) sitting on my lap, tears poured out of me. I held my precious baby close, hugged, and kissed him, and I cried out for what to do. I was not a Christian at that time, but I knew that I needed an answer. All at once, while holding my young son on my lap, I heard a voice so real that I can still hear it today.

"Mama, you love so much my brother, and you want to kill me," the voice said. I started crying desperately, and at the same time a friend who was passing by asked me, "Anna, why are you crying?" I answered her, "I'm expecting a child, and it's destined to die. The doctor told me to abort it, and I have to go in two days to have the abortion." That friend sadly wished me well and said that everything would be OK.

That same night I talked to my husband regarding the situation, but he was not in favor of the abortion, but instead told me to talk again to the doctor and see what he had further to say on this matter.

In the meantime, I talked to another close friend about my situation, and she told me that if the doctor said to abort, then the remorse would be his. After these talks, I made up my own mind and went again to my doctor to tell him that I didn't want to have the abortion. He was astonished. Never in the years of his medical practice had a woman canceled an abortion that was already booked, he told me. Nevertheless, he admired me and gave me words of comfort, assuring me that everything would be all right. "Stay calm, and think positively," he instructed.

Six months later, the baby was born. He was named Nicola, and he was beautiful and perfect in every way. He was in full and complete health. His birth was the joy of our house and the last one of the children to be born to our family.

Looking back on this moment in time, I realize that God had His hand in this situation and had been the one to intervene, even though I wasn't really even a believer in the Lord yet. I am reminded of Psalm 139:13-14 in this situation, *"For You created my inmost being; You knit me together in my mother's womb. I praise You because I am fearfully and wonderfully made; Your works are wonderful, I know that full well."*

God is so good and so faithful.

At the time that this decision needed to be made, I only knew a little bit of catechism, but after three years, in 1973, I had a beautiful personal experience with the Lord and gave my heart fully to Him at that time.

Today I can truly say that God is faithful and rich in love and forgiveness. I feel Him in my heart, and this really is the biggest miracle of all. First the Lord did an operation on my unborn child, and second, He did an operation of the spiritual kind, upon my heart.

With this true little personal story, may you be encouraged, and may you also receive from God the greatest blessing and gift of salvation, that He so graciously bestowed upon me.

## ABOUT THE CONTRIBUTOR

Anna DiGiacinto resides in Hamilton, Ontario, Canada, and has been blessed with ten precious grandchildren.

When she is not traveling to Rome and Italy to visit family, Anna may be found at one of three places: at church; cooking her favorite homemade dishes such as lasagna, gnocchi, or pizza for a friend or relative; or out and about visiting someone and sharing about the wonderful love of Jesus.

# CHAPTER 44

# CROWN OF THORNS MIRACLE

## BRAD FERGUSON

*Who despises the day of small things?* (Zechariah 4:10a KJV)

Two thousand years ago a remarkable man walked this earth who revolutionized human nature. He was called the Prince of Peace. He taught men truth that set them free. And He preached a gospel of love. Yet He told us not to seek after peace, freedom, or love. He said, "Seek ye first the kingdom of God and His righteousness." He promised that if we did so, we should then attain the only lasting peace, freedom, and love.

The place was our town's civic coliseum. The occasion was the 1972 graduation ceremony of one of our city's high schools. I was a sophomore college student sitting in the audience in order to watch my new girlfriend, who had graduated early and was attending college with me, walk across the stage and accept her diploma with the rest of her class. The words quoted above signaled the end of the address by the valedictorian of Tascosa High School. The graduation ceremony was full of pomp, excitement, and poignancy for the students and their parents. It was tedious for those like me, who had few emotional ties to the 750 kids graduating from the high school, which was the chief rival of my alma mater. And yet, the valedictorian had arrested my attention, partly with her listing of the Vietnam War era social and political troubles we were all living through. But primarily it was her unexpected offering that Jesus was the answer to those problems that gripped me.

I had been raised in church but was really just a nominal Christian. And maybe that was why such a public and thinly disguised proclamation of the Savior grabbed me so strongly that I never forgot it.

*They laid Him in a grave and told us He was dead.*
*But He rose again to prove that He had crushed the serpent's head.*
*He has given life to us through the power of His death*
*and in His resurrection won the final victory.*
*Sing alleluia to the worthy Lamb*
*Who was slain and died for us, but rose again to reign.*

It was 1979. By now I was a genuine, spirit-filled Christian. Jeremiah's Commission, a Christian band at Trinity Fellowship, the small church I was a part of in Amarillo, Texas, had just performed "Easter Praise," a song I had recently written. A few weeks earlier a very tough, brawling drug dealer was on his way to prison. He had been led to the Lord by members of the church. This man requested that another song I had written be played at the last service he would attend before being transported to his new concrete and steel room. A deputy sheriff led James into the church and later took him away to jail. The song James wanted to hear one last time was a ballad that he felt reflected his lost, rough life. Unknown to anyone, it also started the birthing of a relationship that had gestated for years and which "Easter Praise," a few weeks later, would give breath to.

Shortly after Jeremiah's Commission finished "Easter Praise" and the congregation was dismissed, a good friend caught me in the church parking lot. She wanted to introduce me to a lovely young visitor to the church named Debbie. This engaging newcomer had heard the song James had requested a few weeks earlier, but after

"Easter Praise," she found my friend and asked, "Who is this Brad Ferguson who wrote these songs I keep hearing?"

"Oh, Brad?" my friend replied as if I were family. "I'll introduce you."

Debbie confessed to me later that when she saw me, I was wearing the ugliest sweater she had ever seen, but that at our introduction something inside her leaped with joy or recognition.

Debbie and I began spending time together, mainly talking. We are both introverts (she more than I), but we can be very talkative when it comes to discussing ideas. She had her master's degree in English literature, and one evening as I was asking about her thesis on C.S. Lewis, she mentioned something from the address she made at her high school graduation. She had been valedictorian. I hadn't known that before and found it very interesting. I told her I'd like to hear her speech, if she had it handy. She found a copy of it on one of several neatly organized bookshelves and began reading it to me. The further she read, the more I began to realize that this was the valedictory address I had heard and been impressed with seven years earlier at my then-girlfriend's graduation. Debbie and I were both caught off guard. This prior connection seemed like a "coincidence" of astounding proportions. Although our relationship was still new, and we weren't certain what implications to place upon our encounter seven years earlier, we believed it was significant.

When Debbie and I met, I was not only between relationships, but also between jobs. I soon took another "between job" as a study hall aide at the high school I had graduated from ten years earlier. It wasn't the kind of job anyone makes a career of, but bringing order to a previously disorderly place brought thank yous from more than one serious student. Although I was unaware of it, God was also bringing order into my life. In my pre-Christian days, I had a short-lived job making jewelry, and I soon learned that the school had a jewelry-making class. I got to know the football coach who taught the class, and he told me that if I had any jewelry I needed to cast, he would cast it for me while casting projects for students. Christmas was just around the corner, and I set about making a pendant for Debbie.

On Christmas day, Debbie was stunned as she held the beautiful pendant I'd fashioned for her in her hands. She had seen a few pictures of my work, but she had only a passing knowledge of the time I'd spent making jewelry. That part of my life, the part before I really came to Christ, seemed far away and insignificant. But it was not insignificant to God. As she gazed at her Christmas present, Debbie suggested that maybe I was supposed to make jewelry for a living. The idea had never really occurred to me. But if I made jewelry now, I wanted to make Christian jewelry. I wanted my faith in Jesus to be reflected in everything I did.

Seeing what I could do, Debbie sat down and excitedly sketched a design on a piece of paper, handed it to me, and asked if I could make a pendant that looked like her drawing. I studied her sketch and replied that I had never made anything like it before, but that I would try. The next day I set my simple wax sculpting tools on my study hall desk and surprisingly quickly, sculpted the master model of our original Crown of Thorns pendant. I know there was something more than my hand at work in the sculpting process. When I first thought I was finished, I had what seemed to me a clever idea—put 39 thorns on the pendant to symbolize the traditional number of lashes Jesus received when He was scourged. I started counting to see how many thorns I needed to add or remove to bring the number to 39. I counted again because I must have made a mistake. No, I counted again. It already had exactly 39 thorns.

I could hardly wait to get off work and take it to Debbie for her approval. She was very impressed. It was exactly what she had pictured in her mind. She did not notice the number of thorns on the pendant and was amazed when I told her my story about the thorns. We were both convinced that God had guided my hands in the sculpting process.

After the Crown of Thorns pendant was cast and polished, we noticed more unplanned symbolism. The pendant was also a circle that intersected with itself seven times. The circle represents eternity. Seven is the biblical number for perfection and completion. Thus, our Crown of Thorns pendant symbolizes God's eternal gift to us, the perfect and complete atonement for our sins that Jesus made through His suffering and the shedding of His blood. Wow. We didn't plan any of that, but we are convinced that He did.

Something in me had attached itself to Debbie because of her proclamation in a high school graduation ceremony that Jesus was the answer to our troubles. Seven years later (perfection and completion), something in her attached itself to me because of my proclamations of Jesus in song. When brought together at the proper time, a picture placed in her mind, and the movement and skill placed in my hands, brought about a powerful symbol of God's love for sinners and His victory over sin.

At the end of the semester, I quit the study hall job and started my Christian jewelry business, Samaritan Arts Jewelry. I set up a small workshop in a corner of a room in the house I grew up in. There were many trials in my effort to get established, and it took 20 years for me to begin to understand the difficulties of owning and running a business. Even though I had a degree in psychology, I was in my forties before I figured out that I was an artist by nature. It took me awhile to say that openly because I had always thought of artists as kooky. It took me even longer to realize that artists are seldom the most gifted businessmen.

Although many people in our church kept urging Debbie and me to get married, it was seven years after we met before we felt directed—or released—by God to marry. We had the longest wedding ceremony anyone we knew could remember. After our honeymoon, Debbie and I set up house together. I continued to struggle financially, and sometimes my attention was divided between my business and pro-life work. Nevertheless, God provided. Sometimes the struggle seemed to be too great, but we would remember the way in which God used us to bring our Crown of Thorns pendant into existence. We would remember the early days when a dying woman sent her son to buy a Crown of Thorns pendant so that she could wear it when she was buried. And we would remember the woman who told me that as she lay dying in a hospital bed that doctors said she'd never get out of, a friend gave her one of our Crown of Thorns, and that whenever she felt it, she remembered that "by His stripes we were healed," and how she rose from that bed with a beautiful testimony of healing. And we would remember missionaries who would wear a Crown of Thorns because they served in countries where wearing a cross could get them killed. And we remembered the cancer patients who bought the pendant because of the testimony of a worker at the local cancer center who always wore a Crown of Thorns. We'll never forget the nonbeliever who bought one on the spot after reading the story about the first one I made because he knew someone who needed something like that.

God brought us together as we heard the other proclaim the Gospel. He enabled me to fashion the picture in Debbie's mind into His Crown. He wove unplanned symbolism into the Crown of Thorns as I sculpted it. And He has chosen to use the Crown of Thorns to again proclaim His Gospel through those who wear it.

## ABOUT THE CONTRIBUTOR

Brad and Debbie Ferguson started Samaritan Arts Jewelry in 1980. There they design and make their well-known Crown of Thorns jewelry, Signet Purity Rings, and True Love Waits rings for young people, Christian wedding rings, and other Christian jewelry. They serve the people of their local area from their store (recently voted the "Best Designer Jewelry" of Amarillo). It is located at 2427 Interstate 40 West, Amarillo, Texas 79109. People from around the world can buy their jewelry via their Website, www.SamaritanArts.com.

# CHAPTER 45

# SONG OF SALVATION

## *The testimony of David Ossenfort as written by Dr. Sherry Anne Lints and David Ossenfort*

*...our Lord Jesus Christ...chose us in Him before the foundation of the world, that we should be holy and without blame before Him in love, having predestined us to adoption as sons by Jesus Christ to Himself* (Ephesians 1:3-6 NKJV).

"*...having **predestined** us to **adoption** as sons...*" Have you ever thought about what this statement actually means? What does it mean to be "adopted" or to be "predestined as sons"? According to the dictionary, adoption is the process whereby one takes responsibility for another and makes one his own. To be predestined means to be predetermined or appointed beforehand. How is this, then, relevant to my story?

Beginning with my father, who was adopted at birth, there was a struggle for identity that undermined the core foundation of my family. Originally born David, my father's name was changed to Arthur to conceal any possible Jewish heritage. Abandoned, abused, and neglected, not only physically but also emotionally, Arthur never realized his full potential as a father, as a husband, or as a man. However, he was still a loving, funny, and caring man—traits that my siblings and I have been privileged to remember and experience. An avid churchgoer, Dad always stressed belief in Jesus Christ as Lord and Savior despite his inner battle of despair, loneliness, and rejection. My father never understood what it meant to be destined for greater things—nor did I. Herein lies the story.

As far back as I can remember, I always knew the hand of Jesus Christ was upon my life. There was an innate spiritual awareness that I had at a young age; I knew that the Lord loved me and was protecting me, especially, when I would sing at church. I could feel *His* presence envelop me to the point of tears when I would sing the hymns and sacred music; I was at home. I felt so free to express praise to my Heavenly Father. I fully trusted Him, and this brought me great comfort. This was similar to the feeling I had when I couldn't wait for *my* father to come from work, pick me up, and just hold me. I knew then that everything would be OK and I was safe.

This all changed as a young teenager when I began to see the inadequacies of my earthly father, specifically his lack of responsibility and good work ethic. Even though Dad stopped drinking before I was born, he traded drinking for gambling and was unable to provide for our family of five, forcing my mother to step up and work three jobs. This created anger and frustration in me, and that anger became a driving force in my life.

Working multiple jobs, excelling in sports, and loving music, I was determined to make a better way for myself. Having played trumpet for several years, my musical interest started to broaden, and I began to further explore the field of music. Through playing an instrument, I was exposed to many styles of music, but deep down inside, I knew that my voice was the *real* instrument that I was supposed to use. My senior year in high school, I performed in *Godspell*, which then led me to studying voice upon graduating. So, I decided to attend Concordia College, a Lutheran seminary, to become a music teacher. While there, I was in the sacred choir, singing classical music, and I discovered a new passion: opera—a world I knew *nothing* about. But finally, I knew that I had found an avenue for my resounding voice and could begin to develop this gift that was in me all along.

Unfortunately, though, during this same time, I was slowly losing the peace that I had as a child and the closeness that I once felt to the Lord. I had a likeable, easy-going personality and a big circle of friends. I wanted more. I started substituting my wants, needs, and desires ahead of His will. The lack of love I felt as a child, because I had a parent who couldn't give what he didn't have, was now coming to the surface. I desired to be close to somebody, and I wanted a relationship that would make me feel good about myself. So, I began to engage in sinful behaviors and relationships, searching for something who made me feel good; this despite the fact that I was a "believer" attending a Christian College. I no longer knew who I was in Christ. Poor self-image set in, and I became a people-pleaser. This was a very easy role to assume because I have a genuine heart of compassion toward people, a spiritual gift. Being concerned with what everyone else thought and what everyone else needed, however, robbed me of my joy and my true calling. The effect this had on my life was soon to become greatly magnified in the opera world.

I decided to take a year and a half off from college to "find myself." I continued to study voice privately while working full-time at a local deli. My chores consisted of scrubbing toilets, cleaning floors, washing dishes, and cooking, as well as doing side jobs, such as landscaping. I was working long hours, and I was physically exhausted. Emotionally, I was becoming angrier and angrier because I felt like I had to be "the man" of the family instead of being the son—the young boy who could run home to Daddy and everything would be OK. The truth is, it would never be "OK" again until I surrendered my way back over to His will. Spiritually, my life continued floundering. Although, I knew Jesus as Messiah, I was not following Him. I even stopped going to church for a little while. I wasn't happy. Still, I knew I had a gift. I knew I loved to sing, and I knew I was still passionate about it.

I returned to school ready to pursue opera as a living. I felt that if I could just make it with my voice, then I could break free from this impoverished living and achieve something of significance. After graduating SUNY Purchase with a bachelor's degree, I began working for regional and national opera companies, believing that, someday, I would "make it big." As a tenor soloist, I sang all over from New York to California to Germany to Alaska. I sang in concert halls, for symphonies, cathedrals, synagogues, and churches. I was traveling and "going places." I was also doing my own thing and found myself surrounded by a world of women, drinking, partying, smoking, cursing, etc. My world was infiltrated with sin. At best, I was practicing watered-down Christianity.

Ironically, the places where I encountered the most opposition to the things of God were the churches and synagogues that I sang for. It was there that I encountered liberal theologies and spiritual apathy. We would sing these sacred pieces about a Holy God and our glorious Lord, yet, live a lifestyle that was anything but glorious or holy. Nonetheless, we would continue to "play the part." Eventually, I became skillful at weaving in and out of roles, wearing various costumes, hats, and masks to portray characters that I didn't believe in. I did what I was expected to do.

As I assumed bigger leads for bigger houses, the frustration increased. I was subjected to more and more intense vocal scrutiny and worked longer hours at the deli to support the increasing demands of my opera career. I was miserable; what I thought would fill my life with happiness was now a great source of pain and heartache. This all culminated after my father's passing and finishing a big "gig" in San Francisco, with no major work ahead of me.

Then, in 2008, by the sovereign hand of God, I landed a job at the most prestigious house in the world—the Metropolitan Opera House. I worked as a cover for one year, but something was missing. I couldn't sing freely like I did when I was a little boy because now I had all this technical stuff restricting me. There no longer was any joy in singing, and I was ready to give it all up. After much prayer, I realized it was time to return to another house—His house. At my deepest point of despair, my Father was beckoning me, His son, back home where I first fell in love with Him and the music.

I know now, as I knew then, that through all of this, He always kept me in the palm of His hand; though I strayed, He was never far. He adopted me as His son. He chose me before the foundation of the world, predestining me to the ministry of healing. At the end of 2008, I was ordained as a minister, and in 2009, was ordained as a cantor for a Messianic congregation. After years of singing in Hebrew in synagogues and not knowing what it meant, it all made sense to me now; both the Old and New Testament are needed to truly understand the heart of God. Every event in my life, desirable or not, has been orchestrated by Him, for such a time as this (see Esther 4:14). I am here to serve Him and to please Him alone.

I am now continuing to study Hebrew but with eyes that have been opened to the fullness of the Gospel, giving me a new zeal for studying God's Word and restoring unto me the joy of salvation. He has taught me to sing a new song (see Ps. 40:3). Once again, I can sing with truth, the words of my favorite childhood psalm:

> *Restore to me the joy of Your salvation, And uphold me by Your generous Spirit. Then I will teach transgressors Your ways, And sinners shall be converted to You. And my tongue shall sing aloud of Your righteousness. O Lord, open my lips, And my mouth shall show forth Your praise* (Psalm 51:12-16 KJV).

So, then, the biggest miracle in all of our lives is salvation—being brought back, full circle, into the fold.

## ABOUT THE CONTRIBUTOR

Born in Long Island, New York, David earned a bachelor's degree in Fine Arts in Opera Performance at SUNY Purchase Music Conservatory. Soon after, David started singing for regional opera companies. He appeared in principal and featured roles with the Roanoke Opera, Anchorage Opera, Opera Birmingham, Opera Theatre of Connecticut, Connecticut Grand Opera & Orchestra, Opera Providence, Sanibel Music Festival, Asheville Lyric and Opera Company of Carolina, and Opera on the James, to name a few. Additionally,

David attended the prestigious Tanglewood Music Center, where he participated in the Phyllis Curtin Seminars and performed numerous leading roles under the direction of Maestro Seiji Ozawa.

Further, he has performed with the American Opera Projects, EOS Orchestra, Cathedral Choral Society at the National Cathedral in Washington, D.C., Duluth Festival Opera, Dayton Opera, New York City Opera, Opera Orchestra of New York, Mississippi Opera, Caramoor, and San Francisco Opera. Additionally, David has sung (and continues to sing) for various synagogues, cathedrals, and churches.

Career highlights include performing as the tenor soloist at the Kennedy Center premiere of Philip Glass' Symphony No. 5 with the Choral Arts Society of Washington, featured soloist in numerous concerts at Carnegie Hall, as well as tenor soloist in Handel's *Messiah* with the Seattle Symphony, guest vocalist in Bernstein on Broadway with the Phoenix Symphony and Minnesota Orchestra and cover for the Metropolitan Opera House.

David was ordained by Tri-Une Healing and Restoration Ministries in 2008 and as a cantor in 2009. In December 2009, David contacted Gordon Mote to accompany him on his first solo project, which is set for a summer/fall release 2010. For information on booking David, his CD release, or for professional voice lessons, please visit www.DavidOssenfort.com. Additionally, if you would like prayer for healing in your life, visit the contact/prayer request page. Shalom and blessings to you.

CHAPTER 46

# I KNOCKED AT HELL'S GATE

## *Debra Pursell*

*Debra was hit by an oncoming car. The next thing she remembered, she was being propelled uncontrollably down a long tunnel of some sort. As she descended deeper and deeper down the tunnel, she began to encounter faces in agony and hands reaching out to try to grab her. Is hell **real?** Debra believes she was headed there, until God heard her cry...*

I grew up in a house—not a home. Maybe you grew up in a "house" too, something like mine. A house is where four walls surround you. Inside those four walls is constant conflict and hurt. There is no love, no hugging, and very few kind words. A home has kind, gentle, warm words of love, a hug now and then, laughter, security, and warmth in relationships. I wish I would have had a *home* like that to grow up in, but it wasn't to be. Nevertheless, I am thankful that I at least had a house to grow up in. Some hardly even have that.

Through high school I was "blessed" with a counselor who essentially convinced me that I would never amount to much. I was continually being reminded that I was slow to learn. Have others somehow made you feel like you are slow and dumb? That is such a lie, because God accepts you for who you are. Don't let anyone try to convince you differently. Trust God to place you around children who need to hear you tell them that they are very special to God, and

God has some special things for them to accomplish during their lifetime. You may not realize what your words of encouragement will do in the mind of a little child.

When I was in the 11th grade of school, my fragile world became even more shattered. My father had been in the hospital for some time. He had cirrhosis of the liver due to alcohol abuse, though I didn't know it until later on in life. Every day after high school, I would go to the hospital and visit him. I loved him so much. I asked Jesus over and over not to let my father go away. He looked so terrible. But I believed Jesus would make him better. At certain times, he would say to me, "Debbie, I love you. I'm truly sorry. I'm really sorry. Please forgive me." I really didn't know what to forgive him for.

My grandmother, whom I also loved very much, painted china, and she helped me paint a plate with a horse on it for my father. I took it to him, and he was greatly pleased with the gift, but he didn't want it kept there at the hospital. He told me to take it home, and he would be coming home soon as well. I believed him.

The next day at school, they called me to the office. The counselor that I admired so "greatly" broke the news to me about as coldly as she could possibly have delivered it: "Your father is dead."

I refused to believe her. I was convinced she was lying to torment me. *I just saw him yesterday. He said he is coming home. He's not dead.* I was almost delirious and near shock.

"No—he's dead," came her icy retort. "Accept it."

I fell over on the floor. The pain was just too much for me to bear. All I could do was ask, "Why, Jesus, why? I loved my dad so much. Why? Everything I love goes away." Have you ever felt that way? After that, I began to think to myself that maybe I shouldn't love.

Years passed, and I managed to graduate from high school and then started attending college. I had a vacuum inside me, though. I wanted someone to love, and someone who would love me. I was vulnerable. Classic. I was attracted to men who abused me. All I had known was abuse growing up. I didn't feel I deserved any better as

I grew older. It's a lie from the devil. It's a total and complete lie. I know *now*. I just didn't know it then.

I became pregnant and was counseled to have an abortion. I knew it was wrong, but the pressure to go through with it was more than I could stand up to. I was taken to an abortion clinic by my soon-to-be husband in Detroit, Michigan. There were a number of women there waiting to have abortions as well. They acted as if it's an every-day thing. I guess to them it was. I felt so alone and so afraid. I felt like I was in an assembly line. I did not want to kill the baby inside me. I was so confused. In my head, I didn't know what I should do. When it was my turn, the nurse took me to a room. I changed into a gown. As I stood there, my heart was racing. I peeked down the hall, sneaked out, and tried to run away. One of the nurses caught me and took me back, saying, "I don't think you should do this."

You see, the money was already paid. I think I remember asking Jesus to forgive me. I know I did later, and that went on for a lot of years. One day someone told me you only need to ask for forgiveness once. Jesus forgets, and the sin is no more.

I married the guy who got me pregnant. I didn't have anyone else to turn to, even though I didn't love him. He went into the Air Force. I became a military wife. We went off to Texas, and I lived there for six weeks. His neglect and abuse of me grew worse. He got an assign-ment in Greece, and we spent two years there. He was a military policeman. He grew more hardened, at least around me. There was more physical abuse, along with the verbal abuse.

When his two-year tour was finished in Greece, he got reassigned to the United States again. I got pregnant with my first child. I had a little girl named Rachael. She was so special. Then a boy came along. We named him Phillip. By the time Phillip came along, the pain in the marriage was nearly at the bursting point.

My husband had an affair, but because I simply refused to believe divorce was an option, I stayed with him. Then he had another affair (that I knew about anyway), and this time he wanted a divorce from me. I refused, but he filed for one anyway, and it went through. He left me and our two children for a while. Then he came back with what appeared to be some compassionate concern. He suggested he take the two children for a month so I could have a rest. I thought it was a good idea, but the moment I stepped off that military base, he got papers filed that I had abandoned my children. They were taken away from me.

Like so many times before, I asked, *"Why, Jesus? Why? What have I done so bad to be treated this way?"* Then in the confusion and hurt, I began to grow bitter at Jesus. I knew it was wrong, but I just couldn't help it. Are you holding bitterness against God right now? It's a carefully orchestrated attack by the devil to separate you from God. I learned that the hard way.

I met some girls and entered the party scene, drinking, and one-night stands. I didn't care about my life. My ex-husband said I was dirt, and subconsciously, maybe I thought I was. My friend and I partied almost every night. All weekend I drank a lot because I didn't care. No matter how much I sinned against God, the next day when I sobered up, I would ask Jesus to forgive me. I would tell Him I loved Him and I was sorry for acting the terrible way I had acted the night before. I'd ask Him to help me. I felt like a piece of a puzzle that didn't belong anywhere. *"Where do I belong, Jesus?"* I would ask this over and over.

I took a barmaid job and began to grow hard. I swore and didn't care. I hurt people and didn't care. I used men and found pleasure in it; I felt power in it.

I had been going with my friends to a palm reader. This palm reader kept telling me things that were going to happen in my life. I believed her. I didn't care about the warnings the Bible gave about doing such things. I was blinded to the fact that this is a gateway to the demonic realm.

I was really tired one night after work. I went to bed early. Around 3:00 A.M., I woke up sharply out of a hot sweat. Two figures stood at the foot of my bed. I rubbed my eyes, said to myself, *"Who is it? Who is there?"*

One figure was all dressed in black with a hood over its head. The other figure was all dressed in white. They were standing quite far apart. The figure in black kept shaking its head back and forth as if to gesture that I was a lost cause. The figure in white was waving to me and smiling. I kept rubbing my eyes because I wasn't really certain this was actually happening. Maybe I was having some kind of delusion. Then in an instant, they both disappeared. I dismissed the whole thing a few days later, though it left me with a very eerie feeling.

I kept living the same rebellious lifestyle after that. I didn't heed the warning. One night, a friend and I left her house to go partying about half an hour earlier than usual. That was very unlike me.

We left the house and went to Dunkin' Donuts. My friend had a bottle of rum in the car. Our usual drink was rum and Coke. I didn't want a lot of rum in my cup because I was driving that night. That wasn't like me, either. Normally it didn't concern me how much I drank while I drove. She didn't care about that, either.

I remember putting on my seatbelt. Then we pulled out of the parking lot of a donut shop and drove down the highway. I stopped at the first stoplight when it turned red. We were listening to music. Then when the light turned green, I moved forward. Then, out of nowhere, a car came at us at high speed. It ran the red light. I remember my friend yelling, "Oh my God!" just before the car hit us.

I left my body. Then, I started going down this long, dark tunnel. It was dark—so dark. I knew I was dead and I was going to hell. I couldn't even see my hand in front of my face. I was yelling, *"I don't want to go yet. I don't want to go yet."* I was falling farther and farther away from the little light at the top of the tunnel above me.

Out of the dark, things began grabbing at me. Long fingernails began to grab and claw at me. They tried to pull me in. I kept screaming, *"No. I don't want to go yet."* Their grotesque mouths were open wide, and their teeth were gnashing at me. There was no sound coming from them, though.

Then I began pleading with Jesus. *"Jesus, no. Don't let me go to hell. I'll do right. Please give me another chance. I'll do right."* I begged and pleaded with Him.

Suddenly my body stopped, and there was a flash of light. It was like I was suspended in mid-air. Then, I felt the impression of hands on my bottom, and the hands pushed me so fast. I saw myself going back toward the light at the top of the tunnel.

The next thing I remember is that I woke up in the hospital, but not in textbook fashion. At first my eyes were closed. When I opened them up, I looked around to see where I was. I was confused. I couldn't figure out exactly where I was. In my confusion, I then heard a policeman say, "Oh—we lost this one. Do you have her name—anything on her?"

I then opened my eyes wider and said, "No, you *didn't* lose me." He jumped back, scared out of his wits. The nurses and doctors came running in, and the place was mass pandemonium. There was blood coming from me everywhere. They were pulling glass out of my body. There was a big piece above my eye. All I could do was lay there and sob. I kept thanking Jesus for saving me from that dark pit I had been in. I had been taken from hell.

After my bad accident, I slowly gave up the party scene and the crowd and friends I hung with. My friends asked me why I was acting different and why I didn't want to party anymore. I told them God gave me a second chance at life. I didn't dare to risk throwing it away anymore. I eventually moved and got back into church. I needed to start living by the principles of the Bible.

Friend, you do *not* want to go where I was headed. You may *not* get the second chance I got. You had better get right with the Lord, because the next intersection might be your next step into eternity. If my only purpose is to be given a second chance at living so I could write this and keep you from going to hell, then bless God and thank Him.

Get right with God, is all I have to say.

Thank you for reading my testimony, and may God richly bless you.

## About the Contributor

Debra Pursell currently resides in Holland, Michigan. She is planning on relocating to North Carolina this summer to be closer to her eldest daughter, Rachael.

Debra has three beautiful grown children. She has one son and two daughters. Her oldest, Rachael, is currently finishing up service in Iraq for the army's national guard. She will be home in June. Her son, Phillip, currently resides in North Carolina, and her youngest, Candace, just recently graduated from high school in June 2009. She is planning on attending college this spring.

In her free moments, Debra loves to decorate with old vintage items and browse antique shops and thrift stores for new and exciting items. In the summertime, she loves to go blueberry and strawberry picking. She also enjoys taking long walks. She is looking for a small- to medium-size dog to go with on her walks this year.

Debra attends a nondenominational church in the Holland, Michigan, area.

Story courtesy and by permission of Debra Pursell and http://precious-testimonies.com/.

Precious Testimonies is a nondenominational evangelistic outreach ministry offering hope, encouragement, and spiritual insights to those who are seeking to know more about the reality of God. They do this by publishing Jesus-glorifying testimonies as well as biblically based writings to help Christians grow in their relationship with God.

CHAPTER 47

# WHERE SHALL I HIDE?

## *Neavei Isaac*

*Therefore, if anyone is in Christ, he is a new creation, the old has gone, the new has come* (2 Corinthians 5:17).

I want to tell you about the single most important event in my life. In doing so, I will have to reveal some things of a personal nature. I guess almost everyone has things in their personal history they would rather were otherwise. There is no profit in dwelling on things that have been cast into the sea of forgetfulness. The events that are recalled here are only to provide some necessary background.

I was born in New Zealand. My mother rejected me for several days, claiming that I wasn't her child. Some days later, she repented and took me home. There I was rejected by my dad. For the most part, he ignored me. But that became more difficult as the months passed. Obviously, I don't remember much of that except that these things were sometimes mentioned as I grew up. I had a very difficult early childhood.

By the time I was school age, my parents had become convinced that I was evil and stupid. Whenever I got into trouble, which was often, they would tell me how evil and stupid I was. Sometimes, Dad would say that Mother should have given me away at birth. Through-out my upbringing, I was treated differently than my brothers and sister. It was not until I was 48 years old that I discovered the reason for all this.

Before Dad died, he told my sister (who later told me) that he believed I was not his son. He said that Mother had been raped, and I was the result. The moment I heard that, many things that had puzzled me fell into place. Bits of overheard conversation and many bewildering comments from relatives all suddenly made perfect sense. Partly heard snatches of conversation, and words like, "love-child," "mamser," and "bastard," now had a context that made them understandable.

Once I understood the truth I was able to have compassion for this man who had been presented with his wife's bastard child. I forgave him for all the unnecessary mistreatment or hurtful words said throughout my life and was able to let go of a great deal of bitterness and resentment that I had been carrying around with me all my life. I want to honor my parents for doing the best they could in a very difficult situation. They were both God-fearing persons, and although they were not taught to understand Scripture, they did rely on Jesus and did their best to honor Him. I have no doubt we will all be together in eternity and have a wonderful relationship that we were unable to achieve on Earth.

By the time I was a teenager, I was a real rebel. I constantly got into trouble of one sort or another. My parents were religious and regular church-goers. The family had to kneel in a circle each evening and chant long, meaningless prayers. Unfortunately, the denomination of Christianity my parents belonged to was strong on dogma and doctrine but weak on teaching understanding and wisdom. The particular church we attended was all empty form and little helpful function. Looking back, I see little evidence of the Holy Spirit, or the love of Christ. Surrounded by cant and hypocrisy, I rejected religion at age 13. I didn't know it then, but I had thrown out the baby with the bathwater.

By then, I was a liar and a thief. I stole a motorcycle and rode it all around the city. Eventually, I was chased and finally stopped by a policeman. He said that if I hadn't been speeding, he wouldn't have noticed me. So it was that at an early age I became a biker and got my first ticket.

Before my 15th birthday, I had left school and started full-time work. Before my 17th birthday I had a motorbike. Before my 18th, I had a fast, powerful bike and a V-8 car.

Early in my teens, I had decided not to take life seriously. I was into V-8s, motorbikes, and girls. At the time I thought I couldn't get enough girls. But looking back, I can see there were far too many, and I treated them badly. As for the cars and bikes, the road was a race-track. Cops were just another hazard to be avoided. Speeding fines were just annoying taxes. Looking back, I am amazed that I wasn't killed or jailed many times. I can see the hand of God protecting me from my own stupidity. Only God knows why He protected me. But I suspect that it was His response to my mother's faith in Him and her prayers for me.

At age 21, I decided that it was time to take life seriously. I began to look for some way to make a fortune. That turned out to be a much harder task than I had imagined. I found that while I could get any number of jobs at the unskilled or semi-skilled level, it was not possible to find one that led to big money. I began to read more widely and began a search for wisdom. That, too, turned out to be a much harder task than I had expected.

After three fruitless years, I decided that I should go to university. There, I thought, I was sure to find wisdom. Since I was looking for wisdom, it made sense to study philosophy. Since I had left school before my 15th birthday, I did not have a solid education and struggled with the academic requirements. The social life was exciting. Most students spent more time partying than studying, and I was no exception. Though I had struggled with my studies, I had proved to myself that I wasn't stupid, as I had been brought up to believe. I also discovered that wisdom was not to be found in the philosophy department, and I suspected that it was not to be found anywhere in the university.

At age 28, I had an education, a house, car, wife, and baby. But I still had neither wisdom nor wealth. There were some good jobs offered to me. They were all long-term propositions. I wanted something with better prospects for the good life before I got too old to enjoy it. One of my brothers, who was a foreman in a factory, had managed to save some money and was also looking for something better. We joined forces and bought a service station and motor repair business. We did very well and soon built a level of affluence that neither of us had previously known. One day the bank manager came calling to ask if we would like to borrow a large sum for a project. We certainly were doing well. Little did I know how soon I was to lose it all.

One day, a beautiful young woman came in to have her car serviced. I just had to have her, and pretty soon we were having an affair. This was not the first time I had cheated on my wife. The others were just out for a good time, too. My wife didn't seem to worry when I was out late. She spent a lot of time with her friends and seemed happy with that. There had never been any passion or romance in our marriage. We were really just companions. Starved for love as a child, I had been looking for many years for love in the arms of women. When my baby daughter came along, I had decided to stop all that, but now I was reverting to my former ways. I never found satisfaction.

Looking back, I can see what a rotten person I was. I was not only a liar and cheat, but also a very selfish person. Knowing from my own admission what a rotten person I was, you may find it very difficult to believe what I am about to tell you. Over the years, I read and heard about several such accounts as this, and I wrote them all off as flights of fancy or delusions. I scoffed at anything that hinted of a knowing, caring God out there. And yet strangely, I was always ready to give credence to tales of ESP.

I suspected that most religions had some truth in them, but not much. I was pretty much New Age in my thinking and outlook. I was such a habitual liar that my mind could no longer distinguish between truth and falsity. If you can relate to what I am saying here, then you know how the mind can be swayed this way and that; it is only flesh, after all. I can only advise that you put your usual mind-set to one side, and listen to your spirit, which knows the truth when it hears it.

One evening when I was with my lover, I had an over-powering desire to completely possess her. I was no longer satisfied with knowing her physically; I wanted my mind to enter her, for my very awareness to be within her. I wanted to know her thoughts and feel her feelings. In order to do that, I forced my spirit to leave my body.

At this point, some of you may be ready to write me off as a fruit-loop. Talk of out-of-body experiences can affect people that way. You need to understand that we all have two bodies—the physical one you are familiar with, and a spiritual "body" that the soul cannot be separated from. This spiritual "body" has no mind of its own any more than a physical body does. Mind is part of soul, along with emotion and volition. I can only tell you that I was familiar with out-of-body experiences, but that I had never before tried to enter another person. Well, I didn't succeed. I left my body, but instead of entering her, I found myself surrounded by featureless grayness. I think at that moment, I died. My friend later told me that she thought I had died of a heart attack. One moment I was with her, fully engaged in what we were doing, and the next moment I was a lifeless hulk. To all intents and purposes, I was lifeless for about 40 minutes. My friend was skilled at first-aid procedures and attempted to find a pulse or breath several times, without success. Of course, I knew nothing of that until she told me later.

I felt puzzled rather than afraid. This was not like anything I had known before. In vain, I looked in every direction but could see nothing at all. I continued to scan, but it was impossible to focus, as there was nothing to focus on. Just as I began to feel panic, I noticed a faint glimmer off to one side. When I looked, I could see nothing, but when I didn't look in that direction I had the sense of a very faint light off to my right. Sometimes when you look at the night sky, you have the impression of stars that are so dim you are not quite sure they are there. It was like that, only there was just the one glimmer.

Suddenly, I wanted very strongly for that glimmer to be a light. I found that I could move toward it, and I did so simply by willing it. I had the impression of moving rapidly, and eventually the glimmer became an undeniable light. At the same moment that I knew there really was a light out there, I realized that I was surrounded not by grayness, but by impenetrable darkness. It is as if one cannot see darkness unless there is some light to measure it by.

As soon as I recognized the darkness as such, I became very afraid of what might be hidden in it. All I knew was to move toward the light, but even that was scary because the light also uncovered me. The light illuminated more and more of the space about me until the darkness had shrunk to a small area behind me. It felt as though the darkness was trying to pull me back, and I had to keep willing myself further into the light.

There came a moment when I was aware of a kind of portal or doorway ahead of me. I could see no door, just an opening. The light was coming from beyond that opening. At the same time that I saw the source of the light, I stopped moving forward. I wanted to go through into the light, as I felt that only then would I be safe. Try as I might, I could not go forward, but I knew I only had to relax in order to go backward. I could still feel the pull of the darkness.

Looking more carefully at the opening, I saw that it had parallel sides but was rounded at the top, having a narrow appearance. The figure of a man appeared in the doorway. I thought the doorway and its occupant were about 50 meters away from me until he stepped forth. Suddenly my perceptions changed, as I realized that He was gigantic in comparison with me and quite a long way from me. It seemed to me that I was no taller than the soles of His sandals. I was terrified. Amazingly, with each step He took toward me, He seemed to shrink.

When He came near me, He was just a little taller than me. He stood there, about ten meters away, and gazed at me. There was nothing disdainful in the way He looked at me, but His gaze contained complete knowledge of me. He saw all of me. He knew everything there was to know about me.

Now I was even more terrified because His revealing gaze showed me what a filthy, rotten bit of muck I was. Every willful and wrong thing I had ever done was revealed for what it was. Every selfish and uncaring word or action, every lie, distortion of truth, or rejection of God and His Word was there to see along with its effects in people's lives.

As I saw myself revealed, I also saw that He was faultless and perfect in every way. Then He spoke, saying, "You know Who I Am."

"But you are not real," I replied. And He just looked at me with that knowing look.

A feeling of great hopelessness came over me as I began to realize that this could be Judgment Day for me. What hope could there be for me? I had been living a life of sin. I had denied Christ for more than half my life and had apparently died when in the very act of adultery.

"What do you want?" He asked. I knew very well that He knew exactly what I wanted, but He obviously wanted me to say so. "I want to go in there where the light is coming from," I said, without any real hope that I would be allowed to enter.

"You can't go in there, and you know why," He said with finality. At that, all remaining hope and strength drained out of me; I was in utter dread.

It was then, at the lowest moment of my entire existence, when there was not an ounce of pride or defiance left in me, that the amazing grace of the Lord took me to the greatest moment of my life. He led me to a low bench that I had not noticed before and sat down with me upon it. Drawing me close to His side, He said, "Neavei, I love you." I knew it was true because He said it, but also because I could feel it. I cannot describe that love except to say that it far transcends anything you can imagine. The most loving feelings you have ever experienced toward your own children pale in comparison.

His love swept through me, touching every part of me. I could not comprehend what was happening. For most of my life I had been denied love, and now the Creator Himself was infusing me with His untrammeled love. Here was I, this vile, mucky creature, being loved by this perfect Lord of All Creation, Jesus. I felt that I was being washed, touched, and healed.

For a time I just bathed in glory. By and by, my wits returned, but just as I began to wonder about the apparent contradiction of being turned away from the door and yet being loved by Jesus, He spoke again. "I am sending you back, for I have work for you to do," He said.

I could not reply, being completely overwhelmed with joy at this reprieve. "There are many on Earth who know of Me," He continued. "But they don't know My Word is true. Many have been raised in confusing circumstances and are deceived. They need to be told the Truth. You are to tell them, 'I Am. I love them. I am coming back soon.'"

The Lord explained to me that being familiar with the biblical stories about Him is not enough. The people have to know that the accounts of His life on Earth, which are found in the Gospels of Matthew, Mark, Luke, and John, are true. He further explained that although He has many servants, there is much to be done. He said there were many people who needed to hear the truth from me. He said He would empower my words to touch people who could not otherwise receive the truth.

When He told me how many people I must reach for Him, I was frightened.

"Lord, I can't reach that many people. I'm only Neavei."

Assuring me that I could indeed accomplish the task He was giving me, He again stressed that many souls depended on the work I was to do. He explained that He could accomplish His will without my help, but preferred to do things this way.

"I must start this work right away," I said.

"You will not begin this work for many years," said the Lord. Then He went on to tell me of many things I would do over the next 20 years.

I was aghast at what He told me. "I won't do those horrible things now that I see them for what they are," I protested.

Realizing the futility of arguing with an all-knowing God, I was filled with shame at hearing of these things I would do. He then explained that I would do these things because I would not remember the truth. I would not be able to remember.

"There is no light in you, only darkness," said Jesus.

Puzzled and fearful, I asked how I would ever be saved, and how I would become an instrument in the salvation of others. The Lord Jesus then explained to me that the day would come when I would call out to Him to save me from the mess I had made of my life. He said that from that moment He would hold me in His hand, and the light would begin to dawn in me. As the light in me grew, memory of these experiences would come to me. Even then, it seemed, I would tarry until the end of days, when time was very short.

"How will I ever manage to reach so many people if I have so little time to do it?" I asked.

"Trust in Me, for My timing is perfect. When the time comes, I will give you the means," He replied.

Even as I heard those words, it seemed I awoke to find myself face down in the back of the car. I remember gasping for breath, and then choking on the dust I had just breathed in. Pulling myself together, I stumbled out of the car, only to be accosted by my friend. She had thought me dead and had been pacing up and down wondering how to get rid of my body without facing awkward questions. She was married too, and was fearful of the consequences should her husband discover what she had been doing. Now she thought it had been a bad joke on my part. I had just been pretending to be dead.

It took me some time to calm her and assure her that I had no knowledge of what had happened. Indeed, that was true. Even as I tried to explain I could remember only that I had been out of my body and had some really great experiences up in the clouds. Thinking that it was only natural for me to be a little confused after being in some kind of coma for more than a half-hour, I said I would tell her everything in a day or two.

Even the vague memories I had awoken with were quite gone the next day. I knew I had experienced something quite mystical, but beyond that, I had no idea what it had been. Many times I tried to recall what had happened that night; I could not. I could remember the occasion and what I had tried to do, but beyond that, nothing, only the conviction that something wonderful and frightening had happened remained with me. So the years passed.

Through the passing of 20 years, I did many things I am now very ashamed of. I have repented of those things and asked forgiveness from all those I hurt. I was degenerate.

In 1992, when my life was at an all-time low, I called out to God. It was a desperate cry for help, but it came out in the form of a challenge.

"Hey there, Big 'G,' I don't know if You are real, but they say You are. I don't know if You can hear me, but they say You can. I don't know if You care, but they say You do. I want to know the truth.

"If You are real, and You are who they say You are, I don't understand why the Creator of the whole Cosmos would care about a nothing hopeless failure like me. I want to know the truth. If You are real, if You sent Your Son Jesus to live as a man and die on the cross to save us from our sins, then reveal Yourself so I may know the truth."

I did not notice any sudden change. I had not expected to. I thought the whole proposition was absurd. Just another sign of the deluded state I was in. I put the matter out of my mind.

Weeks passed, and I found myself sharing a house with a Christian. He had answered my advertisement for a roommate. We had some common interests and enjoyed the same shows on television, so we got on quite well. He seemed an ordinary bloke in most ways, but one night a week, and twice on Sunday, he did something weird. He went to church. He always invited me, but I never went. No way. I was not going to get mixed up in that kind of crap.

About the same time, my children started to talk about the things they were learning at the religious education classes at their school. One night my roommate said, "I know you don't believe as I do. I would like you to come along to church just for fellowship and to enjoy the good music."

I accepted his invitation but was completely unprepared for what happened. To my amazement, there was a church full of people who were obviously enjoying themselves. That was a big enough shock, but soon I was listening to the preacher's message, and something in me was responding. Afterward, my friend asked me if I had enjoyed it. I said I had in some ways, but I didn't want to go back again because it was too uncomfortable.

Months passed, and I would occasionally go to an evening service with my friend, but always with the same result. During this time, I was increasingly engaged with an internal debate. I did not know if I was talking to myself or if this was God I was talking to.

There were changes in my life. I began to care about things I had not cared about for a long time. About that time I visited my sister, who had been a born-again Christian for some years. She witnessed to me and also shared with me some information that my dad had given her. These things had a powerful effect on me. I wanted to believe in Jesus. He seemed to be the answer to so many problems. But was all this just the delusions of an emotional cripple who couldn't make it without some sort of crutch?

One by one, the Lord dealt with the issues I raised. There came a time when I knew that I had to make a decision about the direction my whole future would take. For the greater part of my life up to that time, I had believed that there was no personal God. If there was a Creator, then He had done His work long ago and left the whole universe to fulfill its destiny in some autonomous way. Now I seemed to be discovering that there is a God who knows, cares, and answers. In my search for wisdom, I had looked into the most popular religions, and some cults, and found them wanting. They were all dead, lifeless philosophies that created more troubles than they solved. Now I was being confronted with a sovereign God who takes a personal interest in all who seek Him.

Now I prayed another prayer, "God, if You really are listening, and if You really do care, I want to know the truth no matter what it costs me."

It was as if blinders had been suddenly removed from my eyes. All around I saw evidence of God. In plants, animals, mountains, and especially in people, I saw things I had always been blind to. Previously, I had seen only the natural. Now I saw something of spirit in all creation. It was almost as if I could see the blueprint for each thing as well as the thing itself.

By this time, I felt a great urgency to get the matter settled. One sleepless night, I sat up with the Bible. I could not accept with my mind what I now knew in my heart to be true. Early in the morning, I prayed, "God, I have reservations about what is written in this Bible. There are either contradictions in these books or I lack the ability to understand what I am reading. Show me, in a way I can understand, the truth about just one of these apparent contradictions, and I will take the rest on trust until such time as You may reveal more to me."

Instantly I received an understanding of that particular puzzle. There and then, I gave my heart to Jesus. Over the years since then, many puzzles have been sorted out for me.

Some weeks later, I responded to an altar call, making my new faith a matter of public knowledge. Soon I was baptized with water. Then I received baptism of the Holy Spirit. I was saved, redeemed, and made a part of the Body of Christ. All that happened quickly, but now began the slow process of the renewing of my mind to conform with my status as a child of God. Slowly, I made progress in the things of God. I joined the Full Gospel Businessmen's Fellowship International and fellowshiped with men who knew and loved Jesus.

There came a time when sufficient light was in me for memory of that wonderful event of 20 years ago to come flooding back to my conscious mind. It happens from time to time with anyone who has lived awhile that a particular sight or smell or happening will remind one of a time or place that has not been thought of for many years. When that happens, one is not confused. The memory of that event is clear, and one knows it as memory. Such is the case with the memory I have of those events of long ago. I have recounted them here as accurately as I am able. This is a true account of real events.

The Good Lord continues to improve me as the Holy Spirit deals with me, changes me, and conforms me to Jesus. Praise God for the work He has done and continues to do in our lives. The fact that you are reading this account proves that Jesus has given me the means to carry out the commission He gave me so long ago. I pray that Jesus blesses all who read this testimony and calls them to a closer walk with Him.

*Jesus lives.* The Bible stories about Him are true. Jesus loves us, and will save all who call on His mercy and receive Him into their hearts. These are "The Last of Days."

*Jesus Is Coming Back Soon.*

## About the Contributor

Neavei Isaac is founder of Living Connections Ministries, a ministry that is based on solid biblical teaching and additionally offers a venue for sharing testimonies in the Lord. Living Connections Ministries was established in January 2000, after Neavei experienced a miraculous encounter with the Lord, directing him to establish www.livingconnections.com.

As a resource in these last of days, this highly anointed and blessed ministry of the Lord also offers a prayer and counseling service to those in need.

Neavei Isaac, the author, currently resides in Queensland, Australia. He was born and raised in New Zealand.

# CHAPTER 48

# FREE GIFT

## *Jim Barbarossa*

*Repent, for the kingdom of Heaven is at hand* (Matthew 4:17 NKJV).

Many years ago, my wife and I settled down to raise a family. My wife met some great people at the church where we were married, and I believe this was the start of my receiving the "free gift" that I want to tell you about.

Over the years, our family grew. We had four wonderful children, a fantastic marriage, financial success, and many good friends. Sounds good, doesn't it? Even though it was good, I had many questions:

- Why am I here?

- What is life about?

- Is it possible to live just to die?

- What good is financial success when we must die?

- Why do it?

- Why even be here?

- Why do I feel so confused?

- What is the answer?

- Why, when I have so much, do I have a feeling of emptiness?

For 19 years, I strongly believed that my family was the only thing that mattered and I set out to provide for my family with everything the world had to offer. Almost everything I did was geared to provide for my family and generations of family to come.

Also, during this period of time, I searched high and low, trying many things to fill the emptiness or void I felt: playing softball with the guys and drinking after the games; playing racquetball and drinking after the games; buying campers, snowmobiles, new cars, houses, etc. I tried working extra hours to make more money, buying more worldly possessions, starting a business, investing in and buying real estate, etc. All of these things gave me a very short-lived pleasure or happiness that would not last. It would leave as quickly as it came.

Fortunately for my family, while I was providing for their worldly lives, my wife, Carla, was building a foundation for our eternal lives.

I have always believed there was a god, and I would occasionally pray when things were so far out of my control that I could not fix them. A few things come to mind that caused me to pray—like when my daughter was only weeks old, we had to put her in the hospital, and I feared for her life; also, when my son lay in the hospital with a staph infection; and when my wife was very sick with an infection in her blood system, and the doctor told me that my wife only had a 50/50 chance of survival. The most recent time was when a friend called for our support when his father was very ill. Carla went to help our friend while I stayed home with the kids.

As I lay there in bed that morning, I told God that I felt my friend's father was still needed in this world and that there was much good he could do by teaching God's Word to people like me who still needed help. I asked God to please save my friend's father and to give him the opportunity to help others like myself. In return, I promised to try to follow his path, starting with attending church that coming Sunday.

The following Sunday, I attended church with my wife, and it was a very peaceful feeling. The people at church all seemed so happy and full of life that it made me want to return the next Sunday.

As the service was ending on my second visit, I felt very relaxed and was in no hurry to leave. After searching for the answers to my earlier questions, I came to the conclusion that we could not possibly live just to die. There was no other answer or reasoning to my problems and questions other than believing in God and having enough faith to accept His Son, Jesus Christ, in my life; so I did.

The love I saw in all the people "hit me," and it was like nothing else I have ever felt in my life. At that time, I was not sure if it was Jesus filling the empty place in my heart or just all the love of the people reaching out to me, but whatever it was, I hoped it would never stop. And if I could have one prayer answered, it would be that all God's people have the opportunity to share the same experiences that I have come to enjoy, need, and want.

Looking back, I know that the Lord was with me every step of the way, and the path He was leading me down was to teach me about the values of the world and temporary happiness versus complete and total joy and the values of the Lord.

The Lord blessed me and my family by enabling us to make the right decisions on what I called my "gut feeling," but now I know it was my inner spirit leading me to worldly prosperity so that I would someday be able to testify that the things of the world are temporary and that worldly happiness will slip away very quickly.

Even though I was blessed with prosperity before being blessed as a Christian, being a Christian means more to me than anything the world has to offer. Recently, my wife and I were approached by a lady we did not know, and she asked us to pray for her heart problems.

She said she could see that we were Christians. Being recognized as a Christian was one of the best moments in my life.

In 1990, I had to quit my job of almost 20 years due to a rare blood disease. The doctors did not know what caused it and said they could do nothing for me. In January 1994, the Lord told me He was going to heal me of that rare blood disease. In March 1994, I took the same blood test that had led to the diagnosis that I had the rare disease. This time the results were negative. My blood had been cleansed by the Blood of my Savior. By His stripes I was healed. Praise God.

Up to this point, everything you have read occurred 14 years ago. Today, I am still healed. My blood is normal. To the glory of God, I have shared this story of God's healing power all over the world.

God has called and sent me as an equipping evangelist to the Body of Christ (the Church) to speak into and bring change in four specific areas:

1. To identify, release, and establish the Ephesians 4 gift of the equipping evangelist in churches around the world.

2. To call the 97 percent of Christians who refuse to share their faith to repentance and then to train and equip them to witness for Christ.

3. To raise up and equip an army of shofar (the ram's horn originally used by the Israelites) blowers around the world.

4. To teach Christians how to handle their finances according to God's plan, not the world's plan.

At the writing of this book, Carla and I have been married 35 years. We now have four children and nine grandchildren.

If you have any questions or problems like I had, don't try to weather the storm on your own; come in out of the rain and let the Son of God, Jesus, meet your every need. Let Him lead you and guide you, through the Holy Spirit, from now to eternity. Since I accepted Jesus as my Savior, the empty place in my heart has been permanently filled with the love of Jesus Christ, the Holy Spirit, and God, our Father.

God can meet your every need and will if you do your part. I urge you to read God's Word daily, pray daily, praise the Lord's name daily, and go to church every time the door is open.

*If ye abide in me, and my words abide in you, yet shall ask what ye will, and it shall be done unto you"* (John 15:7 KJV).

Receive the "free gift."

May the Lord bless you.

## ABOUT THE CONTRIBUTOR

Jim Barbarossa and his wife Carla are apostolic equipping evangelists, and are the founders of both Step by Step Ministries and theshofarman.com. Jim and Carla have been called by God to prophesy to the dry bones to reach the 9 out of 10 Christians who never witness and then teach those willing how to witness, while at the same time releasing and raising up the gift of the Ephesians 4 equipping evangelist in the local church.

Their evangelism training materials and outreach tools won first place in a contest advertised in *Charisma Magazine* in May 2007. These evangelism tools and training materials are now being used in over 90 countries worldwide, resulting in the establishment of evangelism outreaches in 20 countries, with over 70 new churches being planted, and over 600,000 souls coming to Jesus in the last four years.

Between Jim's gifting in teaching and Carla's worship anointing at services, the move of God can be felt mightily in their conferences and is evidenced by the numerous miracles, signs, wonders, deliverances, and salvation that occur.

Jim is also a member of A.F.C.M. (Association of Faith Churches and Ministries).

Jim and Carla have been happily married for 35 years and have four children and nine grandchildren. You can visit their Website at www.step-by-step.org or www.theshofarman.com. Please also visit their home church's Website at: www.jubileeworshipcenter.com.

# CHAPTER 49

# THE MIRACLE OF LOVE; GOD'S AMAZING GRACE

## *Dawn Johnson*

*I shall not die but live, and shall declare the works and recount the illustrious acts of the Lord* (Psalm 118:17).

*And as for your birth, on the day you were born your naval cord was not cut, nor were you washed with water to cleanse you, nor rubbed with salt or swaddled with bands at all. No eye pitied you to do any of these things for you, to have compassion on you; but you were cast out in the open field, for your person was abhorred and loathsome on the day you were born. And when I passed by you and saw you rolling about in your blood, I said to you in your blood, **live**. Yes, I said to you still in your natal blood, **live*** (Ezekiel 16:4-6).

I have wondered many times while reading God's Word, what does grace really mean? Little did I know the Lord would reveal this to me through a precious little bundle. In 2004, we applied for adoption, and the process began. There was much to be accomplished, especially for international adoption. It is a miracle all by itself of how the money to adopt little Gracie was given to us so abundantly. And one year later, we were on our way to Ethiopia to pick up our daughter.

Her testimony was life changing for me. Baby Grace was found abandoned in a field, a field that was daily visited by vultures and hyenas. She was tucked under a bush with a cloth draping over her newborn naked body and a rope tied tightly around her neck. She lay there helpless and vulnerable, a victim open to the elements. The odds of survival certainly were not in her favor. The blood diseases that had overtaken her infant body were so intense that they encouraged us not to adopt her, knowing she would not recover. The chances of her recovery were less than 5 percent. But there was one who heard her cries two days after she was abandoned in the open field who came to her rescue and took her to the nearest hospital. God made a way, and she was rescued just in time. She was taken to an orphanage, where they nurtured her back to health. She was handed over to us at 11 weeks old. Her nine-pound body was tiny and frail and fighting to live.

As I held this precious bundle and gazed into her beautiful eyes, the love within my heart felt as though it would burst. I was hands on witnessing a miracle of love. We were elated to receive this priceless gift, and excited to take her home and claim her as ours.

Twice, medical records showed no hope, but God stepped in, and within two months of bringing her back to the United States, we attended a healing crusade in Detroit, Michigan. That night our little girl was healed. Though it was not immediately visible to the natural eye, we knew all was well. The scar around her neck where the rope had threatened to take her life began to heal, along with the rest of her. The miracle process from beginning to end has left many with hope, joy, and encouragement for life. The full story can be read in the book titled: *God's Amazing Grace—Once Destined to Die; Now Destined to Live*, purchasable through www.hopeharvest. net or Amazon.

These past five years she has brought such joy and love to our family and those who have crossed her path. God's grace and love is evident in her life. Every day our little girl wakes and we hear the giggles from chasing after a butterfly, the excitement of picking Mommy pretty flowers, or the continuous praise songs coming forth from her heart, our precious reminders of the love and favor her Heavenly Father has bestowed upon her. She is a living testimony of God's amazing grace.

But I have a word for you. That same love and favor our Lord Jesus bestowed upon baby Grace is also for you. Just as he heard Gracie's cry, came to her, and rescued her in desperate state, our Lord Jesus will hear your cry and come to your rescue, too. God is no respecter of persons; all He's waiting for is to hear you cry out to Him, and it's there He will meet you. Give to Him your heart, your pain, and your sin, and allow Him to give to you His joy, His love, and His forgiveness. You are of great value to our precious Heavenly Father. He loves you so much that He gave His only son to die on the cross just for you. To God be the glory.

## ABOUT THE CONTRIBUTOR

Dawn Johnson resides in Nekoosa, Wisconsin. She is a home-maker and the mother of seven children. She continues to speak and give God's testimony of His amazing grace, etc. She has written a book on Gracie's story, including many more of the miracles in Gracie's life, titled *God's Amazing Grace*. This book can be purchased through www.hopeharvest.net or www.gabrielhope.org, and she can be contacted by calling 715-323-0733 or 616-307-3080.

# CHAPTER 50

# A Testimony to God's Faithfulness

## *Allison C. Restagno*

*The Lord is my strength and my song; He has become my salvation* (Exodus 15:2).

It's difficult in some ways to know where to begin writing this testimony out. God has been so good to me in my life so far, and I know that I am where I am today because of His love and His faithfulness toward me.

Perhaps, then, the very best way of sharing what the Lord has done for me is to retrace, or highlight, some of the past instances where the Lord has shown Himself faithful to me through the occurrence of some of the various miracles in my life. So, if you will allow me, I would like to share just a few of some of the miracles that I have been so blessed as to have experienced in my life thus far.

## Reflecting on the Faithfulness of God

When I was in my mid-teens, in high school, and still living at home with my parents and younger sisters, I had what I believe was a definite miracle in my life.

I remember that it was a Saturday morning because I had (as a typical teenager), decided to sleep in a bit on this particular Saturday. Well, I had decided to sleep, but the Lord seemed to have other plans.

I woke up early, and all that I could hear was a constant hum from a neighbors' lawnmower. I tried initially to get back to sleep, but I couldn't. It was at this point that I had the strangest feeling, and sudden urge, that I must pray for that neighbor who was cutting his grass, and that I must pray right now.

I was still half asleep, but the thought was so strong that I knew that I needed to pray, and so I did. As soon as I had finished a prayer of protection for whoever was cutting his grass at the moment, I heard the lawnmower turn off. Then I fell back fast asleep peacefully for about another hour or so.

I thought nothing more of this prayer until dinnertime. It was while my mother, two younger sisters, and I were seated at the dinner table and ready to start our suppers that my dad came up the stairs and into the kitchen. He told us that we were not to use the lawnmower until it could be fixed.

I asked him what had happened with the lawnmower.

My father replied, "This morning I was cutting the lawn, when I felt electricity-like charges going up my limbs, but then right at that moment, the lawnmower just quit."

I put my fork down, and sat there stunned. I realized two things. First, it was my dad who was out cutting the lawn that morning and second, the lawnmower didn't just "turn off"; it was somehow "cut."

As I listened more to what happened, I was really taken aback. My father said that when he went to unplug the lawnmower and inspect it, he found that the cord had been nicked. He had accidentally run over the cord. Somehow, though, he said it had just "cut," and right at the perfect moment. He was just starting to feel a shock going up his body and into his arms and shoulders when this lawnmower had stopped working.

I told him that I had awakened just before that exact moment and felt a very unusual urge to pray for the person who was cutting their grass. I knew then that the Lord had specifically prompted me to pray that morning.

I've chosen a second story because of the impact that this miracle had on my life professionally. Again, I was in my teens, and I remember my father coming home from work one day and telling the family that he had been laid off from his job. The whole family was naturally upset. I remember being very concerned about this for my father and for our entire family, and I was also silently disappointed because I knew that as my father was now laid off, my music lessons would need to be temporarily halted.

As a budding young musician who loved practicing the piano any chance that I could get, this was quite the upset. But I understood, and therefore when the time came for my next lesson, I went, knowing that it was my last for the time being.

Later that week, to take my mind off of music lessons, I decided to accompany my younger sister and father to an after-hours veterinarian's clinic. My sister's new pet had become quite ill, and needed to be treated right away.

While I was waiting to find out about how my sister's new pet was doing, a pleasant older gentleman struck up a conversation with us.

"Are any of you musical?" this nice older man said, while looking at my father and myself, who were sitting near him, and also waiting in the waiting area. I remember thinking how unusual it was that a complete stranger would ask a question like this as a first question to someone.

The first thing that I thought of was, *Does Dad have something musical on, like a pin, or something on his jacket?* I looked up and noticed that neither my father nor myself were wearing anything musical, so I wondered what would make him say this to us.

I never really did find out, but my father started talking to this man, and he did tell him that yes, both of us loved music, and both of us played the piano.

This is when the gentleman told us with a deep sigh that he had a piano at his home and that no one really played it anymore, and he really would just love if perhaps we could come over and play something on it for him sometime.

Although we didn't really know this gentleman, we both felt very strongly that, for some reason, we should go over to his home one afternoon, meet with him, and fulfill his special request and play his piano.

We left the veterinarian clinic, and the next weekend we found ourselves at his house, getting to know him, and trying out his piano for a few hours. We had a wonderful time meeting with him and his wife.

When we got home, we talked about how nice this man and his family was, and what a really great time that we had also. Then the phone rang, so my father picked it up. When my father hung up the phone, I asked him who had phoned.

Without knowing anything about us, and definitely without knowing anything about my father being laid off, or my music lessons being cut, this wonderfully kind stranger who we had just spent the afternoon with, had phoned to say that he had just felt that he wanted to purchase music lessons for me. As a result, he had gone ahead and pre-paid for a year's worth of music lessons with an acclaimed teacher, whom I later learned was a music professor at an internationally recognized university, as well as a music critic for a very well-known newspaper.

The gift, he had told my father, was to be used or would be wasted. He absolutely refused to take no for an answer and that is why he had gone ahead and pre-paid this music tuition for me. I was so deeply thankful, and I never have forgotten what the Lord, and this kind gentleman, who was prompted by the Lord, did for me that day.

Now my third story is related somewhat to the previous one. I was now 18 years old, and although I had really enjoyed a few years of pre-paid music lessons and had moved forward musically, I had not applied to go to university for music. I was still thinking about what to do career-wise and hadn't fully made up my mind yet. The spring of my high-school graduation year, to help out a friend, I accepted her request to learn her accompaniment music and back her up for her university music audition on the piano. She was to play the trombone. Everything went smoothly. She did well, and I felt that my job was now done. As such, I was expecting to be excused from the room where she was being auditioned, when the auditioning professor, with a doctorate of music, turned to me, and asked me when my audition for university was, and where I had applied.

Well, I conveyed to him that I hadn't really applied to any university music programs. I told him that I was thinking about doing an A.R.C.T., possibly with private lessons, but that I hadn't completely made up my mind yet. He then spent a few more minutes asking me a few specific questions. Before I knew it, he had collected my contact information and told me that he would like to set up an audition for me. There would be a performance audition, a written entrance exam, and an ear training exam, and it would be arranged with another faculty member shortly. He stressed to me that he would really like me to consider this opportunity.

This, I knew, was quite unusual, as this was months past the normal deadline for university audition applications.

I was up and down for a few days and not really sure if I should pursue this or not, but in the end, I decided that it wouldn't hurt to audition anyway and see what happened. I wasn't sure if they would accept me, but they did. I spent four years at that university, and graduated with a degree in music.

Looking back now, I realize that this was God. If God hadn't stepped in, I wouldn't have continued my piano lessons when my father was laid off, and my piano lessons would have temporarily stopped. Instead, I received advanced training. If God hadn't stepped in and arranged for me to do a favor for a friend and provide accompaniment for her audition, I wouldn't have been a music teacher at all.

At present, I have been teaching music now for more than 20 years. I started out teaching with just two students at the time: my father's bosses' wife, and a high school music teacher who also wanted lessons. When word got around that I was teaching, my teenage music teaching "business" took off from there.

Over the past years instructing, I have had the opportunity to teach many students of many ages, levels, and walks of life. It has been highly rewarding, and very much a blessing. For whatever reason, the Lord has placed me in these students' lives, and I am most thankful.

I chose my fourth story because this was another pivotal moment in my life. It was a very important time but for a very different reason. I will back up a bit to when I was in my mid-twenties, and was teaching music full-time, part-time from a private school of music in Burlington, Ontario, and part-time from my parents' home on Saturdays and few days and evenings during the week.

I remember one Saturday morning; everyone had plans to leave the house very early. Everyone left, and I remained at home to instruct some music lessons. This is a long story, but through the Lord's total protection, I lived through the experience of a home invasion. At one point during this ordeal, while praying to the Lord after the main phone line wasn't working, and my cell phone battery had died, I just literally felt that I should just grab my keys and run as fast as I could out of the house. I was able to run quickly down the long staircase from my second floor bedroom and out of the front door of the house without being harmed. That was a miracle in and of itself.

I grabbed my keys and was in my car before I knew it. I had no idea where to go, but I knew that I needed to phone the police. I remember just praying to God and asking Him to help me get help, and for some reassurance. It was at that moment that I had a strong thought that I should go a certain direction, turn right on a certain street, and then turn right into one of four parking lots, on a particular street corner. I remember pulling into the lot. There must have been a hundred or perhaps two hundred or more parking spots, and I just prayed for the Lord to show me where to pull in. I had it in my mind that if I pulled in, I would immediately park the car, and ask a store clerk if I could use the phone, and dial the police.

As soon as I pulled in, I looked left out of my drivers' side window, and into the faces of two people inside the vehicle, in the parking spot next to where I had parked my car.

It was my mother and one of my sisters, and they had just pulled in when I had pulled in, perhaps 30 seconds earlier. Could this have been mere coincidence? I didn't believe so. God knew that I needed them that day, and He placed them there, as well as directed me to that particular street, plaza, and exact parking spot, when I could have easily ended up in any of a number of plazas or businesses in the area to use the phone. God's timing was perfect. I had reassurance and comfort just when I needed it most. Thankfully, I was not alone for the remainder of that weekend. By the end of the weekend, we had had a professionally installed alarm system.

All of our family slept better, especially me. I felt better just knowing that God had not only protected me, but had also directed me to precisely where I needed to go to be able to phone the police, and also to get some much-needed family comfort that I needed at that particular moment in time.

My fifth and final miracle story is similar to the last one in that it involves another time when our family was protected. I was still living at home and going through university. On that particular night I was up late working on a few class assignments due for the next day. I was just finishing up, at about 2:30 A.M. or so, when I started sensing a strong need to pray urgently and immediately for the protection of our family, and over our property, and also specifically for our vehicles parked in the driveway.

I remember dropping my pen, holding my notebook on my lap, and praying to the Lord to take this uneasy feeling from me, and that if there were any people that shouldn't be lingering around our house, that there would be angels sent to scare them off. I continued to pray for God to protect us, our vehicles, and the property right then, in Jesus' name. Very shortly thereafter, I felt much better. I put my books away and fell into a peaceful sleep.

The next morning, when I came down for breakfast, my father was just coming in the house. He looked upset, and I asked him what he was doing outside.

He told me that he had just finished up giving a report to a police officer. Our family vehicle had been broken into sometime in the night the evening before.

Neither the vehicle nor anything inside the vehicle had been stolen. The burglar had prepared the ignition to steal the vehicle. The officer was at a loss to explain why the thief, who he deemed to be "a professional" and who was moments away from making his getaway, had simply abandoned his attempts to steal the vehicle and had fled. He said that there was no reason in the world why they hadn't been able to take our vehicle. The officer commented, "They had to have been spooked by something."

I now knew why I had been burdened with such an urgency to pray for protection.

Countless miracles such as this have occurred in my life. Many have unfolded after I was married, and in the last several years as well. For now, I will just conclude my story by saying that God is good. He is faithful, and He can be trusted.

He will truly never leave you nor forsake you. Even through your battles, He will be right by your side, with you at all times. Cast all of your anxieties on Him, because He truly cares. He truly does listen to you when you ask anything according to His will and purposes for your life.

I also had to learn to trust God day by day, through my receiving of a progressive physical healing. I encourage you to do the same with whatever you are facing. Sometimes it may not feel like it, but God really does care. He really has the ultimate best purpose in mind for your life. Just trust Him to lead you on, and you will find that He not only can but that He will: May the Lord be your richest source of joy and comfort, as you walk out your days, with Him by your side.

# CONCLUSION

In closing, I have to say that I truly do not know what I would have done if it weren't for the Lord helping me, leading me, and guiding me truly every step of the way. I can't imagine walking through life's battles without the Lord by my side. He has done so much for me, and I just want to thank Him for everything.

I have so many blessings in my life and so much truly to be thankful for, but without Him by my side, I don't think that I would really have a proper vantage point to see all of the many blessings that I do have in this life.

Would you too like to know that you have someone who will walk through all of life's battles with you? Someone who truly will never leave you nor forsake you? Someone who truly does have only your absolute and best long-term interests at heart and in mind for you? He's someone who even knows you right down to the count of the precise number of hairs on your head. He's someone who loves you so much that He plans to give you hope and a future. Then when you have completed your life's mission and purposes, He is someone who will give you an expected end to your life here on this earth. The most important thing is the security of knowing that you have an eternal place reserved for you in Heaven when you finally die in your earthly body and leave this home.

If so, and you would like this eternal assurance and to have a brand new life, filled with pages of many miracles in your own life as a testament to the Lord's faithfulness and from out of the Lord's genuine mercy, and goodness, then the person you are looking for, and the person you may have been searching for your whole life up to this point in time, is Jesus Christ of Nazareth.

Jesus is still alive and well. He is still not only the worker of miracles as seen in Bible days, but he is also a worker of miracles today. The best part, though, is that He can be your best friend if you will let Him in. You can come into a new and wonderfully exciting personal relationship with Him now if you so choose. What do you have to lose? Nothing at all, but you have everything eternally to lose if you don't choose Him now and you are wrong in your assessment and opinions of Him and His existence and relevance to your life today.

Jesus, I believe, is alive and well, and He is asking you to draw nearer to Him and to come into a personal relationship with Him for all of eternity. Starting now, right now, please, don't wait a moment longer to make this decision. Life doesn't offer us any guarantees. You may not have tomorrow, or even these next ten minutes, but if you have Jesus, you will have eternity, and an eternal destiny, and home awaiting you forever.

The choice is then yours to make, and this decision is all up to you, and no one else. No one will ever force you to make this decision to give your heart to Jesus. But I can tell you that it will be the best decision that you will ever make. Jesus is waiting for you. Won't you choose Him, and the brighter path that He has marked out for your life? Choose Jesus, and you will be so eternally glad that you did.

Just remember, there is no one past the point that Jesus could accept him or her. You are not the exception to any rule. Jesus came for anyone and everyone willing to accept Him. Even if you believe that you are beyond God's hope, or the worst sinner alive, if you will turn from your past sins and open your heart to Him and allow Him to come in and change you, He will. He will wash you afresh and anew. He changes even the innermost part of your heart, giving you a new heart—His heart—and the mind of Christ. He will teach you

His ways and lead you in the way that you should go, the way that is best from this point forward for your life.

Let Him do that for you. Give Him a chance, and if you are willing to start this brand new life, with a brand new hope in Him, just repeat this simple prayer after me. You will have this assurance of this new life that He is offering to you.

Please say this prayer from your heart, and you will have a new life in Christ:

*Dear Jesus, I admit that I am a sinner and have fallen from Your ultimate perfect plan and perfect purposes for my life. I know in my heart that You did come to earth over 2,000 years ago and lived and died a horrible death on the cross just for me to take away all of my sins and give me this gift of eternal life. I recognize that You rose on the third day and ascended into Heaven, and that You are coming back to earth one day again.*

*I want to be right with You and want to start fresh with you from this day forth. So please, dear Lord, forgive me of all of my past sins and failures, and come into my heart. Cleanse me from the inside out. Wash me clean, and make me a new creation in You from today onward. Help me to spend the rest of my life serving You. Help me to know You better, and also to do Your perfect will and purposes that you have predestined for me from before the foundation of this world were established. Lord Jesus, I accept You into my heart now fully. I ask that You start to work in me, from this moment on. Send the Holy Spirit to me and into me right now.*

*In Jesus' name I ask all of this right now, Amen.*

Now if you have just prayed that prayer with me today, be reassured that Jesus has come into your heart. He has completely forgiven you of any and all of your past sins. Your old life is forgotten and is under His blood. He will remember this no longer, and from this moment on, you are a child of the most High, a child of the King, and an heir to salvation. I trust that you will feel a completely fresh spirit from within, and will also notice shortly both a new song in your heart and a new bounce in your step.

Remember that you are never alone, and you are never beyond God's care and compassion. His mercy and love are new every morning, and His compassion for you will never fail you. All that is left for you today is just to enjoy the new gift of salvation that the Lord has given you. Develop a stronger relationship day by day with Him by going to a good, Bible-believing church, and spending time in prayer, and in communion with Him. Then, finally, let the new light that He has placed within you shine forth so brightly.

I believe that as you walk forth in your new life, having taken your first, but most important, step today in receiving the gift of your eternal salvation, that today will be a better day. Jesus hasn't promised that you are going to be exempt from all suffering and pain in this world because you are now a Christian. But you can be assured from this moment on that when the storms come, you will always have Jesus walking hand in hand by your side.

In closing, just remember that God loves you and that you are never alone. Your sins have not only been forgiven today, but you are also on the path to a better life. You will be living your life for others. Live each day for God and you will be reaping eternal rewards and joys.

You are His heavenly representative now. Go out and find that good, Bible-believing church, and start from this moment on, serving the Lord.

Walk forth in joy and expectant faith.

Your God is a wonderful, powerful, miracle-working God, and He loves you very, very much.

God Bless You,

Allison

P.S. The Lord also put a new song in my heart (see Ps. 40:3). While going through my valley experience, He gave me the words and lyrics for a song I entitled "God Will Guide Me Every Step of the Way." It is just a very simple song, but prayerfully has encouraged others who may be going through a valley experience of their own.

God may not always remove us from the valley immediately, but when He does it is for our good, in His perfect timing, and for His total glory. In the meantime, I believe that He often allows these times of great trial and tribulation to test us, and to use us in an even more impactful way for His glory and His purposes. God always has bigger plans than we can see when we are on top of the problem. When we step back, sometimes even years later, we can more clearly see the bigger picture and the good that He has intended to truly come out of our momentary pain.

If you are waiting for a miracle of your own, just place your trust in Him and hold on for the ride. It may be a tough ride, but when it's over, you'll come forth as gold. You will be all the better spiritually for having endured the battle.

Keep the faith, and keep going on. Your day is not over yet. In fact, it's just beginning.

# THE SINNERS' PRAYER

*Lord, please forgive me for all of my past sins that have separated me from You and Your wonderfully loving presence.*

*I repent of all of those past sins today and ask You to come into my heart and wash me as white as snow.*

*I confess with my mouth today that I believe that You are the Son of God, and that You were sent to earth and died for me to save me from eternal punishment and eternal separation from you.*

*I believe that on the third day, You arose from the dead and were lifted into Heaven and now sit at the right hand of the Father.*

*Jesus, I give You my life now and ask You to come and fill me with Your presence. Please send Your Holy Spirit, the Comforter, to fill me with Your reassuring love and peace.*

*Jesus, from this day on, I dedicate my life to You and willingly serve you with all of my heart.*

*Please come into my heart now, and give me a new and bright future filled with Your presence, and many miracles and blessings to come as I learn to go forth as a new creature in you from this day onward.*

*I praise and thank You, Lord. I ask all of this in Jesus' name, praying and believing that I have received this free and eternal gift of salvation. Amen.*

Name _____

Date _____

Committed life to Christ with the assurance of eternal salvation.

*Note: This is the best insurance policy you will ever have. Keep it in a safe place; tuck this away in your heart. Be blessed.

# MORE ABOUT
# ALLISON RESTAGNO

Allison Restagno is a music teacher, and happily resides with her husband, in Waterdown, Ontario, Canada.

She has compiled this collection of fifty short miracle stories at the Lord's leading, to encourage, uplift, and inspire each reader to an even greater level of expectation through faith with the Lord. She has personally experienced many miracles in her own life, and encourages others to reach up in faith, and to expect the same: "All things are possible to those that believe in the Lord. Just hold on to your faith, and trust God. No matter what the circumstances, God is on your side. Just trust the Lord, believe, and have faith. That is truly what life is all about."

To contact Allison Restagno for a faith-building speaking engagement through her powerfully faith-building testimony of God's love and faithfulness, or to order books, please see her ministry Website: www.moderndaymiraclesbook.com or email her at ARestagno@sympatico.ca. She inspires faith and trust in the Lord!

The book *Modern-Day Miracles* by Allison Restagno can be purchased at special reduced rates for special church projects, ministry, and charity fundraisers. Please email the author directly at: ARestagno@sympatico.ca for volume rate discounts.

# IN THE RIGHT HANDS THIS BOOK WILL CHANGE LIVES!

Most of the people that need this message will not be looking for this book. To change their life you need to put a copy of this book in their hands.

> *But others (seeds) fell into good ground, and brought forth fruit, some a hundred-fold, some sixty-fold, some thirty-fold* (Matthew 13:3-8).

Our ministry is constantly seeking methods to find the good ground, the people that need this anointed message to change their life. Will you help us reach these people?

> *Remember this—a farmer who plants only a few seeds will get a small crop. But the one who plants generously will get a generous crop* (2 Corinthians 9:6).

## EXTEND THIS MINISTRY BY SOWING
### 3-BOOKS, 5-BOOKS, 10-BOOKS, OR MORE TODAY,
#### AND BECOME A LIFE CHANGER!

Thank you,

Don Nori Sr., Publisher
Destiny Image
Since 1982